DANCE

ABOUT THE EDITORS

LYNNETTE YOUNG OVERBY is an Associate Professor in the Department of Theatre at Michigan State University, and an Adjunct Professor for Lesley University. She earned her B.S. degree from Hampton University, M.A. in Dance Education from George Washington University, and Ph.D. in Motor Development from the University of Maryland. Currently, she teaches courses in Creativity, Creative Dance and Dramatics, and Children's Theatre; and directs the Young People's Touring Company, The Program for Interdisciplinary Learning Through the Arts, and Artsbridge.

Dr. Overby has published both research and practical works. Some of her publications have appeared in *The Journal of Mental Imagery; The Journal of Physical Education, Recreation, Dance; Cognition, Imagination and Personality;* and *Dance: Current Selected Research.* She recently co-authored a book, *Interdisciplinary Learning Through Dance: 101 Moventures*, with Beth Post and Diane Newman. In 1996, she received a Teacher Scholar Award from Michigan State University; in 2000, she was named the National Dance Association Scholar/Artist; and in October, 2004, she received the Leadership Award from the National Dance Education Association.

BILLIE LEPCZYK is an Associate Professor in the Department of Learning Sciences and Technology within the School of Education at Virginia Tech. She holds Dance Notation Bureau certifications as Professional Notator, Laban Movement Analyst, and Labanotation Teacher.

At Columbia University, she was a Teachers College Fellow and is currently a Fellow of both the International Council of Kinetography Laban and the Research Consortium of the American Alliance for Health, Physical Education, Recreation and Dance. Honors include the 1998 National Dance Association Scholar/Artist Award and Excellence in Teaching Awards from Virginia Tech; Southern District AAHPERD; and the Virginia Association for Health, Physical Education, and Dance. Dr. Lepczyk conducts research in movement analysis.

DANCE
Current Selected Research
Volume 5

Edited by
Lynnette Young Overby
and
Billie Lepczyk

With the Cooperation of the National
Dance Association

AMS PRESS
New York

DANCE
Current Selected Research
Volume 5

ISSN 0894-4849

Series ISBN: 0-404-63850-3
Vol. 5 ISBN: 0-404-63855-4
Library of Congress Catalog Card Number: 87-47814

All AMS books are printed on acid-free paper that meets the guidelines for performance and durability of the Committee on Production Guidelines for Book Longevity on the Council on Library Resources

AMS PRESS, INC.
Brooklyn Navy Yard
63 Flushing Avenue – Unit #221
Brooklyn, NY 11205-1005
USA

MANUFACTURED IN THE UNITED STATES OF AMERICA

CONTENTS

CONTRIBUTORS

Karen E. Bond, Ph.D., Department of Dance, Temple University, Philadelphia, Pennsylvania

Theresa Purcell Cone, Ph.D., Brunswick Acres Elementary School, Kendall Park, New Jersey

Jill Green, Ph.D., Department of Dance, University of North Carolina at Greensboro

Judith Lynne Hanna, Ph.D., Senior Research Scholar, Department of Dance, University of Maryland

Diane B. McGhee, M.S., Arts for Children Interdisciplinary Program, State University of New York at Brockport

Lynnette Young Overby, Ph.D., Department of Theatre, Michigan State University,

Mila Parrish, Ph.D., Department of Dance, Arizona State University, Tempe, Arizona

Byron Richard, Department of Dance, Temple University Philadelphia, Pennsylvania

Michele Root-Bernstein, Ph.D., Independent Scholar, East Lansing, Michigan

Robert Root-Bernstein, Ph.D., Physiology Department, Michigan State University, East Lansing, Michigan

Susan W. Stinson, Ed.D., Department of Dance, University of North Carolina at Greensboro

PREFACE

This fifth volume of *Dance: Current Selected Research* presents a variety of invited papers that are concerned with various aspects of dance education. The criteria for the consideration of such papers for publication consisted of: (1) original manuscripts on topics for which valid techniques in experimental, historical, ethnographic, clinical research have been applied in the collection of data with appropriate analytical treatment of the data; (2) state-of-the-art research reviews on topics of current interest with a substantial research literature base; and (3) theoretical papers presenting well-formulated but as yet interested models.

It is the intention of the editors and AMS Press, Inc. to continue to provide dance researchers and students with a series reporting original investigative research that is important to the advancement of knowledge in all aspects of dance. The volumes are intended to supplement and support journals and annual reviews reporting on similar topics.

This series should contribute to communication among those who represent the various aspects of dance. Each volume is meant to serve as a reference for educators investigating similar topics. Courses of study considering topics on dance should find this series useful as a supplement to required readings.

A volume of this nature would not be possible without the cooperation of many individuals. In this regard we wish to thank the contributors for presenting their work for evaluation. The enthusiasm and support of the National Dance Association continues to be important to the contribution of this series.

TEACHING ETHICAL DECISION-MAKING TO PROSPECTIVE DANCE EDUCATORS: AN ACTION RESEARCH PROJECT[i]

Susan W. Stinson

This action research project involved development, implementation, evaluation, and reflection upon a process for teaching ethical decision making to undergraduate prospective dance educators. Central to the process were six ethical dilemmas drawn from real experiences faced by dance educators; each was correlated with relevant principles from a state-mandated Code of Ethics for teachers. Most of the dilemmas presented a conflict between multiple principles in the Code, so that the "right" course of action was not completely clear. Students were assigned to discuss the action they would take in each situation and the basis for each decision. Students responded to the dilemmas three times, recording their responses in electronic format, facilitating data collection. Built into the process was a small group component in which students read the responses from peers before revisiting the dilemmas. In successive stages of the process, the instructor gave further prompts to facilitate students' questioning of their thinking; one of these included presentation of Kohlberg and Gilligan's theories of moral development, with a suggestion that students examine their thinking in relation to these theories.

The data consisted of three sets of written responses from each student. The researcher examined student responses in terms of the basis for student decision making (ends-based, rules-based, or care-based, as defined by Kidder, 1995) and the degree to which students were able to question their thinking. Most students were more successful at defending their decisions than questioning them, although they improved during the process. Presenting the dilemmas next to principles from the Code of Ethics facilitated rules-based thinking, although there was significant presence of care-based thinking in student responses.

As is the case in all action research, this study offered an opportunity for the researcher's critical reflection on ethical issues that arose within this project, as well as her own personal and pedagogical values. The findings further reveal the value of this assignment in terms of student engagement and learning about ethical decision making in dance education. The researcher concludes with a number of suggestions for refining the assignment in the future.

I have been writing about ethics in dance education and research for 20 years. Up until now, most of this writing has been in the category I would call the theoretical or reflective essay, looking at my own values in relation to professional literature and practice. What I had not studied was the ethical thinking of the undergraduate dance education student I taught at the University of North Carolina at Greensboro.[ii] I knew that I wanted my students to become ethical practitioners, but what was ethical practice in teaching, and was it even possible to teach it?

While I was accustomed to presenting students with case studies that required ethical decision-making, I did not emphasize the decisions as ethical ones and doubt that my students perceived them that way. However, all teacher educators in my state are expected to make sure that our student teachers are familiar with and abide by the Code of Ethics for North Carolina Educators (1997) when they go into public schools. This code was developed by the North Carolina Professional Practices Commission in consultation with North Carolina educators, and was adopted by the North Carolina State Board of Education in 1997.

I admit that the first time I read the Code I thought that the guidelines seemed relevant but also obvious. For example, it seemed evident that teachers should do as much as possible to protect students from harmful conditions and discipline students in a fair and respectful manner. My dance education colleague Jill Green and I dutifully informed our students that they were responsible for reading and following the Code, but never addressed it otherwise. In an informal survey of teacher educators in other departments at my institution in fall 2003, I found that hardly anyone was giving the Code any more attention than this. Even though I questioned how successful any formal code might be in ensuring ethical behavior, I wondered if, by explicitly teaching the Code of Ethics and studying the process, I could learn something that would improve my own teaching and possibly inform others as well, even those teaching in situations where there is no formal code.

Review of Literature

It is clear from the literature that the development of codes of ethics has as much to do with political concerns as with ethical ones. Charles Rudder (1999) writes that, when trying to determine the right thing to do, "there are two subconcerns, ethics, and politics. Problems pertaining to morality are taken as ethical when they are individual and political when they are collective" (p. 42). He argues that:

Efforts to establish and enforce professional policies pertaining to both the protection of persons and professional competence are often misidentified and misdirected because they are not functionally ethical but political and may actually inhibit the exercise of sound professional judgment. (p. 42)

Another political dimension related to codes of ethics is their use to help establish and justify teaching as a profession. Citing Katz (1988), Nancy Freeman (1998) wrote, "Social scientists' definitions of 'profession' invariably include adherence to a code of ethics on their short list of prerequisites" (p. 32).

In a 1992 publication, Gerald Fain discussed ethics in the fields of health, physical education, recreation, and dance. He recognized how problematic it can be to have no code of ethics:

When there is no instruction from the profession, the practitioner alone determines what to do. In that case, practitioners use their reasoning, intuition, and/or practical experience with matters of right and wrong.... In searching for guidance, the practitioner gains no benefit from the collective experience and knowledge of colleagues. As a result, the basis for determining good practice is invented by each solitary practitioner and the opportunity for building a unified profession becomes impossible. (p. 3)

The importance of a professional code of ethics goes beyond the justification of teaching as a profession. According to Freeman (1998),

In the increasingly pluralistic, multicultural landscape of modern society...decent, well-meaning, conscientious colleagues can disagree about issues of morality and personal conscience. They may take opposing positions in discussions about abortion, the defensibility of the death penalty, or matters of personal behavior as private as birth control, but these differences are unlikely to interfere with their success in the classroom. When they work together, however, and share the same profession, they have an explicit responsibility to embrace the same professional ethics. (p. 31)

Despite this significance, Freeman noted that, in her own field of early childhood education, "if ethics is taught to early childhood educators at all, three hours or less is likely to be devoted to instruction" (p. 34). When ethical decision-making is taught, it is clear that a case study or narrative approach is favored by teacher educators and teacher education researchers (Colnerud, 1997; Corrigan & Tom, 1998; Freeman, 1998; Luckowski, 1997; Patterson & Vitello, 1994; Schwartz, 1998; Sottile, 1994).

Sottile (1994), drawing on an informal study of 30 teachers, found that the three most common ethical situations they faced in the classroom were ones relating to psychological (emotional) abuse, confidentiality, and physical abuse. A more formal study of 31 teachers by Daniels, Plant, Kalkman, and Czerny (1996) had a longer list, under categories of teacher-student relationships (complaints, risky behavior, cheating, lying, allocation of time, support), teacher-teacher relationships (unprofessional conduct toward student, parent, colleague, or school), teacher-parent relationships (school work, children's needs, mediation), teacher-school policy issues (such as inconsistent rules and standardized tests), and other (including violation of copyright laws).

Freeman defines ethical dilemmas as ones in which "teachers have to take action that will benefit one party at some expense or inconvenience to another. Resolving dilemmas forces teachers to prioritize among the conflicting wants, needs, or interests of students, parents, colleagues, or the larger society" (1998, p. 32). Daniels and colleagues (1996) identify three components in "moral conflicts or ethical dilemmas": "rules or values in conflict, confusion about the relevant questions to be asked about a unique circumstance, and problems identifying foreseeable effects and viable alternatives" (p. 33).

Rushworth Kidder (1995) clarifies further when he identifies the difference between two kinds of choices, the most obvious being a choice between right and wrong. He proposes several tests to determine whether a choice is wrong, the most obvious being whether or not the case involves legal wrongdoing. Three others are the *stench test* (Does it make your stomach turn?), the *front-page test* (How would you feel if what you are about to do showed up tomorrow morning on the front pages of the nation's newspapers?), and the *Mom test* (If I were my mother, would I do this?) (p. 184). Kidder notes that:

> right-versus-wrong choices...are very different from right-versus-right ones. The latter reach inward to our most profound and central values, setting one against the other in ways that will never be resolved simply by pretending that one is "wrong.... If we can call right-versus-right choices "ethical dilemmas," we can reserve the phrase "moral temptations" for the right-versus-wrong ones. (p. 17)

To simply call such situations "right vs. right," however, implies that it does not matter which choice we make, rather like "win-win" solutions. If that were the case, they would present no difficulty. In reality, making one right choice in an ethical dilemma means that we cannot make another, which is equally right and equally important.

Kidder goes on to say that there are four paradigmatic ethical dilemmas, and the existence of any of the four can be an indicator that one is facing a right vs. right choice. He named the four as conflicts between truth and loyalty, individual and community, short-term and long-term, and justice and mercy. He pointed out that, in resolving such conflicts, sometimes an opportunity is available, a "middle ground between two seemingly implacable alternatives" (p. 167), which he referred to as a "third way" in a "right-right" dilemma.

A number of sources identify different ways to think about ethics, and these have consequences for how we teach ethical decision-making. It is clear that no framework is value-free, and that there is no single way to understand what is "good." One of the best known is the developmental theory of Lawrence Kohlberg (1981), who identified six different stages in ethical development; in his framework, the highest stage is one in which individuals use abstract universal principles such as equality and justice as the basis for making ethical decisions. Carol Gilligan (1982), noting that women in Kohlberg's research tended to be categorized at lower levels of development when compared to men, identified stages of ethical development based on research with women. She described a progression that begins with selfishness/individual survival, progressing to a stage where self-sacrifice in caring for others is seen as goodness; the highest stage for Gilligan is one in which women include themselves along with others as ones to be cared for.

Examination of additional literature provided ways of conceptualizing ethical theories not based on cognitive development. A widely cited study by Coles, Seel, Becker, and Hunter (as cited in Jarrett, 1991), based on a survey of 5000 Girl Scouts ages 9-18, identified five different orientations, listed here in "descending order of frequency":

1. *Civic Humanist*, in which decisions are based on what will serve the common good.
2. *Conventionalist*, following order and accepted moral practice.
3. *Expressivist*, "going with the flow" of feeling and needs.
4. *Theistic*, obeying religious admonitions.
5. *Utilitarian*, deciding on the basis of their own interests.

Howe and Miramontes (1992) identified two categories, which they called "virtue-based" and "principle-based." Virtue-based ethical theories start by describing an ethically virtuous person, and then "evaluate ethical choices in terms of how well they exemplify the deliberations of the ethically virtuous person" (p. 18). Theories based on principle are of two kinds, consequentialism and non-consequentialism. The former affirms that "one principle will suffice for the whole of ethics: *Actions or policies are right when they maximize the total good*" (p. 13). In contrast, non-consequentialism holds that other principles, especially justice, are more important.

Kidder (1995) identifies three principles to use in resolving ethical dilemmas (p. 154):

1. "Do what's best for the greatest number of people" (ends-based thinking); this is comparable to consequentialism.
2. "Follow your highest sense of principle" (rule-based thinking); this is comparable to nonconsequentialism.
3. "Do what you want others to do to you" (care-based thinking); this connects most closely to Gilligan's work (1982), as well as Nell Noddings' discussion of an ethic of care (1984). It asks that we put ourselves in the place of others when making ethical decisions. However, care-based thinking is made more complex when we identify multiple "others," sometimes with conflicting interests.

If I had discovered some of this literature before designing an assignment to teach the Code of Ethics, I might have made some decisions different from the ones described below. Instead, it has served my action research in other ways, informing both my analysis and ideas for revising my pedagogy in the future.

Methodology

In exploring my questions about how to teach ethical decision-making to my students, I was entering a realm known as "action research," also referred to as teacher research, practitioner research, or insider research. The most distinctive feature of action research is that the practitioner is studying his or her own practice, sometimes in collaboration with another researcher, sometimes alone; the goal is not the discovery of any universal truths, but the improvement of one's own practice. A major justification for action research seems to be a political one: the desire to make teaching more "professional." As Clarke and Erickson note,

For teaching to assume the mantle of a profession a central tenet of that practice is the ability and willingness of its members to inquire into their own practice; into ways of improving and developing their practice consistent with the unique contexts in which they work and with an appreciation of current trends in education…. When a teacher ceases to be inquisitive about his or her practice—inquisitive about how students learn—then his or her practice ceases to be professional. Without inquiry practice becomes perfunctory and routinized. (2003, pp. 3–5)

While the purpose of action research is quite clear, the ways of going about it are less definitive. Some sources (Tomal, 2003) emphasize a problem-solving approach, in which one identifies a problem, collects and analyzes data, then develops, implements, and evaluates an action plan. Such an approach closely resembles Ralph Tyler's (1978) approach to curriculum planning. Another way of thinking about practitioner research is favored by Schon (1987), emphasizing reflection on one's professional practice as a way of facilitating teacher development and thus better practice. A third orientation is put forth by Patti Lather (1991), who considers it a form of social action. Similarly, Carr & Kemmis (1986) emphasize action research as a form of critical educational science; they write that "action research, by linking reflection to action, offers teachers and others a way of becoming aware of how those aspects of the social order which frustrate rational change may be overcome" (pp. 179–180). While I have engaged in significant critiques of practices in education and dance education in my previous work, my orientation in this study was directed more towards expanding my own consciousness and enhancing my pedagogy.

Context and Procedures

Like most educators, I am constantly studying, or at least evaluating, my own teaching. Taking this to a more formal level in which the words of my students would be part of a study that would be published and presented to others, however, brought up its own ethical dilemmas, of particular significance in a study about ethics. I had never used my students as subjects in my research, and was concerned about the conflict of interest between my role as a teacher and that of a researcher. Green (1999) raises many of these in relation to a study in a course, which was developed solely for purposes of emancipatory research, or changing students' consciousness; she notes the importance of being self-reflective and continually seeking discrepant cases.

In my case, my primary concern was to avoid even accidental

coercion in seeking informed consent. My university requires approval of all research using human subjects, and the guidelines of the Human Subjects Review (HSR) Committee (University of North Carolina at Greensboro, n.d.) were helpful. I could give whatever assignments I wished, in which all students would participate, and was restricted only in use of student material that would be shared with others through publication or presentation. Following HSR guidelines, I presented the overall project to the students prior to the assignment, including my desires to use anonymous portions of their assignments in the paper I would write. During this presentation, two assistants not enrolled in the course were present, one who collected the statements of consent from the participating students and kept them until I had turned in grades from the semester; the other served as a witness to the procedures.

I conducted my study during fall 2003 in an undergraduate course, the first in a sequence for K-12 dance education. Twenty students, all women, were enrolled in the course; of the 16 students whose responses I analyzed for this project, five were African American, and the rest were European American [iii]. Fifteen of the students were traditional-aged college students, most in their third year of four at the university, while five were older students returning to school. Most were working towards a license for teaching in North Carolina public schools. The range of intellectual development in the class presented a challenge for me as instructor, with only a few students able to demonstrate abstract thinking skills. Several of the previous assignments had required that students raise reflective questions regarding their observations, a task which challenged many of them; it was clear that they thought being a student should be more about receiving and giving answers than about finding their own questions. Further, they had a difficult time seeing that questions might be anything other than a request for factual information. In addition to teaching them appropriate course content, I hoped to help students develop skills in thinking critically and reflectively about dance education.

The Assignment

Before I decided to connect this project to the Code of Ethics, I had begun recalling and writing down ethical dilemmas that I had faced in my own practice and ones that colleagues and former students had reported. A decision to use this opportunity to teach the Code of Ethics led me to revise the dilemmas so that they more clearly related to the guidelines in the Code, ultimately creating six scenarios. While I wanted them to be grounded in real life, just as important to me was that they be ones which would engage students and "trouble" their thinking (Loytonen, 1999; Lather and

Smithies, 1997), as my own had so often been troubled. I correlated each scenario with two to three Code guidelines, attempting to have the scenario fall in between them so the right course of action would not be completely clear.

Because I wanted to understand how students were thinking, not just what decisions they would make, I directed them to explain not only what they would do in each case, but also the thinking which got them to that decision. Part of their grade would be based on the degree to which they questioned their own thinking, an issue to which I will return later in this paper. In the assignment, I clarified what I meant by questioning their own thinking through an example:

> This description would get a lower grade: "I would do this because this is what I have been taught ever since I was a child."

> This description would get a higher grade: "I realize that I have been taught to do this ever since I was a small child. However, I don't still follow all the guidance I was given as a small child. Instead, I have rejected some guidelines from my family but kept others. I guess this principle is one that most of my friends would agree with; I think my friends now are a greater influence than my family, because I can't think of any area where I would disagree with them. I wonder if I choose my friends because I think like they do, or I choose my friends for other reasons and then adopt their thinking."

The assignment occurred in three "rounds." In the first, students were asked to respond to the six scenarios, telling what they would do, then describing and questioning their thinking; they sent their answers to me electronically. I then divided them into groups of 4–5, and posted the answers from each student in the group in an electronic discussion board, after deleting students' names; I tried to mix the groups demographically and also to split up students I knew were close friends. For Round 2, the students read the responses of others in their group, then considered whether any of their own answers had changed, and, if so, why; they were asked again to describe and question their own thinking. Although I had considered making this stage an online discussion, I eventually decided against it; I will discuss this decision in my concluding reflections.

Next I held a class session in which I presented the stages of moral development according to both Lawrence Kohlberg (1981), in more detail, and Carol Gilligan (1984), in less detail. I explained their conceptions of stages of development and provided a handout summarizing the stages and also web sites for students who wished to review the material in more detail. Following that, students completed Round 3. Although my original intent for Round 3 was for students to assess their own stage of development according to one or both of the models (Kohlberg and Gilligan), as well as discuss any changes to their responses, I did not completely follow these plans.

Like other action researchers, my first responsibility was as an instructor, not as a researcher. I was more interested in helping my students become engaged with important issues and learn from them than I was in objectively comparing strategies for effectiveness. Since I was grading students on their work, I wanted to give them whatever assistance was appropriate in order for them to be successful. Thus, during the project I responded to instructional needs that I perceived, just as I would have if no research project were in progress.

When I reviewed Round 1 responses, it appeared that most students were looking for solutions that avoided any conflict with other people as well as with their own thinking; they wanted to be "right," rather than question themselves, and most did not seem to understand what it meant to question their own thinking, despite the example I had given in the instructions. Because of this, prior to Round 2 I discussed in class potentially problematic aspects of the scenarios which I thought no one had considered, and gave students many examples of questions they might ask themselves. One student at that point noted that she had not been asked in other classes to reveal her questioning, but only the final results of her thinking, which she then had to defend. She was not challenging the assignment, but marveling at the newness of it.

Round 2 responses were quite diverse in length, ranging from five and a half pages single spaced, to a couple of sentences. Two students who were the briefest simply said that they had read their peers' responses to all questions, and found no reason to change any of their own. Many students acknowledged good solutions proposed by their peers and a very few changed their decisions about what to do. A few noted issues brought up by their peers that did not make them change their decisions, but gave them new perspectives they had not considered before. Some used this as an opportunity to defend their original positions, while others used it as an opportunity to question themselves. Following Round 2, I again gave many examples of questioning one's own thinking. This was the same session in which I presented the Kohlberg and Gilligan constructs. By this time, I had realized that my original idea to have students classify their own ethical thinking according to stage of development would be beyond the capacity of a number of the students in the class, unless I spent considerably more time teaching these theories. Even more important, this task no longer seemed especially significant. I was more interested in having students use these theoretical constructs to ask themselves questions about their own thinking, just as Kohlberg and Gilligan had asked questions of their subjects in order to classify their responses. I thus provided an optional modification in the Round 3 assignment.[iv] Several students, ones who had struggled with higher order thinking during the class, confided to me that they really did not understand the stages of development or how to apply them to their own thinking.[v] I also returned their Round 1 and 2 responses during this class, with notations of where I thought they were questioning their own thinking, and encouraging those who had done little really to push themselves. In Round 3, many students who had done little questioning added a lot more and responded again to individual scenarios. Others, especially those who had done a lot of questioning already, picked only a couple of the scenarios to reexamine. A few students really looked at the bigger picture of their own thinking throughout the assignment, engaging in the kind of metacognition I had hoped for.

Analysis of Findings

I will now look in more detail at the student responses and what I learned from them. Because of space restrictions, I have chosen to review their responses in detail to only two scenarios, with a more brief summary of others.[vi] Following the analysis, I will reflect upon the findings, problematize my own thinking, and propose how I might teach this material in the future.

A Father Punishes His Son

This scenario asked students to consider three directives from the Code of Ethics, to:

Protect students from conditions within the educator's control that circumvent learning or are detrimental to the health and safety of students.

Discipline students justly and fairly and not deliberately embarrass or humiliate them.

Acknowledge diverse views of students, parents and legal guardians as they work...to shape educational goals, policies, and decisions...

The specific dilemma was drawn from an incident related to me by a former student:

You are teaching in a summer arts program for low-income children. One child in the class, a 10-year-old boy, has been

Susan W. Stinson

consistently disruptive in your class. You have repeatedly removed him from the class for "time out," and spoken with the supervisor. The supervisor calls the parent, and the boy's father comes in for a conference. He tells the supervisor, "I will take care of this. You just let me know if my boy acts up again." As he leaves the school with his child, you see out the window that the father is hitting his child. You take your concern to the supervisor, who says, "That's just the way these families do things." What do you do if the child is disruptive in your class again? Describe your thinking that leads you to make this decision.[vii]

In terms of "rule-based thinking," this dilemma brings into conflict two rules, one protecting children and one protecting family diversity—definitely a "right-right," although it does not appear to fit any of the four conflicts identified by Kidder. As a parent and teacher strongly opposed to corporal punishment but doing my best to respect family diversity, I felt considerable conflict when thinking about this situation, and hoped that my students would as well. By asking students to consider what they would do if the child were disruptive again, I was asking them to consider the consequences of their decision. In terms of "care-based thinking," this scenario presents a conflict between caring for (protecting) a child and protecting a father, or, at least, the father's right to determine how to discipline his child. Most of my students revealed care-based thinking, although there was evidence of thinking based on both rules and consequences.

Round One responses. A number of the students reacted most to concern about hitting a child, certain that it is wrong, if not abusive. Their first response was to protect the child. Care-based thinking seemed to predominate in responses like this one:

> To suspect that a child in your class is being abused by a parent is one thing; however, witnessing the abuse is another. I would be letting that child down if I did not do something. I think that if he were to be disruptive again, I would continue with the time outs but I would not contact the father. My frustration with the student would shift from having to control his behavior, to anger and frustration toward his father who is damaging his son physically, mentally, emotionally and now intellectually.

Other students recognized that, in trying to protect a child (care-based thinking), they might actually make matters worse rather than better. Here are two of these responses:

> I would keep an eye on the boy, and ask other adults do so as

well. If there were any signs of being abused, I'd take action immediately. I'm not sure if I would go to the home and speak to either of the parents or the neighbors, or notify a social worker to come and help. My concern is that the father in particular, and mother out of denial and fear, may get defensive and mad. Plus there's a chance they could punish or threaten the boy even more, thinking that he had told someone...I thought about sending home a good report to the father, but I fear that he will see his hitting his son as a successful means of changing his behavior, and I don't want him to continue this in the future.

Before the student would even have the opportunity to misbehave again, I would feel it necessary to contact social services to be certain that the child is safe in his home. This may end that particular problem if the child was removed from his home. However, if the boy's living conditions did not change I think I would have to search for a way to deal with the problem between the two of us. Perhaps a conference with him might help...Although I do not think keeping his behavior problems from his father would actually help his living situation in the long run as he will probably be hit many more times in the future, I feel it is important not to contribute any further excuses for his father to strike him. I have been educated against any form of domestic violence and, although many families believe in spanking, I think there is a very fine line between a spanking for punishment and beating a child. I am worried that his...behavior would not improve with only my actions alone and I am going back and forth as to how ethical it is to keep something hidden from the parents. However, I think I would be willing to try almost anything to keep him from being hurt again.

Like the student above, several others were so concerned that they were willing to initiate action that might eventually lead to removal of the child from his home. This student focused on caring for the child, yet was also considering rules:

I feel I would not be keeping that student safe [if] I witnessed the abuse and shrugged it off because that is how "some of these families are".... I think abuse happens in all kinds of families from very low to very high incomes. Would contacting the police be unethical? I might contact them anonymously if the school would not support my taking action to remove the boy from the home.

Other students, like this one, would support such action, based apparently on rule-based thinking:

Regardless of whether or not the child is disruptive in my class again ethically it would be my responsibility to contact social services and discuss the potential physical abuse of that child. This is in accordance with the very first Code of Ethics for Teachers in North Carolina: "Protects students from conditions within the educator's control that circumvent learning or are detrimental to the health and safety of students." If a student is being [abused] at home that will not only have an effect on his learning capability but also on his behavior.

While these students were concerned with the ethics of child abuse, others (and sometimes the same students) were able to look through the eyes of a parent as well. In some cases, this meant agreeing with the parent that physical discipline was appropriate. The following two students seemed to reach their conclusions through considering both rules and consequences for the rest of the class:

I think the key word here for me is, "hitting"; hitting is abuse and should be reported to the proper authorities. "Spanking" however is not illegal in any state that I know of. Part of acknowledging diverse views is respecting this parent's choice to discipline his child in the way he sees fit. Also by not automatically passing some sort of judgment just because it isn't the way you may handle the situation with your own children. In this situation I would first look to see if the father's choice of discipline was causing the child any detrimental harm, if it wasn't and there was no immediate danger, then I would look at whether or not this form of discipline was achieving the desired goal. Obviously not if the boy continues to act up. Allowing the boy to be disruptive is not an option because eventually, his behavior will unfairly affect the attention given to other students. I would call the boy's father in again, and tell him that what we've been doing isn't working and that we may want to consider some new options, other disciplinary tactics. The parent may or may not be responsive but I will have at least made every effort to give him alternatives.

The next student agreed, stating that she prioritized the directive to acknowledge:

"diverse views of students, parents and legal guardians as they work...to shape educational goals, policies, and decisions..." I grew up in a family where if I acted up in class my mother would spank me and I would not do it again. If the father beat the child in public then the child is obviously used to getting spanked and it is not like he is really abusing him. If the child were really being abused he would be terrified to act up in class because he would be afraid of what his father would do to him when he found out. So I would acknowledge the fact that that is the way father raises his child and even though I don't agree I can't let this kid disrespect me and act up in my class just because his father spanks him.

Other students, too, seemed to consider consequences, in terms of protecting the right of other children to learn in class. These students appeared to see the disruptive behavior of the child, rather than the behavior of the father, as the biggest problem, and thought that physical punishment would be an effective deterrent. Here is one example, from a student who brought up cultural differences and biblical injunctions:

I have been in a ton of situations similar to this one. Working at schools for lower income students, you see this sort of thing all the time. I have talked to a child so much that I had to bring the parent in; the parent spanked the child and the child hardly ever acted up again. Different families discipline their children in different ways. Being an African American, I grew up with spankings on a regular [basis] that is how a lot of us were disciplined and discipline our own. Other families of different backgrounds may just do time-outs or talk to their child. I know that just talking does not work for every child. If the child had gotten beat or was hit [inappropriately], I would have taken it to a higher power in charge, even higher than the supervisor. If the child just got spanked, like parents are supposed to do and are advised through biblical text, then I don't see the problem, other than doing it someplace private. Some times being…spanked is a great solution for a disruptive child, as long as it's not abuse. If the child [were] to act up in my class again, I would give him ample opportunity to [straighten] up before I ask him if he needed me to make another phone call to his parents. I would then decide what to do based on his reaction to my comment.

This student agreed, but proposed some parenting education as well:

If the student continues to act out in class, I would try to put the responsibility on the student and remind him that he has a choice…he can either follow my directions and participate in class without disturbing the other students, or he can choose to disrupt. I would make it very clear to him that if he does choose to disrupt the class, it will be his responsibility to call his father on the phone and explain his negative behavior. My thinking in handling the situation in this way is that parents have the right to know what their child's progress is in school. Many parents want to contribute to their child's education and want to assist the teacher whenever or however they can. In the event that parents believe in spanking as a form of discipline (which many do), I may set up a conference or a phone conference with that parent and find other ways for myself and the parent to reward their child in the classroom and at home for positive behavior. Hopefully the disruptive behavior will decrease or even be eliminated when the child realizes that the focus is on the positive.

A number of students also focused more on the disruptive behavior of the child, but did not support the parent's behavior; they wanted to understand the child and reward him for good behavior rather than punish him. The following is an example of this kind of response:

After seeing the child being beaten by his father, I realized that yelling and hitting will not solve his disruptive behavior in class. It's quite apparent that no matter how many times the child is reprimanded for his behavior, he continues to be very disruptive. Maybe yelling and hitting is not the answer. I am starting to think that maybe the child needs attention.... I would try to handle this situation differently by talking to him after class to see what the problem is instead of yelling at him. Another way I could solve this problem is to speak to the child and find out what his interest and hobbies are.... By speaking to this child about his hobbies and interests, I am showing that I care about something going on his life. Maybe he will open up to me and I can now explain to him what it means to show respect towards others. Hopefully he will learn to respect me as a person and will stop being disruptive. This method will definitely take time but I think…it better than yelling at him. I have seen this method done in the past by my dad. He often works with kids who are considered "the problem child" in society. He gets to know them and becomes role models to these children. I believe that children often act out because they are not receiving attention. By using this method, I saw my father drastically change lives. This may not work for every child. Also, there might not be enough time for me as a teacher to actually get to a have a one on one session with a student.

While this next student recognized that the child might need attention, she had a different approach; it appears that she was considering primarily the consequences, in terms of the child's behavior:

I would try not to give him as much attention as usual, because maybe that is why he is acting up, to get attention. This situation is hard because he is not a permanent student. I only get so much time to get to know him; it may not be enough time to solve the problem.

Two students wanted to build a relationship with the child, but thought that some form of punishment was still appropriate; they too were focusing on the child's misbehavior, rather than the parent's discipline, as the problem. Here is one of the similar responses:

If the kid disrupted my class again and I had already witnessed the father's actions of punishment, I would ask the child to wait for me after class so we can talk…I would ask the child to think of ways that he should be punished. By allowing the student to pick their own punishment, the process could be more effective. As the teacher, I would judge the student's decision and decide if the decision was appropriate in the situation. I would make sure that he understood fully how his actions could not continue to be a problem. My concerns for the child would depend in the severity of the hit. Some parents spank their kids and normally does not leave a [scar] or cause serious damage to the kid, but if the parent hits their kid with all the force they had then I would be [wary]. This in turn could lead to the issues of child abuse, which I would have to report to the right authorities.

A complex response in Round 1 came from this student, who considered both care and consequences:

The question is whether or not the parent's methods were effective. If the child was immediately disruptive then I would want to have a conference with the boy's father and an expert in discipline to discuss strategies and student history. Is the disruptive behavior new for the child or has it been a consistent pattern? If it was a consistent pattern perhaps we could agree to "catch" the boy being cooperative and report to the parent the number of cooperative incidents rather than disruptive incidents in order to increase desired behavior. Some people are disruptive because that is the only way they know to get attention. Talking with the parent might uncover a temporary situation that could be addressed with counseling or other means. I do not consider physical discipline in itself harmful to a child although current thinking may have research that proves otherwise. This is where an expert could provide accurate information to the father. Information he might be ignorant of and could change his choice of discipline. I think it is great that the parent is taking an active interest in the child and this should not be discouraged nor is it appropriate for me as the teacher to try to protect the child from parental discipline by failing to report misbehavior. It does raise the question of how much our society broadcasts "bad behavior" and ignores cooperation and consideration. If the parent's discipline was effective, long lasting and the child did not appear to suffer from child abuse I would tell the supervisor again if the child started to misbehave. I do worry that physical punishment teaches people many things such as "might is right" and I do not like the societies that have been based on that concept. I also know that there is a level of moral behavior that is only motivated by fear of punishment. Allowing the child to continue to be disruptive is not an option as it is not responsible to the rest of the children.

Round Two responses. The above student did not change her response to this particular scenario in the second round. There were two students who did not change their thinking about any of the scenarios as a result of reading responses from their peers. The students below also did not change anything in their thinking by reading the responses from their peers, relying on their "moral instincts based on personal experiences and convictions" (Freeman, 1998, p. 31); the second one also brought up the concept of "duty":

I think that I would try to talk to the student about the severity of the "beatings" and how frequently his father hits him. Sometimes, problems at home make a child act out in school. Maybe talking to the child about what's going on at home would help him to get his feelings out in a different way. Of course, if it seemed to be a very serious matter (from what the child told me) I would need to call child protective services. I know that people have an issue with people calling CPS [Child Protective Services] every time they discipline their children but no child deserves to be beaten.

I understand that certain families deal with discipline in different ways, but to me hitting in ANY sort of way is inappropriate and as a teacher it is my duty to watch out for my students' health and safety.

In general, however, reading the responses of their peers to this scenario, more than any of the others, enabled many students to expand their thinking, even if they would not change their action. Perhaps my reminder of the need to question their own thinking helped a few more students raise questions in this round. While most Round 1 responses recognized only one constituency (the child, the parent, or the rest of the children in class), by Round 2, many students began to expand their vision and raise some questions, often while reaffirming their original decision, as in these examples:

> After reading the other responses from my group I would try to include more positive reinforcement for this child and possibly meet with the parents to encourage that idea in their own home. However, I am not sure how ethical it is to keep a child's behavior secret from his family, especially after the father specifically asks you to let him know about the child's progress. In fact, I am fairly certain it is not ethical. I am not certain how to decide which is the more important idea to follow. My parents used to spank me and I don't feel it has had an overall negative impact on my life. Not all children spanked turn out to have major psychological problems, however, I have always known that I will not choose to spank my own children. I think this might be a gut feeling worth following, and so should also be applied to this situation, especially since I do not know how far the spanking goes. No matter what, despite the ethical dilemma of withholding information, I would do my best to keep the child out of harm from his father.

> I still think that I would try changing my style of discipline and try to be more positive with the child.... I found it interesting that some of my peers had no problem with the parent's style of discipline, although they seemed not to agree with what this teaches children. I would want to try my hardest to be a positive influence for the boy...there are better ways to teach...children the difference between good and bad. If the boy is [consistently] disruptive...this is a sure sign that he needs positive attention. It is also a sign that his home life does not provide the proper attention he needs.... It also tells me that the parent's style of discipline is not working. My only concern is that after the parent hit the boy, will the boy be responsive to my efforts of changing my approach to him? He may hold against me that I got him in trouble with his Dad. That is why I think it is important to talk to the boy...to try to let him know that I am on his side.

> I still feel the same way about handling this situation. (I would set up a meeting with this child...and discuss ways to deal with the situation as well as meet with the parents/father. I would want to find ways for the parent to reward/discipline his child at home without spanking if possible....) I liked the idea that another student said about trying to find out the child's interests or hobbies and sharing some things about myself.

I understand that this method [spending more time with the child] may not work. There is a possibility that this child may not want to spend time with me. I could also give this child more attention and he can still continue to be disruptive. I don't know the right answer to this situation but I do know that spanking this child is not solving the problem because he continues to do the same thing. I was reading someone else's idea about having a conference with the father, which I thought was a very good idea. It's apparent that the father cares about his son's behavior because he continuously comes to the school whenever we call. Maybe we could come up with something collectively to solve this problem...Maybe we can decide to take away something that he really cares about when he decides to be disruptive. I know whenever I was a child and I have done bad things, I couldn't watch television for a month or couldn't go outside and play.... Taking things away from him can back fire also. But I feel that as a teacher, it is my job to solve this problem to the best of my ability.

The greatest shift came from those students who began to question their initial assumption of child abuse:

When I read this scenario I assumed that the father actually hit the child with some sort of force.... I think I reacted based on the thought of child abuse. It didn't even register that some families believe in spanking, and because we don't know anything about the "hit" I guess it could have been a spank.... While I don't plan on spanking my children, I can't say that it makes someone a bad parent...because I'm going to tell my children that hitting is wrong, it would be hypocritical of me to spank them as punishment. The thought of violence bothers me a lot.

I stand by my opinion if the child is being abuse[d], however I do need to find out or distinguish between hitting and spanking before calling social services. Regardless of my personal views on discipline I have to respect the parenting styles and choices of others. One question I would have to answer for myself is, is this a one time event or is it more on going. Also, what kind of impact does it have on the child as a whole? My initial reaction would be to question whether the child [would] be more than happy to be taken out of his/her home. However children do not [necessarily] know it's in [their] best interests.

As the child's teacher, I would want to try and respect different cultural beliefs on forms of discipline, but I do not feel I would be able to be satisfied with seeing a parent use physical discipline...I understand some people believe in spanking their child, but how do you know the difference in spanking and abusing?.... I still believe I would try to punish the student myself, so that I know he is learning from his mistakes and not being abused because of them. I liked the idea of allowing the student to come up with his own form of discipline from the teacher.... Also, should you really consult the child about his father's actions? Wouldn't that make the student feel uncomfortable and embarrassed?

After reading her peers' responses, the next student began to rethink her initial assumption of child abuse, as well as the need to care for other students in the class by assuring them a positive learning environment. As a result, she began to identify possibilities other than simply reporting the father's actions to legal authorities:

A couple respectable points raised my awareness in this topic of child abuse. I assumed that the father was hitting his son with his own hands, humiliating his son in public, and breaking the boy's character because of disruptive behavior in class. I did not question the type of hit or take the time to categorize, which hits were abusive and which were disciplinary. I understand that parents choose how to punish their children and that it is hard, as an outsider, to interject when it is none of my business because I am not in the family to see how they do things. But then again, I think I am involved at this point because the student is disrupting my class and it takes my attention and energy from teaching the other students to put him in time outs. He is acting out for a reason. Is it because he wants help and his motive was for someone to see how he is treated at home? Is this "normal" in his daily life and he acts out for attention even if it is negative attention? If it is "normal" living with being hit, is it right to step in and change that because I see it as abusive behavior? I think ethically and morally it is my responsibility to bring attention to this parenting behavior. If my job is to teach and try to give the very best and safest learning experience to each student, then it seems to be my job to protect this student from his father's abuse, whether it is contacting the police or maybe other family members. My opinion stays the same to take action, but my methods might be less invasive or accusing, by being involved with the students' well-being first and foremost.

One of the most thoughtful Round 2 responses came from a student who revealed her struggle and questioning, as she attended to her own experience as a child and newer values coming from a religious conversion, drawing on care-based, rule-based, and ends-based thinking:

I originally thought that as long as the hitting was not abusive [then] it was the parent's right to [discipline] their child in the way they deemed appropriate. However, it occurs to me that some may consider any form of physical [discipline] abusive. Regardless of the [legality] of the issue. I've thought about the subject a lot. I have joined a faith different from that of my parents. My new faith prohibits ever [striking] a child. Though I have no particular opinion that spanking is [necessary] to raise unspoiled children, I also have never raised a child or dealt with the trials that that [entails]. I also, know that I was spanked as a child, out of a sincere, loving [belief] that it would help me become well adjusted. And in some ways I guess it did, it certainly made me afraid to misbehave, and a little afraid of my mother (I guess some would say that having your child fear you is a bad thing but I honestly don't know). Either way I don't think I'm worse off because I was spanked. My faith would recommend that I treat the situation as abuse, but my past personal experience would give a lot more leeway with the father. So I listen to neither, in particular. I would literally review whatever standard had been set for abuse and carefully determine if this man has crossed that line. If not, then I don't [hesitate] to call him in again if the child is disruptive. In this situation, there can't see a middle ground. I would rely on the standards because, suppose that I personally [believe] it's abuse, but it would not be deemed so by the appropriate [officials]. If I report it anyway, and nothing happens, I risk alienating the father, the child, and perhaps putting a stop to the child's [involvement] in the program for nothing.

Round Three responses. Many students chose to rethink only a couple of the scenarios for Round 3; most of them included this one about the father hitting his child. Based on this, I can assume that this dilemma was especially troubling to them. Many of the Round 3 responses were similar to those in Round 2, as students continued to expand their perspective on the situation to include other constituents, to include more of the three ways of thinking (rules, consequences, care), and to consider other possibilities for action that might have more possibilities and fewer limitations. This student raised many questions:

I discover that it's very difficult to consider every point of view in a possible scenario.... In scenario one if I had acted rashly and not consulted with my co-workers before calling social services my action could have cause emotional scarring for this child. Due to being [removed from] his house and [placed] in a foster home...I thought of one way I could deal with this situation...I would see if he has a favorite teacher and see if maybe they could spend some additional time together in which the student could talk about anything that was bothering him. Well...what if I was his favorite teacher? Should I still go about my plans and spend additional time with him or should I go about it another way? Or if I spend extra time with him would I get emotionally [too] close to him and should I step back from this?

Based on Kohlberg's stages of moral development, I would say my thinking process for the first part of the ethics assignment was at stage 5. Stage five is based on individual rights, and throughout my first paper for the ethics assignment, I focused on each individual's rights in the different scenarios.... For example, in scenario one, I did not agree that the behavior of the father was appropriate. When the principal said it was just how parents handle their children around here, I completely disagreed with him. Therefore, I said I would not take the child's punishments to higher authority anymore in fear that his father would have to be involved again. I would deal with the child's punishment myself and try to help him understand the consequences he faces because of his behavior. I would not contact his parents anymore; because I feel it is wrong for parents to hit their child, no matter how hard or soft.... Is this wrong to be concerned with the child's safety over punishing the child fairly? Also, would I need to treat every child in my class this way?

Concerning the first situation I realized I was thinking the worse. Maybe the father did not severely hit his child...I was raised not to be violent; I was never spanked or slapped, so when I witness such an act I am shocked. I do realize that not all people feel the way that I do. So one question I have is how do you know when to draw the line between abuse and discipline? How are you supposed to draw that line without letting your own personal beliefs get in the way?.... This is a situation, that as a teacher I would continue to pay close attention to...if I did begin to notice a change in the boy's attitude or begin to suspect child abuse I would go to some sort of superior. Who would be the appropriate person to go to for this sort of situation? I guess after looking at this scenario for the third time I would change some of my thinking strategies. I realized that maybe the worst is not always what is happening, and that maybe I need to take a closer look at situations. However, there are some things that I would not change. I still believe that any act of violence is morally wrong. I just need to find a way to distinguish between violence and discipline.

While students tended to write the longest responses to this scenario, and to struggle with it all the way through Round 3, some of the other dilemmas also provoked strong feelings and personal connections.

The Colleague and Her "Personal Trainer"

> One of your middle school students has told you that her brother, a high school athlete at a neighboring school, is helping the dance teacher at his high school by meeting her at 6am several days a week to serve as her "personal trainer." Your student thinks something more is going on and so do you—you have met this teacher, and she seems flirtatious and seductive. You have no other evidence. Should you stay quiet or say something? If you decide to say something, to whom will you say it? Describe your thinking that leads you to make this decision.

The guidelines from the Code of Ethics document were clearly connected to this scenario:

> *Maintain an appropriate relationship with students in all settings; do not encourage, solicit, or engage in a sexual or romantic relationship with students, nor touch a student in an inappropriate way for personal gratification, with intent to harm, or out of anger.*

> *Take action to remedy an observed violation of the Code of Ethics for North Carolina Educators and promote understanding of the principles of professional ethics.*

In presenting the analysis of student thinking about this scenario, I will depart from the pattern in the previous section, and report the data from individual students through each round of the assignment.[viii]

This scenario seemed to raise issues for many students, reflecting a question by Kidder: "When, in the face of a perceived injustice, do we speak up to correct obvious wrongs, and when do we remain silent to protect ourselves and others from abuse?" (1995, p. 65). There were only a few students who initially perceived an "obvious wrong" and indicated that they would report it to authorities. Just two of these made any reference to the welfare of the student; in both cases, legal requirements guided their thinking. One of them wrote,

> I absolutely say something. I would be liable for the young man's safety, if I...ignored misconduct, just the same as if I had committed the misbehavior myself. If the situation comes out and people find out that I looked the other way, I could lose my job and besides being detrimental to me, the school system and

the students would lose an otherwise responsible teacher. I tell my principal first, and on their [advice] I tell whoever the proper authorities are and [cooperate] fully with any investigation.... If nothing comes of the investigation then I drop the issue. The burden is not on me to prove or find out anything, I only report reasonable suspicion. [Round 1]

After Round 2, while not changing her mind about the appropriate course of action, this same student was able to articulate its problematic aspects:

I'm still [absolutely] convinced that I should report the situation [immediately] to the proper authorities. When thinking [about] the other teacher, I can sympathize with not wanting to [endanger] my career. And I might also be helping to create an environment where teachers feel uncomfortable dealing with students as anything other than students. I know personally, I have had female teachers take me out to dinner, take me plays and concerts, because they thought I would [benefit] from exposure to the arts, a male teacher with the same sincere intent may not have felt as comfortable and a [student] like myself might miss out. But inevitably, you have to go back to the standards and if they say report, regardless of personal feeling, I report.

A second student in the class echoed this approach in Round 1, finding some comfort in turning the situation over to the principal: "It is then in his/her hands and he/she can research the problem." This student indicated in Round 2 that she would "suggest to my student that she discuss her concerns with her parents so that they can also get involved." Even by Round 3, she affirmed,

If this was my son, I would want to know what was going on. A lot of personal training involves touching parts of the body...which could lead to sexual feelings. I feel it is inappropriate for a teacher and student to behave this way.

Two other students also thought they should report the situation. The next one raised issues other than the welfare of the young man, focusing on rule-based thinking in following the Code of Ethics:

What is that teacher thinking! Obviously she is not thinking. I would not hesitate to speak with a supervisor about this behavior. It seems ridiculous to "train" at 6 in the morning with a student.... This is common sense to me. I don't think proof of physical contact in a sexual way is needed to stop the activity. If this teacher were following the code of ethics, she would know this behavior is inappropriate and would have never met with the student. I would let my supervisor know immediately that other students have informed me of her behavior. If the students think that it seems strange, it probably is. [Round 1]

In Round 2, this same student disagreed with her peers; she held to her original decision and found additional reasons for it. I found evidence of ends-based thinking in her desire to do what she thought best for a larger population:

> If a student comes to me and has the sense of sexual behavior existing between a student and a teacher, then it is not gossiping or catty to investigate. The reputation of the student, the teacher, and the school is at risk. I would go straight to the top at that school to get the ball rolling...I would not be involved from then on, and I would hope the problem was confronted and resolved quickly. Is it ethical to not get involved when you know that the possibility of unprofessional behavior is happening? If this other teacher is a dance teacher, then she is representing all of us. I would not want this kind of behavior labeling me or my colleagues. If the situation turned to out to be false, then the teacher accused would be able to defend herself and the student. I think it is responsible to look out for your peers, but my focus is the students and what they see and think matters most. I don't think I would ever ignore this problem, so my opinion stays the same.

In Round 3, the student affirmed that she was using rule-based thinking, when she classified her thinking according to Kohlberg's six stages of moral development:

> I think I am responding at level 4 and level 5. "Emphasis on obeying laws..." and "what is right... has been agreed upon by society- code of ethics" respectively. Am I underestimating this teacher? Why would she put herself in this situation? It is illegal for teachers to be physically (sexually) involved with their students. Why would she need a student to train her? It seems sneaky and suspicious.

Another student who stated in Round 1 that she would report the situation to her principal indicated her misgivings in Round 3. She, too, was concerned about her reputation and that of other dance educators:

> In my high school we had a couple of teachers do things with students that are not ethical. Then once one student found out the

rest of the school would know. Then the teacher was either fired or the [principal] never found out. However the teacher was then frowned upon by the students. I almost feel like a tattletale for going to my higher up but it is in the best interest of the other teacher. She may not know that other people know and her career could be ruined. I do not know if I really would care so much but it kind of makes us other dance teachers look bad and I don't want to be blamed for something someone else did. Then again why do I want to help the other teacher out it's not my business what she is doing. Then again all of us dance teachers have to stick together because there is not a lot of us out there so we need to stand beside each other.

I was surprised to see how many students were clearly less focused on the student's welfare and more focused on the teacher's reputation and the dangers of spreading rumors; for them, ethical imperatives to respect the privacy of peers and avoid spreading rumors were higher than the ones in the Code of Ethics. To resolve this conflict with the Code, many found a persuasive reason to decide that the guidelines did not apply: Since they had not "observed" the unethical behavior (as stated in the Code of Ethics), they would feel more unethical reporting anything. The following Round 1 response reflects this point of view, as well as a desire to protect the writer's own reputation; she was demonstrating care for herself and her fellow teacher rather than care for the young man:

> There is no real evidence to what is being assumed. I have...been taught that you should not make assumptions about someone because it will only make you look bad. If I went and told someone about it and it wasn't true then it would make me lose [credibility] as a teacher. Until there was real evidence that I could back up...I would just leave it as gossip.

By Round 2, this student had found more reasons to support her reasoning, but also began raising questions:

> I still would not get involved with the rumor that my student told me. Maybe the kid became upset with her brother and was trying to get him back and didn't...realize how bad her accusations were. Maybe it is true and it does need to be stopped and dealt with. How do I assess the situation without causing problems with privacy of a student and another teacher.

Round 3 brought only another way to avoid taking any responsibility for the situation: "I still would not get involved. I would tell my student to talk to her parents about it and let them deal with the situation."

For the next student, the imperative to "stay out of others' business" was very strong; she would, in fact, try to teach this lesson to the sister who had originally confided in her:

> I am the type of person who tries to stay out of others personal business, especially if they have not spoken with me about things going on in their life. If I had no other evidence to expect the teacher was having intimate relation with one of her students besides a student telling me this and her flirtatious and seductive personality, I could not accuse her of any wrong doings. I would, however, be more aware of the situation brought to my attention, and if I caught any more evidence of the rumor to be true, I might be more comfortable about opening the issue to higher authority. As for the student in my class, I would explain to her that she should try to avoid talking about the matter, because she does not have any real evidence of the situation. I would also teach her to not get involved with others personal lives until she has full evidence. Then, she should bring up the issue to...me, and I would take it to higher authority. [Round 1]

In Round 2, she affirmed this position, disagreeing with her peers who would report the behavior because "I don't feel it is my place to explain to a grown up what is right and what is wrong." She did, however, question herself a little: "I guess my major question is where do you draw the line of staying out of others business and interfering with something that you know could be morally wrong?"

The next lengthy response reveals another student's disinclination to get involved, as well as her struggle with this stance; she seems to be considering rules, but also, to a certain extent, putting herself in the place of several of the "others" involved:

> I do not think you can assume they are fooling around just because a middle school student thinks so, and you know she has a flirtatious personality...There is a huge difference [between flirting with] grown men, and high school students. I would ask what it was that the boy had done or said to make his sister believe that. Because if he made a comment about how attractive this dance teacher is to a friend over the phone or something, I don't think that is reason to believe there is something going on. It's not unusual for a high school student to have a crush on a teacher. However, it is unusual and wrong for there to be a sexual relationship...until he expresses being uncomfortable by this situation, there are no grounds to accuse either one of them. Or, in the case that he is taking advantage of the dance teacher, there has to be substantial evidence of something he said...to

investigate. I think it would be a horrible mistake to accuse either of them because reputations can be ruined for good. If he has told his sister, or she has heard him say to a friend that he is uncomfortable then I would address the other dance teacher and question her intentions about this personal training. It's very possible that there are other people in the gym at this time, and nothing is in fact going on, which she could clarify. If not, she'll at least know that word got back to you and maybe she'll stop seeing the boy so that rumors do not get spread.... I would not go straight to the parents or the school system because that can cause a lot of drama, which would likely ruin or at least question both of their reputations. I would tell the sister not to talk to any of her friends at school about it because it's not something that should be made public amongst middle school kids. She doesn't want to be responsible for starting a rumor that isn't true about her own brother.... This is not to say that I do not believe her and am not concerned. I think I would speak to the dance teacher before I would speak with anyone else, because I hesitate to get directly involved because I don't want to be responsible for any part of this. I myself wouldn't go straight to the parents, unless I was sure that there was something fishy about all of this...and create a huge mess for the boy, teacher, school district, and community. Something similar to this happened at my high school, and while I believe something could have been said on one occasion, both the student and teacher agreed that no harassment or inappropriate behavior occurred but that didn't stop the rumors from flying. [Round 1]

The same student in Round 2 brought up other interpretations of the situation, but still affirmed her desire to stay "out of it":

The more I thought about it, it's very likely that the middle school student could misinterpret or misunderstand something she heard. At first I assumed she heard it from her brother but how do we know she didn't hear it from another kid.... Also, as said in one of the responses, I never considered that the high school student could be making it up. I'm trying to picture the situation. If his buddies were teasing him and they were all fooling around, something they may have said jokingly could have been misinterpreted by the sister or another witness. While all this is very true, I wouldn't ignore my student's concern because there is always a possibility that something seriously wrong could be occurring. As much as I want not to involve myself, I would feel so horrible if anything came of it and I hadn't listened to my student.... It's not that I don't think it can occur, but I have a tendency to defend people in situations where they look bad.... I didn't think about speaking with the high school guidance counselor. That would keep me out of it, and place it in someone else's hands.

Her Round 3 thinking brings up the "golden rule" that is the basis of care-based thinking; she wanted to treat the teacher as she wanted to be treated: "In the teacher/student affair scenario, I was thinking in stage two. I didn't want to jump to any conclusions, because I don't want others to jump to conclusions about me."

In contrast, the transformation between Rounds 1 and 2 for the following student was notable. In Round 1, she was thinking in a way that revealed caring for the teacher:

> I think every attempt should be made to gather evidence before mentioning the situation to anyone. I initially thought of going to the principal of my school, however, even if proven innocent, such allegations of sexual misconduct would ruin a teacher's career. I know this from watching it happen in my own high school. I would speak with the high school teacher to find out about this student as a physical trainer to see if I could get some sessions with him or work with the two of them to see her reaction and see what their working relationship is like. Unless there is any concrete evidence I think the only complaint that could be filed would be that I find this teacher to be overly flirtatious and sexual with her students in general. I think I would make this complaint to the principal of my school, leaving it up to him or her to contact the principal of the other school...going straight to the principal of the other school seems very attacking and, without evidence, out of line.

In Round 2, she referred to the class discussion, in which I had pointed out that most students were expressing concern for the teacher's welfare, but not the student's. She continued, revealing how troubled she was about this dilemma:

> I think [Sue] is absolutely right and I cannot believe this is true. While in high school, I had a teacher who continuously behaved inappropriately with me. Although his advances were not desired, I never reported him out of fear of what would happen to me and what my peers and parents would think of me. However, had someone else taken the initiative to find out what was going on I would have gladly cooperated. It was a matter of someone else saying something first. It is possible that this student feels the same way. It seems from this description that he is willingly involved in whatever may or may not be happening so he may not cooperate in any investigations. Thinking about all this, for days now actually, I still don't know if I should say anything without evidence. False accusations could ruin both the

teacher and the student. But if I wait to get evidence, is it worth the risk that the student is continuing to be harmed? I think the best possible solution that I have come up with in the past few days is to suggest the girl express her feelings to her parents and speak with my principal. I would simply tell him or her that I had a student who seemed deeply concerned about the situation, that I had no evidence to think she was either right or wrong, but I felt it appropriate to pass on her concerns to be dealt with as the principal wished. Then...I would look into the situation myself with discretion.

It was surprising to me that the student above had not drawn on her previous experience receiving the unwanted advances of a teacher until this point. This made me wonder if she and other students might have responded differently if the teacher in the scenario had been male and the student trainer a female. Perhaps students just assumed that a male high school student was not likely to get into a sexual situation with a female teacher if he did not want to be there. I wish that I had thought to bring up this consideration during discussion.

The following student revealed consequences-based thinking as defined by Kidder, justifying her decision based on causing the least harm (if not the greatest good) for the largest number of people, and seeking a "third way," that is, investigating or stopping the behavior without making an accusation, a decision she reaffirmed in Round 2 after this initial statement in Round 1:

I would not take immediate action on this situation. I feel as though there is a lot of material I am unsure of, and...it is unfair to make a judgment before I am positive about what is going on. I could ruin the teacher's career as well as the lives of the student and his family. I would not ignore this accusation because there could very well be something happening between the student and teacher that needs to be stopped. Perhaps I would ask the high school teacher if it would be alright for me to come in a work out with the both of them one morning. I would say it in a non-accusing way so that she does not get offensive or think I am accusing her of something.

Speaking to the teacher was chosen as an appropriate action by several students, including this one, who considered more options and raised some questions during subsequent rounds:

[Round 1] I will absolutely tell someone but it will be in the form of confronting that teacher personally. Basically recommend to her that she should find another personal trainer and try to avoid situations that could be misread. I will go and tell her if it continues that I will speak to her supervisor on the matter.

[Round 2] I would consider approaching the teacher in a more subtle [way] so it would not come across as being an accusation. If the teacher has nothing to hide then she will not behave in secretive manner. However, if she appears anxious then this may indicate that there really is foul play occurring between the teacher and young man. This maybe a little deceptive however, I think sneakiness would be essential [in] uncovering the truth.

[Round 3] I originally decided to confront the teacher and recommend to her that she...find another personal trainer. Well what if the student told me a lie about the teacher because she didn't like her? Then I would be embarrassing myself confronting the teacher. What if I couldn't tell which one was lying to me and giving me false information? How would I go about the situation then? Should I pretend the student didn't tell me and ignore what happen? Should I investigate some information about the teacher before confronting her? Should I go and work out with her and the "personal trainer" to see for myself if anything is strange going on between the student and her?

Most other students raised the same issue (concern about spreading rumors and damaging reputations) and solutions (speak to the teacher, ask the sister to tell her parents, or, with misgivings, report the tale to the principal or another school professional as a rumor that needed to be investigated). I was surprised by the number of students who thought that it was acceptable for a teacher to have a personal training relationship with a student at her school, as long as they were not having sexual relations.

At the same time, this was a scenario that generated a lot of thought, especially by Round 3. This student whose Round 1 and 2 responses emphasized asking for advice from others, especially the school counselor, reveals a great deal of questioning in her third round, mostly reflecting concern for her own reputation and welfare:

First of all, why would a dance teacher need to have a student for a personal trainer? Would not a professional be a better option for her? These questions seem to make it clear to me that the relationship is taking place. This would give me reasonable suspicion of her. My other question is how would it affect my reputation as a teacher if I were to "tattle" on her? It would be hard to handle it professionally. I think going to the counselor first is still a good plan. The other thing is if my student is telling me this, rumors will likely be going around. Eventually the relationship may come out into the open without my doing anything. In the end, if I did not speak up, could I be criminalized for keeping it under wraps? This makes it seem like a lose/lose situation, maybe I would be better off not saying anything at all. Maybe I should tell my student that it is really none of my business and direct her to the counseling office if she feels someone needs to know. Would this make me seem uncaring? I think not, if put to my student in the correct manner. I could end up being the good guy for directing her to someone who would be more capable of helping than I. Now, when I think about it I feel that trying to get too involved with the situation would be out of my jurisdiction and would create too much unneeded drama for myself.

One student, who had considered every possibility in Rounds 1 and 2, was able to reflect on her own thinking and what was underlying it in her Round 3 response. While many of the other students were especially concerned about their own reputation as a gossip or tattle-tale, and the reputation of dance teachers in general, she indicated that her decision to talk to the other teacher (rather than do nothing or report the situation to a higher authority) was based on solving what she saw as "the following problems inherent in the scenario":

1. Protecting a fellow teacher
2. Protecting the school system
3. Protecting other children
4. Follow the code of ethics and rules agreed on by our society.

I think I am operating in level five [Kohlberg] as I am motivated by what is good for society as a whole. In talking to the teacher I am trying to treat others the way I would like to be treated.

Summary of Responses to Remaining Dilemmas

I selected these two scenarios to discuss in more depth because they were the most successful in facilitating the kind of thinking that I had hoped for. Next I will briefly summarize the responses to the remaining scenarios, with the exception of the one labeled E in the assignment.[IX] The remaining three scenarios seemed to be less successful as ethical *dilemmas*, as this is defined by Kidder (1995).

The Father's Offer

The Code directs educators to:
Evaluate students and assign grades based upon the student's

demonstrated competencies and performance.

Refuse to accept significant gifts, favors, or additional compensation that might influence or appear to influence professional decisions or actions.

This is a situation that does not exactly fit the ethical principles above, but is related:

> You have been hoping for years to take your advanced dance students to an international dance festival. It will be expensive, and some of your students have told you that they cannot afford to go. The parent of one of your wealthier students offers to provide scholarships for all students needing assistance if his daughter gets the solo role in the piece you will show at the festival. She is a good dancer, but not the best for the role. The student you want to cast is one of those who need financial assistance. Should you accept the father's offer? Describe your thinking that leads you to make this decision.

I realized when I read Round 1 responses that students perceived the situation as a right-versus-wrong situation. Not unsurprisingly, every one of the students in the first round indicated that they would reject the father's offer, because they would see it as a bribe (the second guideline quoted in the scenario above). Some expressed outrage at the offer. Some also brought up the first guideline that was quoted, and did not want the father's daughter to learn that she could win rewards based on anything other than merit. Some expressed concern for the young person who was best suited for a solo role, and wanted her to receive the reward she deserved, while others thought that solos were inappropriate in a high school setting. Some were concerned about making some parents feel bad if they found out that another parent had funded their child's participation. They were very determined to act as a model of integrity.

I wish I had included a statement that "You have tried every fundraising opportunity, and have raised some of the money, but it is not close to enough, and there is no time to raise more." Without this limitation, students saw an easy "third way" to avoid accepting the offer or disappointing their student dancers: Hold fundraisers in the community so the participants could earn the funds they needed. Only one student substantially questioned herself in Round 1, indicating that she would:

> not be attached to my choice of who dances a particular part because that sounds like I am trying to build my ego by trying to make "my" dance look as good as possible for personal gain. I

would need to examine the value of the international festival for myself and my students. Who benefits and why?

Since peer response did not bring up diverse perspectives, I offered more in class, raising issues that I thought complicated this scenario. I pointed out that the father was not offering the money to the teacher for her own use, but to benefit all of the students; I asked if it was still a "bribe." I also brought up the principle of "the greatest good for the greatest number," which I had expected might complicate their thinking. Students still rejected accepting the father's money, although several looked for still another "third way," especially creating a work without a solo and trying to convince the father to fund the trip even without his daughter getting a solo role. One suggested telling the father that auditions for the solo would be held to determine the best-qualified student.

By Round 3, few students even bothered to mention this scenario, much less question their thinking about it. One who did wrote,

> In scenario two maybe I shouldn't [have] refused the father's offer because it could help other students out to go on the trip. I could try to talk to the father into donating the money to help other students go on the trip, but it wouldn't guarantee his daughter the solo part. What if the father doesn't accept this offer I give him? I guess it wouldn't be fair if I don't give him something in return. Is there anything I could offer him except his daughter getting the solo part? Would it be [ethical] to offer the father something in return for him donating money?

The following student maintained her position in Round 3, but recognized what was problematic about it:

> What I said about not taking the bribe still goes. If fundraising is not possible. Then: No one goes if I feel that the opportunity would have given unfair advantage in my class to the students who would have attended. Only the children who can afford it go, if it's deemed as an extra-curricular activity. Both of these are [problematic] the first because even if it's not fair, wouldn't if be better for some children to have the experience than to be held back by those who could not afford it. The second solution is [problematic] because now you've taken the lower income children out of the mix and the daughter of the man with the bribe might be the best for the solo. She might get it anyway and so now the girl who should have gotten the solo is not only passed over for the solo, but so won't even get to go. Again nothing is perfect, in fact both solutions suck. This sounds weird but sometimes being fair, just isn't fair.

The Young Mother and the Test

> One of the students in your high school class tries very hard, but is struggling with some very difficult personal situations. She is a single mom of an infant and has some serious chronic health problems. She has returned to school to try to graduate. She has minimal assistance from her family. You have given a written exam in the class; few did really well on it, but she is the only student who failed it. When you asked her if she had studied, she said that she had, but her baby was up most of the night before the class. Should you offer to let her retake either the test, or a different version of it? If so, should you put any conditions on it (i.e., should you deduct points from her final score because she is getting another chance?) Should you extend this offer to all students? Describe your thinking that leads you to make this decision.

I thought this scenario was connected to these guidelines:

Acknowledge the worth and dignity of every person and demonstrate the pursuit of truth and devotion to excellence.

Strive to maintain the respect and confidence of... students...

Protect students from conditions within the educator's control that circumvent learning

I was still uncertain about my own response to a similar situation, in which I had gone through all of the same internal arguments that my students raised about fairness to the student as well as fairness to the rest of the class. Unlike them, I had framed my own argument in terms in the tension between equity and equality (is *equal* treatment always *fair*?).

To many of these students, the greater ethical issue was not what to do about one student who failed, but what to do about the poor performance (more about this later) of all students. Half of them took responsibility for the performance of the students and most proposed a retest for all students and/or an opportunity for additional credit. The following responses were typical of Round 1:

> I think that out of compassion this student should be given a chance to bring up her grade. Knowing her circumstances and how easy it would be for her to give up completely, I think giving her any help I could, would be the right thing to do. However, she has to learn that not everyone is going to be willing to give her a break and so I would not completely ignore

the first test, but average that score with the new score on a different test. I also think that it is not ever a good idea to play favorites even if that is not the intention. I could assume that if the other students who did poorly stayed up late by choice or simply did not put forth any effort, but until one knows everything there is to know about their home situations I cannot assume such a thing. They could have special circumstances as well that I am not aware of. I debated over this because if there was a special circumstance behind a bad grade, more than likely the students would tell the teacher to try and help their grade. However, if a student was embarrassed of the reason they did poorly (such as their drunk parents fighting all night, etc.) he or she might not say anything. Every student should be given the opportunity that this student is given.

My ideas of tests are not for my benefit to see who passed and who failed, who knew the material and who didn't. I feel tests are for the students to engage their knowledge on things discussed in class and try to take the important concepts from class with them. If most of my students did not do well on the test I had given, I would offer a retest on the material so the students and I could make sure the information in class was taught and learned...The student who failed...would have a chance to bring her grade up to passing. I do not feel that tests should be the biggest part of a student's grade in a class. Participation and obvious gaining of knowledge on the subject being taught should be most important; therefore, my tests would not be that strict.

I wondered how much students' responses might have been related to my own actions earlier in the semester: With a previous assignment in this course, I had publicly taken responsibility for not having worded it clearly, and adjusted the grading criteria accordingly. Because of this, the grades were actually higher than for any other assignment. At the time, I also told students that they would face similar issues as teachers in creating new assignments, that sometimes they would realize that an assignment was problematic, and I hoped they would take the same kind of action I was taking to be sure that students were not penalized. I also spoke with them about my own position of wanting to facilitate learning, rather than punishing students for not learning, and I made available opportunities for additional credit to encourage this. Although no one mentioned it, I wondered if students were following my lead in their answers to this question.

Some students also struggled with the conflict between teaching young people about compassion and about responsibility, as was the case with these two students:

Telling the student that she can retake the test is saying that it's okay to not study for a test because you can always make it up. She will feel that whenever she misses a deadline on an assignment or fail another test, it's okay because she knows I will give her an extension. I can remember times when I was in high school and I would often refer to certain teachers as the "the one I can get over on". I don't want her to feel like she can get over on me. Is it my problem to care about whether or not she has a child at home? After all, everyone has problems day to day but we still have the responsibility to complete work on time as well as learn how to prioritize our lives. It also bothers me that she will wait to the last minute to study for an exam when I am quite sure that she knew ahead of time when the exam was. If I tell her no she can't take the test over, will I be looked at as a teacher with no compassion?

I will...explain to the students that I really care about how well everyone does on these exams. But this will be the only time I allow them to retake another exam. I will explain to them the importance of time management and that they don't always get second chances in life. I can talk about the importance of deadlines and meeting certain criteria explaining to them that when they get a job in the future, their boss doesn't care about their personal issues when it comes to taking on a big responsibility at work. They have to learn to prioritize.

In Round 2, after reading responses from their peers (and, in many cases, speaking with others), more questions were generated by a few of the students, including this one:

It was brought up in the responses that if I give this student another chance she would come to expect second chances in life. I don't know if this is true. Life is going to be very difficult for this student. By giving her the option of a second test am I feeding an illusion that it will be easy and she can always try again? I think this might be true, but also, doesn't the fact that she is a teenage mother show that she is probably aware of her lack of second chances? Knowing how hard her life is going to be, I still think it is best to offer a brief moment of kindness and compassion. Maybe when times are rough she will be able to look on my kindness and push through. Maybe she will one day offer kindness to someone else. Maybe the other students will also learn a lesson in compassion, a lesson many kids do not learn.

Before Round 2, I tried to help students problematize this situation, by asking them if they thought it was always the teacher's fault if students did not do well. The next student responded to that idea; she may also have been indicating how she felt about the extra credit opportunities I had made available in the course:

> How did I forget about extra credit? ... I think that's because I feel as though offering extra credit (and not giving another test) is saying that I am ok with the results from the last test and there's no reason to address the poor grades to the class. It's not always going to be the teacher's fault for the entire class doing poorly, but that is what I had in mind when I read this scenario. With that in mind, I feel as though blowing off the test is like not admitting that you may not have taught it well and punishing the class by keeping the low-test grades. Providing extra credit after they have already spent time studying is nothing more than making them do more work for only a few lousy points when they are already discouraged.... I feel it is the teacher's responsibility to clarify the material that everyone missed.... It's very frustrating having to guess what material the teacher will be testing and not knowing exactly how demanding the questions will be.

In a further attempt to help students question their own thinking, I suggested before Round 2 that they might consider how much time it would take to create and grade a new exam or assignment; what if they, too, had a child? Before Round 3, in my presentation of Gilligan's stages of moral development, I related this situation to the stage of caring for oneself; I shared my own dilemma when caring for my students means spending so much time on them that there is little left for caring for myself, and I pointed out that this, too, is a moral issue. Only one student responded to this perspective, and only in Round 2:

> As a teacher, this might add more work to an already full load, but the students will benefit from rereading and rewriting the material.... I had other things happening, maybe the students would remember to stay flexible for me if I didn't get grades back at a certain time.... You raised some interesting points about how re-designing the test and work would effect my time, but I think if I have learned anything in this class...it is to remain FLEXIBLE!!! My opinion hasn't changed, but the reality of the possible hassle the extra work could be on my life opens my eyes to how hard it is to remain that flexible without getting walked on.

I realized after reading Rounds 1 and 2 combined that almost two-thirds of the students in the class had made some statement about most students doing poorly on the exam. I went back to the scenario and reread the wording, which stated only that no student had done "really well." In class, I suggested that no student doing really well might mean only that no student had earned an *A*, but many might have earned a *B* or *C*. I further suggested that students might consider why they had interpreted the scenario this way, and what, if anything, this might indicate about their own interpretation of grades. No student really responded to this issue in the third round.

The Colleague Dominating Discussion

> The dance teachers in your district are developing a new curriculum. One of the teachers, not the chair of the group, seems to monopolize the conversation, and this teacher is steering the process in a direction that you do not agree with. Every time you speak up about an alternative, this teacher engages in verbal put-down that makes you feel silenced. Other teachers have stopped trying to say much. What should you do? Describe your thinking that leads you to make this decision.

I would not have thought of this kind of situation as an ethical dilemma except for these guidelines for North Carolina educators:

> *Acknowledge the diverse views of...colleagues as they work collaboratively to shape educational goals, policies, and decisions...*

> *Participate actively in professional decision-making processes and supports the expression of professional opinions and judgments by colleagues in decision-making processes...*

Even more than the other dilemmas, student responses to this one seemed to focus on practical solutions rather than ethical considerations. One of the students even wrote, "I honestly don't see the ethics dilemma in this one as I do the others." However, it was the kind of situation all students had experienced, and most of them found it frustrating to have one person "take over" what was supposed to be a shared task.

The primary evidence of ethical thinking I could find was in their desire to treat even the "difficult" colleague respectfully. One of the most common responses was to suggest talking with the colleague outside of the meeting, trying to reason with her or him. A few acknowledged that the individual might not be responsive, or that an argument might ensue, and several indicated that they preferred to avoid verbal confrontations.

Another response chosen by many of the students was to go to the chair of the committee and, if that person would not take action, to go to a higher authority. Several thought it would be helpful to make this a collaborative effort with others on the committee, while others did not like this idea. As one student stated in Round 2, "Despite needing the support of the other group members, I wouldn't want to come off as a gossip."

The third most common response was to take responsibility to stand one's ground and not be silenced. The following student, in Round 2, managed to include all of the responses above, and indicated that she was willing to question her own motives:

> I would have to get over my feelings of being silenced and speak out after talking to some of the other teachers to determine if my observations were accurate or I had a position bias that was coloring my views of the other teacher's behavior. After searching my motives and getting confirmation from others, my first approach would be to confront the other teacher directly by inviting her out for tea and letting her know in private how I felt and what she was doing specifically that caused it. If she continued to do it, I would talk to the chair of the meeting privately and express my concern. If the chair didn't take any action I would bring the issue up in the meeting before she was abusive again and determine what the group believed the appropriate rules of behavior were and whether or not it included personal put downs. This would then give me the support of the group to challenge verbal put-downs if they later occurred. If the group continued to sanction verbally abusive behavior I would resign from the group and depending on how important the groups decision-making was to things I care about I would escalate the behavior of the group up the chain of command asking that the chair be replaced. I hold the group and the chair of the group responsible for the standards of behavior in the group and I see my self-responsible as a group member to create an atmosphere conducive to work. I always like to talk to people individually first because I assume people are well meaning but ignorant including myself. I do not have all the answers. What is important is that the group process be safe enough to include everyone's thoughts.

There were several other suggestions for how to solve what was viewed as a practical, rather than an ethical, dilemma. These included an idea box (so that all ideas could be put forth even if teachers did not feel able to speak during meetings), forgoing the committee and instead giving everyone a task they could work on independently, or developing a plan that would mandate equal speaking time. One student even suggested that she would "kill this teacher with kindness," as a way of breaking down the problematic behavior, adding, "Though she is rude to everyone, I would speak to her with the utmost respect, all while doing my research and making sure my suggestions [were] positive, helpful and significant to the curriculum and the conversation."

Discussion

At the conclusion of an analysis, any researcher must ask themselves the "So what?" question. Since the goal of action research is pedagogical knowledge, I have to ask myself what I learned from my first experience of formally teaching ethics to undergraduate students in dance education. I will discuss practical considerations and ideas for revision of this unit, and also reflect on some of the bigger issues that arose for me, ones for which I do not have clear solutions.

On Problematizing—Seeking Questions or Answers

During the first discussion in class, when I became aware that most students seemed to want most of all to find the "right answer," and I continued to tell them that there was not one, I wondered if I was simply confusing the students by having them consider situations which clearly could not be solved just by applying the Code. If I had just wanted to get them to read and understand the Code, wouldn't it have been better to come up with right versus wrong situations which could clearly be solved by applying one or more of the Code guidelines? Was I just teaching them to discount the Code by bringing up situations, which raised more questions than they answered?

Further, even when their responses indicated that all of my students would have made what I also considered an ethical decision (in the scenario about the father's offer), why was I disappointed? Why did I want them to question a decision, which even I agreed was ethically sound? Considering these questions brought me to the realization that I aspired to more than just having my students follow the rules in the Code. While I needed them to understand the Code of Ethics to fulfill licensure requirements, I wanted them to go further. I wanted them to think about complexities, not just look for the right answer. I wanted them to look at a situation through the perspectives of all the constituents. I wanted them to question deeply their own thinking, not just to defend it.

For these teacher education students who need to learn to think ethically, isn't this a precarious position? Why do I think questioning oneself, and entertaining the possibility that one might not be right, or the possibility that there might be more than one "right," better than just learning to follow the rules, even when the rules are ethical ones? I realized that I want my students to recognize that sometimes the rules may be wrong, and sometimes the only moral response is to disobey authorities, despite the consequences. Indeed, some students came to this realization during a class discussion, with the recognition that the Code was written by people like themselves, people who had no more direct access to the truth than they did. When a student asked if they could lose their job over disobeying an immoral order, I told them that I hoped each of them could think of some rule or law they would feel so strongly about that they would rather lose their job than obey it.

And yet I recognized that my scenarios were sending "mixed messages" to the students. By setting the scenarios up against the Code of Ethics, I was implying that the solution to the problem was simply to follow the Code. This led some students to attempt a rule-based decision. By requiring that they then problematize their decisions, I was implying that following the Code was not the answer. However, without going any further, students might have perceived that it doesn't matter which solution one chooses, since all are problematic. By not telling students which decisions I would have made (no one asked), and by telling them that there were no clear right answers, I was perhaps encouraging a relativist position, which I regret. In some ways, I wondered if I could be guilty of teaching students that ethics is little more than an engaging intellectual activity. Kidder warns that ethics is:

> not mere analysis. It doesn't come from woolying around with apparently insoluble dilemmas or arguing endlessly and inconclusively over case studies. Unfortunately, some ethics training these days does just that. It leaves ethics in the realm of analysis—no conclusions, no resolutions, no ways forward, just a lot of fun talk. (1995, pp. 59-60)

I hope that, when I teach this material the next time, I can stay even further away from relativism. However, I never got the idea that students considered this assignment simply a matter of "fun talk." To the contrary, they seemed deeply engaged in a struggle to figure out what to do in situations they realized they might face some day. It was clear to me that the students took the assignment seriously, both inside and outside class; it was not "just a lot of fun talk." Despite some very vocal complaints about the workload in the course earlier in the semester, most students wrote far more than I had anticipated and suggested. One student who had complained the most wrote the most—13 single-spaced pages. I heard their struggles in their words. The assignment became something that engaged them beyond the requirements of the class, as they discussed the dilemmas with friends and family.

44 Susan W. Stinson

In addition to my concern about relativism, I recognize another limitation to my value of questioning: it can lead to paralysis, or the inability to make any decision. One student asked me at one point one decides to stop questioning and make a decision. I affirmed that we as teachers do need to make decisions, and we must often do so even when we are not certain that our decision is the right one or the only right one. Rather than stop questioning, however, I prefer to make decisions with the consciousness that I indeed might not be right, that I may think about it more and make a different decision next time. This, of course, is an uncomfortable place to be; certainty feels so much more secure.

Despite this discomfort, asking difficult questions of myself about my own thinking, making myself highly uncomfortable in the process, has always been the most generative path to growth for me (see Stinson, 2001), so it is logical that I wanted my students to engage in this activity as well. I had initially thought that my one carefully crafted example about how to question their own thinking would be sufficient to trigger their own questioning, especially since I had been coaching them on finding good questions in previous assignments, and had repeatedly told them that finding one's own questions would be a key to ongoing professional development once they graduated. Because this assignment was being graded, students had substantial incentive to engage in questioning, and they all got better at it by the final round of the assignment. Despite my distaste for assigning grades, I am convinced that this motivated some students to raise questions, and wish that I had asked them to evaluate the effectiveness of the grading criteria. However, I wondered if some students just tried to come up with anything that ended in a question mark, rather than allowing the questions to really trouble their thinking. I knew that, the next time I taught this material, I didn't want them to ask questions just for the sake of questioning; instead, I wanted to provide a foundation which could help them see its value as well as get better at it.

On Finding a "Third Way"

I was initially slightly frustrated that some of my students seemed to be looking for solutions that did not require them to make tough choices; this happened especially in the scenario about the father's offer. I wanted them to have the courage to take a stand even when a decision was simply the least bad of two problematic alternatives. At first, I thought I should have created dilemmas that did not allow an easy option to avoid a difficult decision. I eventually realized my *own* tendency to seek desperately for what Kidder calls a "third way" to resolve a dilemma. Kidder writes that:

sometimes that middle ground will be the result of a compromise between the two rights, partaking of each side's expansiveness and surrendering a little of each side's rigidity. Sometimes, however, it will be an unforeseen and highly creative course of action that comes to light as the heat of the struggle for resolution. (p. 185-186)

While I could be critical when my students seemed to want to find a solution that would avoid their having to make a difficult choice, I could be similarly critical of myself. It was somehow a comfort that Kidder identified such a course as revealing creativity rather than a lack of courage. However, I am going to make the "father's offer" more challenging the next time, and will try to promote discussion of both creativity (in finding solutions that avoid problematic decisions) and courage to make difficult decisions when necessary.

Activities Most Effective from the Students' Perspective

I invited students to rank the significance of several aspects of the assignment, in terms of the value to their thinking. Because they had mentioned talking with family and friends, I added this activity to the list of five others: the process of writing, reading the Code of Ethics, reading responses from a small group of peers, my comments during class discussion, and learning about stages of moral development (Kohlberg and Gilligan). Only nine of the 16 students ranked the activities. Because it was both possible and relevant to objectively gauge how students valued these activities, I did so, finding that the activities considered most valuable were writing their answers, talking with friends and family, and the instructor's comments during class.[x] Their judgments confirmed for me the value of having students write their answers, as opposed to just discussing them in class, and I was pleased that students recognized that writing often generates more reflectivity. The high value attached to "talking with friends and family" was a special pleasure. While I had not thought of it ahead of time, I gave an immediate positive response when a student first asked if this were okay. Next time, I will encourage it from the beginning, and will also use this opportunity to discuss when seeking assistance from others should be considered "cheating" and when it should not: another opportunity to discuss ethics.

While three students indicated they would have liked more class discussion, I was quite aware that there were some students who almost never spoke in class, but they could not similarly "hide" their ideas in this assignment. I have previously noted that I had considered online discussion to become part of the process, but decided against it. I had been concerned that there is no way to guarantee anonymity in online discussions, using the Blackboard technology that is available at my institution.[xi] Students in this course were in many other classes together, and would be in future classes together. There were clear cliques among the student population, and some were perceived to have greater status (often based on their performing skill). While I thought that asynchronous online discussion would help develop student thinking, and I found persuasive the argument that professionals have to be able to defend their decisions in discussion with peers and superiors, I came down on the side of encouraging responses that were honest rather than ones that might be viewed more favorably by their peers. However, I will try online discussion next time, and will evaluate the outcomes.

As I have previously indicated, I concluded that most students did not learn enough from a 45–minute discussion of Kohlberg and Gilligan to be able to classify their own responses. Of the 16 students whose responses I analyzed, only eight mentioned anything at all that arose from the discussion and only five attempted to classify their own thinking, with mixed success. Yet I want to expose students to theoretical perspectives on ethics, not just situations and conflicts, and I want to facilitate their intellectual development as well as their ethical development; because Kohlberg's and Gilligan's frameworks are based on a model of cognitive development, I had thought that they might facilitate such development. However, my brief presentation and discussion did not do them justice. I will discuss below an alternative for the next time I teach this material.

In response to my request for other ways to teach the material that they would have found helpful, two students suggested role-playing the scenarios, and two suggested a debate; while these might have been engaging activities, I am not sure that they would have led to the same depth as reflective writing. Two students thought that it would be helpful to talk with current dance educators about ethical decisions they have faced; I will incorporate this suggestion into a later course.

On Effective Outcomes

In an earlier presentation of this project to colleagues, one asked how I knew whether or not this assignment would affect my students' decision making as future professionals. Such a study as this one cannot provide any such evidence. I can look, however, at two other pedagogical experiences for clues since, prior to this assignment, I gave a related one in two other courses.

With a different undergraduate course (further along in the dance education sequence), I simply asked students to read the Code of Ethics and reflect upon which guideline they thought they would find most challenging to follow, and why. Almost all students picked the guideline about evaluating students and assigning grades; their concerns were practical, not ethical ones, when they discussed the difficulty in figuring out how to be fair and objective in grading student work in dance. This made me realize that students will not necessarily foreground ethical dimensions of decisions unless these are called to their attention.

In a graduate dance education course, where there had been a great deal of emphasis on questioning one's own thinking, I gave the assignment online during a week I was unavailable for class. I asked students to read each other's responses and respond to each other online; because I was away, however, I did not challenge their thinking through class discussion like I did in the undergraduate course, and the assignment was not graded. The graduate students had useful ideas, but did practically no questioning of themselves, despite their much greater practice and facility at it. Their answers were brief and included little reflection; this made me realize that even students who are capable of reflective thinking may not engage in it without significant encouragement to do so.

Based on these two experiences, I am convinced that the kind of process I used for this study encouraged deeper reflection about ethical issues. It would be interesting to follow up with these students once they are professionals in the field, to see if they perceive that it has made a difference to them.

Revising the Process

As I conclude the preparation of this paper, I am simultaneously preparing to teach the course in which I will repeat a variation of this assignment. One decision I have made is to reduce the number of scenarios to four (A–D in the attached assignment), with minor modifications. After reading them, students will record their first, intuitive response to each. I will then present in class three different approaches to ethical decision-making (rule-based, ends-based, and care-based); students will work in small groups to apply each approach to the different scenarios, comparing the decisions that would result and the questions that are generated.

Their next writing assignment will ask them to rethink their decisions to each scenario: "Considering the different decisions that could be reached through different approaches to ethical decision making, select the one you think is best, and articulate why." The third round will be an online (asynchronous) discussion; I am asking students to:

conduct this discussion as though it were a professional

conversation among educators…In your discussion, you should
ask questions of your peers to try to better understand their
positions, revealing your respect and depth of thought. You are
free to agree or disagree, as long as you are respectful, but don't
avoid controversy just to be "nice." Avoid simply defending
your position as any kind of a final truth.

The assignment will conclude with an in-class discussion and an
evaluation of the assignment.

By ensuring that students will look at the same situations
from different perspectives, I hope that they will become better
able to generate more of their own questions in future situations
they will face, both during their teacher preparation program and
beyond. At the same time, I do not think that I have found any kind
of "ultimate solution" for teaching students to think critically or
ethically, and know that I will continue revising what and how I
teach for as long as I teach.

One Final Ethical Dilemma

As an institution approved by a national accrediting body
for teacher education programs, we are required to assess student
"dispositions" in making decisions about whether or not students
are allowed to continue in a teacher education program, student
teach, and be licensed. While the organization leaves it up to each
institution to name these dispositions and determine how they are
to be assessed, it is clear that a disposition toward ethical behavior
is to be expected. The assignment I have been studying offers an
opportunity to understand a student's ethical disposition. It is
foreseeable that a student's responses to the scenarios might
provide evidence that could be used against them during a review.
This brings up issues regarding confidentiality as well as punishing
a student for honesty. My own response to this dilemma would be
to seek a "third way," and use a problematic response as an
opportunity for further dialogue. However, if continuing
conversation with the student brought up serious concerns about
their capacity or willingness to act ethically in their relationships
with young people, I would feel compelled to consider this in
making a decision regarding a recommendation for licensure.
Ultimately, I have to prioritize protection of young people in
schools over career needs and desires for my own students. Of
course, I would not reach such a decision on my own, and I am
thankful that an appeals process exists for students.

Conclusions

In concluding this paper, I realize that I am simply concluding the first phase of what will be a continuing project for the rest of my career. I find myself with more questions about teaching ethical decision-making than I had when I began. More than anything else, I have learned how much I value formal preparation of students for the ethical dilemmas that all teachers face. I am delighted that considering issues of ethics both challenges students and engages their interest, two criteria on which my own teaching is evaluated. Further, this project has affirmed for me that thinking about teaching—what, how, and why—is one of the most engaging pursuits possible, and how fortunate I am to be part of a profession which encourages it.

REFERENCES

Carr, W., & Kemmis, S. (1986). *Becoming critical: Education, knowledge and action research.* London: Falmer.

Clarke, A., & Erickson, G., Eds. (2003). *Teacher inquiry: Living the research in everyday practice.* London: Routledge.

North Carolina Professional Practices Commission. Code of Ethics for North Carolina Educators (1997). Retrieved January 26, 2004, from http://www.ncpublicschools.org/teacher_education/ethics.pdf

Colnerud, G. (1997). Ethical conflicts in teaching. *Teaching and Teacher Education, 13* (6), 627-635. Abstract retrieved January 23, 2004, from ERIC database.

Corrigan, S.Z., & Tom, A.R. (1998). The moral dilemmas of teacher educators. *The Educational Forum, 63* (1), 66-72.

Daniels, D., Plant, M., Kalkman, D., & Czerny, D. (1996). Preparing teachers for moral issues. *Thresholds in Education, 22* (3), 33-42.

Fain, G.S. (1992). *Ethics in health, physical education, recreation, and dance.* (Report No. EDO-SP-91-4). Washington, D.C.: Office of Educational Research and Improvement. (ERIC Document Reproduction Service No. ED342775). Retrieved January 23, 2004, from http://web5.silverplatter.com/webspirs/showFullRecordContent.ws

Freeman, N. K. (1998). Morals and character: The foundations of ethics and professionalism. *The Educational Forum, 63* (1), 30-36.

Gilligan, C. (1982). *In a different voice: Psychological theory and women's development.* Cambridge, MA: Harvard University Press.

Green, J. (1999). Somatic authority and the myth of the ideal body in dance education. *Dance Research Journal 31* (2), pp. 80-100.

Howe, K.R. & Miramontes, O.B. (1992). *The ethics of special education.* NY: Teachers College Press.

Jarrett, J.L. (1991). *The teaching of values: Caring and appreciation.* London: Routledge.

Katz, L.G. (1988). Where is early childhood as a profession? In B. Spodek, O.N. Saracho, & D.L. Peters, Eds., *Professionalism and the early childhood practitioner* (pp. 192-208). New York: Teachers College Press.

Kidder, R.M. (1995). *How good people make tough choices: Resolving the dilemmas of ethical living.* NY: Fireside (Simon & Schuster).

Kohlberg, L. (1981). *Essays in moral development.* San Francisco: Harper & Row.

Lather, P. (1991) *Getting smart: Feminist research and pedagogy with/in the postmodern.* New York: Routledge.

Lather, P., & Smithies, C. (1997). *Troubling the angels: Women living with HIV/AIDS.* Boulder, CO: Westview.

Loytonen, T. (1999). *Researching one's own professional practice: Problems and possibilities.* Panel presentation at conference of the Congress on Research in Dance. Claremont, CA.

Luckowski, J. (1997). A virtue-centered approach to ethics education. *Journal of Teacher Education, 48* (4), 264-270. Abstract retrieved January 23, 2004 from ERIC database.

Noddings, N. (1984). *Caring: A feminine approach to ethics and moral development.* Berkeley: University of California Press.

Patterson, S.M., & Vitello, E.M. (1994). *Instructional strategies for implementing ethics instruction in health education courses.* Paper presented at annual meeting of the Association for the Advancement of Health Education. Denver, CO. Abstract retrieved January 23, 2004 from ERIC database.

Rudder, C. (1999). Ethics and educational administration: Are professional policies ethical? In D. Fenner (Ed.), *Ethics in education* (pp. 41-66). NY: Garland.

Schon, D.A. (1987). *Educating the reflective practitioner: Toward a new design for teaching and learning in the professions.* San Francisco: Jossey-Bass.

Schwartz, G.E. (1998). Teaching as vocation: Enabling ethical practice. *Educational Forum, 63* (1), 23-29. Abstract retrieved January 23, 2004, from ERIC database.

Sottile, J.M. (1994). *Teaching and ethics.* (ERIC No. ED378174). Abstract retrieved January 23, 2004, from http://web5.silverplatter.com/webspirs/showFullRecordContent

Stinson, S.W. (2001). Choreographing a life: Reflections on curriculum design, consciousness, and possibility. *Journal of Dance Education, 1* (1), 26-33.

Stinson, S.W. (2004). Teaching ethical thinking to prospective dance educators. In L. Rouhiainen, E. Anttila, S. Hamalainen, & T. Loytonen (Eds.), *The same difference? Ethical and political perspectives on dance* (pp. 235-279). Helsinki, Finland: Theatre Academy.

Tomal, D.R. (2003). *Action research for educators.* Lanham, Md.: Scarecrow Press.

Tyler, R. W. (1978). Specific approaches to curriculum. In J.R. Gress & D.E. Purpel (Eds.), *Curriculum: An introduction to the field* (pp. 239-254). Berkeley, CA: McCutchan.

University of North Carolina at Greensboro (n.d.). Procedures for research activities involving human subjects. Retrieved May 26, 2004 from http://www.uncg.edu/rss/IRBProceduresHuman Subjects.pdf

APPENDIX A

Original Assignment

1. Read the North Carolina Code of Ethics for Educators in the Teacher Education Handbook (www.uncg.edu/soe/updated_site/teachersacad _home.html. Click on Teacher Education Handbook. To get to the Code of Ethics, go to page 33 (top of page) or page 45 (shown at the bottom of the computer screen). Make a note of any items that you do not understand; send me an e-mail telling me which ones they are.

2. The discussion is divided into 6 sections, A-F. In each case, I have selected portions of the North Carolina Code of Ethics (in italics), and then posed a scenario that you might face as a dance educator in a school or community setting. Write your response under each of the items. There are three "rounds" to this assignment.

   a. Round 1: Due by November 18. (Points will be deducted if your response is not posted by this date.): Answer the questions in each scenario. If you need to give conditions, do so. (In other words, If you would contact the parents if the student said x, but not if the student said y, explain this.) Be sure that you describe your thinking that led to this decision; keep in mind the grading criteria (below). Post your responses in your individual discussion board.

   b. Go to Blackboard Groups and find the discussion item "Code of Ethics." Round 2: Due by November 25. (Points will be deducted if your response is not posted by this date.). Read the responses of all of your peers in your discussion group. (I will have copied your responses onto the discussion board, deleting names.) On your own Discussion Board, add to the discussion for each scenario: Do you still agree with what you originally wrote, or have you now changed your mind? Indicate why you have or have not changed your mind. Keep the grading criteria in mind.

   c. On December 2, we will discuss (in class) these scenarios and the process of making ethical decisions.

   d. Round 3:

      1) Original assignment: Due by December 8. Post on your personal discussion board the answers to these questions: Based on the stages of development in ethical thinking presented in class, how would you describe your own ethical thinking in these scenarios; give the basis for your decisions, keeping in mind the grading criteria. Did your thinking change during this process? If so, how did it change? What suggestions do you have for the next time the topic of ethics is included in a dance education course?

      → Your grade for this assignment will be based on

      1. Whether or not you answered all of the questions in all three rounds by the dates they were due.

2. Whether or not you described your thinking thoroughly, and questioned your thinking.

2) Alternative to round 3 above: Due Dec. 8 by 5pm: Posted on Blackboard (personal site) or e-mailed: Write 1-2 pages on the first two questions. (Write 2 pages if you did less questioning in rounds 1-2.)

1. Considering the discussion on 12/2 about stages of moral development, what other questions arise for you about your own thinking about the 6 scenarios? (You do not have to identify your own level of moral development.)

2. Did your thinking about what you would do in the scenarios change during this process? If so, how did it change?

3. Rank the following (1 is highest) to show what you found most useful in helping you think about the right thing to do as a dance educator. (If you have comments, I hope that you will give them.)
- Reading the NC Code of Ethics for Educators
- Individual writing in response to the scenarios
- Talking with family and/or friends
- Reading online what some of your peers said
- Hearing the instructor's comments/suggestions in
  class
- Learning about stages of moral development
- Other:

4. What did we not do that might have helped you think more about moral situations you might face as a dance educator?

→ Your grade for this assignment will be based on

1. Whether or not you answered all of the questions in all three rounds by the dates they were due.

2. Whether or not you described your thinking thoroughly, and questioned your thinking. (up to 7 points)

3. Your ability to communicate using correct spelling, grammar, and sentence structure.

→ Example of questioning:

- This description would get a lower grade: "I would do this because this is what I have been taught ever since I was a child."

- This description would get a higher grade: "I realize that I have been taught to do this ever since I was a small child. However, I don't still follow all the guidance I was given as a small child. Instead, I have rejected some guidelines from my family but kept others. I guess this principle is one that most of my friends would agree with; I think my friends now are a greater influence than my family, because I can't think of any area where I would disagree with them. I wonder if I choose my friends because I think like they do, or I choose my friends for other reasons and then adopt their thinking."

Please note that there is no "right answer" that I am looking for, and your grade is not dependent on what you think is the right thing to do.

APPENDIX B

The North Carolina Code of Ethics for Teachers states that an educator following the Code of Ethics:

A. *Protects students from conditions within the educator's control that circumvent learning or are detrimental to the health and safety of students.*

Disciplines students justly and fairly and does not deliberately embarrass or humiliate them.

Acknowledges diverse views of students, parents and legal guardians as they work...to shape educational goals, policies, and decisions...

You are teaching in a summer arts program for low-income children. One child in the class, a 10-year-old boy, has been consistently disruptive in your class. You have repeatedly removed him from the class for "time out," and spoken with the supervisor. The supervisor calls the parent, and the boy's father comes in for a conference. He tells the supervisor, "I will take care of this. You just let me know if my boy acts up again." As he leaves the school with his child, you see out the window that the father is hitting his child. You take your concern to the supervisor, who says, "That's just the way these families do things." What do you do if the child is disruptive in your class again? Describe your thinking that leads you to make this decision.

B. *Evaluates students and assigns grades based upon the student's demonstrated competencies and performance.*

Refuses to accept significant gifts, favors, or additional compensation that might influence or appear to influence professional decisions or actions.

This is a situation that does not exactly fit the ethical principles above, but is related:

You have been hoping for years to take your advanced dance students to an international dance festival. It will be expensive, and some of your students have told you that they cannot afford to go. The parent of one of your wealthier students offers to provide scholarships for all students needing assistance if his daughter gets the solo role in the piece you will show at the festival. She is a good dancer, but not the best for the role. The student you want to cast is one of those who needs financial assistance. What should you do about the father's offer? Describe your thinking that leads you to make this decision.

C. *Acknowledges the worth and dignity of every person and demonstrates the pursuit of truth and devotion to excellence.*

Strives to maintain the respect and confidence of ...students...

Protects students from conditions within the educator's control that circumvent learning

One of the students in your high school class tries very hard, but is struggling with some very difficult personal situations. She is a single mom of an infant and has some serious chronic health problems. She has returned to school to try to graduate. She has minimal assistance from her family. You have given a written exam in the class; few did really well on it, but she is the only student who failed it. When you asked her if she had studied, she said that she had, but her baby was up most of the night before the class. Should you offer to let her retake either the test, or a different version of it? If so, should you put any conditions on it (i.e., should you deduct points from her final score because she is getting another chance?) Should you extend this offer to all students? Describe your thinking that leads you to make this decision.

D. *Maintains an appropriate relationship with students in all settings; does not encourage, solicit, or engage in a sexual or romantic relationship with students, not touch a student in an inappropriate way for personal gratification, with intent to harm, or out of anger.*

Takes action to remedy an observed violation of the Code of Ethics for North Carolina Educators and promotes understanding of the principles of professional ethics.

One of your middle school students has told you that her brother, a high school athlete at a neighboring school, is helping the dance teacher at his high school by meeting her at 6am several days a week to serve as her "personal trainer." Your student thinks something more is going on and so do you—you have met this teacher, and she seems flirtatious and seductive. You have no other evidence. Should you stay quiet or say something? If you decide to say something, to whom will you say it? Describe your thinking that leads you to make this decision.

E. *Protects students from conditions within the educator's control that circumvent learning or are detrimental to the health and safety of students.*

Acknowledges the diverse views of students [and] parents and legal guardians, as they work collaboratively to shape educational goals, policies, and decisions; does not proselytize for personal viewpoints that are outside the scope of professional practice.

Select <u>one</u> of these scenarios:
A distraught 16-year-old student in your class has confided in you regarding a personal dilemma. In keeping with her family's cultural heritage and religious practice, she will be married in a few months to a man selected by her parents. She will have to drop out of school to serve the needs of her husband. What should you do? Describe your thinking that leads you to make this decision.

One of your students has confided to you that she is pregnant, and tells you that her parents will disown her, as they did with her older sister, if they find out. This means that she will have to drop out of school and give up her dreams of college. She wants to have an abortion, although she and her family are members of a religious faith that strongly disapproves of abortion. What should you do? Describe your thinking that leads you to make this decision.

One of your students has confided in you that she is sexually active, but her family's religious faith strongly disapproves of both premarital sex and contraception. She tells you that her family will "disown" her if they find out. You sense that she is questioning her faith on matters other than contraception. Should you invite her to visit your church (with more liberal views on such matters) or talk with your minister? Describe your thinking that leads you to make this decision.

F. *Acknowledges the diverse views of students, parents and legal guardians, and colleagues as they work collaboratively to shape educational goals, policies, and decisions...*
    Participates actively in professional decision-making processes and supports the expression of professional opinions and judgments by colleagues in decision-making processes...

The dance teachers in your district are developing a new curriculum. One of the teachers, not the chair of the group, seems to monopolize the conversation, and this teacher is steering the process in a direction that you do not agree with. Every time you speak up about an alternative, this teacher engages in verbal put-down that makes you feel silenced. Other teachers have stopped trying to say much. What should you do? Describe your thinking that leads you to make this decision.

NOTES

i. This research was prompted by my participation in a project housed at the Theater Academy of Finland, "Making a Difference in Dance." An earlier version (Stinson 2004) was published in the anthology produced by the project. I acknowledge the important contributions to this work by Dr. Jane Harris, who provided assistance in instructional technology; Dr. Jill Green, who affirmed the integrity of the early analysis of two of the scenarios; and Dr. Eeva Anttila, who provided critical yet collegial critiques of several drafts.

ii. In my state, licensure for teachers in all subject areas, including dance, is required at the undergraduate level; advanced (masters level) licensure is available in most subjects, but is optional.

iii. Two students chose not to participate in the "formal" research project, meaning that they did the assignment but their data is not included. Also excluded from the data for this publication are responses from two students who completed course assignments after the end of the semester, due to personal circumstances. They happened to be among a small number of students I judged to be more advanced cognitively, based on the depth and complexity of their thinking in class; this was borne out in their responses to this assignment. However, since they had the advantage of hearing all the class discussion before writing even their first responses, I was unable to evaluate the impact of the assignment on their work in the same way.

iv. The option allowed them to simply raise questions stimulated by the class discussion, rather than classify their previous responses.

v. One student told me that she realized that many other students in the class had been asking questions all semester that she had never imagined, and she wondered if something was wrong with her. (I assured her that individuals develop at their own rate, that she was not finished developing yet, and that I was confident she would continue to grow into a strong teacher. I was thrilled when her Round 3 responses showed a breakthrough in questioning!)

vi. Although I include in the analysis only a small portion of the material written by students, I have attempted to include all viewpoints represented. I have corrected spelling errors when necessary for purposes of clarity, shown in brackets in the text, but have not otherwise made changes in the students' words.

vii. I intentionally described the parent's behavior as "hitting," rather than "beating" or "spanking"; I thought use of either of the latter words would make it too easy for students to make their decision.

viii. If there is no mention of a student's Round 2 or 3 response, it is because they did not mention this scenario during that round.)

ix. In Scenario E, regarding a high school student who confided in her dance teacher, I offered two options in addition to the original one involving abortion. Living as I do in a state where many individuals hold fundamentalist religious beliefs, I was afraid, in a required assignment, to put my own students on the spot regarding this very controversial issue, even though I knew that it was one most would face. The complication of three choices, however, meant that it was more difficult for me to interpret much about students' ethical thinking.

x. I calculated the average score of each activity by determining the sum of the ranked numbers, and dividing it by the number of students who had ranked that item. With a score of 1 indicating the most important activity, a low score was better. Activities that they scored as most valuable were writing their answers (average rank 2.667; four students ranked this as highest in value), talking with friends and family (2.667; three students ranked this highest), and the instructor's comments during class (2.7; only one ranked it highest). Scores for other activities were 3.9 for reading the North Carolina Code of Ethics for Educators, 3.7 for reading the responses of peers online, and 4.8 for learning about stages of moral development.

xi. Students had to remember to "uncheck" a box to have their identity withheld. In a small group (no more than 5-6 students in a group is the recommendation for online discussions), if a few students either forget to uncheck the box or decide that they want their peers to know who they are (and I could imagine some of my students making this decision), the anonymity of remaining students in the group would be severely compromised, especially in a group that knew each other.

2

DIGITAL IMPROVISATION: INTERACTIVE MULTIMEDIA FOR DANCE EDUCATION

Mila Parrish

This research looks at the complexity of components surrounding multimedia for dance education and sheds light on the issues surrounding the teaching and learning of dance using computer-assisted instruction (CAI) found in the Discover Dance CD-ROM. Case study methodology was used to determine the effects of the Discover Dance CD-ROM on fifth graders' ability to make dances, perform dances, and inquire in the dance domain.

Participants for this research study were 15 fifth-grade students attending a two-week summer dance and technology workshop at The Ohio State University led by the researcher. The students were instructed in dance using the Discover Dance CD-ROM and studio activities for a total of twenty hours, two hours a day for two weeks.

Data was collected from multiple sources including student journals, interviews, focus groups, and dance making. In the data collection, emphasis was placed on description and interpretation of the elements rather than measurement and predictions. The students were active co-researchers in this process.

The results of this study reveal information about the issues of learner diversity, knowledge construction, communication, and constructivist approaches to learning. Data reflected that when using the Discover Dance CD-ROM, students were engaged, focused, and intent on learning. The workshop students and outside evaluators characterized the Discover Dance CD-ROM as a valuable resource for self-discovery, choreographic inspiration, understanding and clarifying difficult concepts, useful for outlining and recording their thinking, and encouraging students' active investigation, self-reflection and productive dance thinking.

At the onset of the new millennium, American society is experiencing rapid and profound change, as information traveling at the speed of light transforms the way we live, communicate, form communities, and educate our children and ourselves. In short, we have become an information-rich culture.

National reform efforts have challenged educators to "improve learning by creating interactive, high-performance learning environments" (U.S. Department of Education, 1998). The department's plan is based on the potential for information technology such as multimedia and telecommunications that can improve learning. Since then, the U.S. Department of Education has required the integration of technology in all subjects, including dance. In the last few years, the majority of dance educators I have spoken to at conferences and workshops in the U.S. and abroad have shown interest in including technology within their curriculum. At the same time, they have complained that they have few, if any, resources to assist them in creating quality dance experiences for their students.

As a dance educator in U.S. public schools for five years, I became aware of the challenges of dance instruction in our schools, limited as it is by time, classroom space, finances, administrative support, or teaching style, among other factors. The integration of instructional technologies can impact the type and kind of dance education delivered. But with what approach and to what purpose? Harrington (1991) cautions, "How technology is incorporated and used may significantly impact what education becomes" (p. 54).

In order to address the application and utilization of technology in the dance curriculum, attention must be placed on the dynamic partnership formed by the student, teacher, and computer technology. Over the last eight years, I have been investigating the use of computer technology in dance education and have developed an interactive, multimedia-teaching tool for children, a CD-ROM called Discover Dance, to meet the needs of teachers and students. This CD-ROM was designed to supplement classroom instruction in dance with computer technology. It blends the physical experience of dance (choreography, improvisation, and, performance) with computer technology (digital video, databases, Internet links, and printing capabilities) to enhance students' skills of dance inquiry, analysis, and choreography. The Discover Dance CD-ROM is not limited by style of pedagogy; rather, its focus is to enhance students' experiences and exploration in dance, and expand their understanding of dance.

Especially in dance education, the development of media technologies has remained untapped; and hindered by the lack of meaningful evaluation of technology; educators struggle to meet equivalency requirements as they search for new paradigms in technology education. This CD-ROM fills a void in the field of K-5 dance education, where computer-assisted instruction (CAI) has been nonexistent to date. A definite need exists for meaningful discussion between technology developers, teachers, students, and researchers, and for formative evaluation of the emergent CAI. Students and teachers can test CAI product design in the classroom to see how they match up to their specific curricular needs.

In this article I provide an overview of the research methods employed in testing the Discover Dance CD-ROM and present the analysis of data, conclusions, and recommendations.

Statement of the Problem

The development of media technologies has remained completely untapped in dance education. I have undertaken this research and development of the Discover Dance CD-ROM for children because computer-assisted instruction (CAI) is nonexistent to date in the field of K-5 dance education. In all fields of elementary education, there is a need for technological field-testing and research in "real" classroom environments where technology is used to enhance learning (Carlson, 1998). In order to improve existing methods for instruction, teachers, researchers, and technology, developers can learn from one another to best capitalize on CAI.

Numerous research initiatives propose educational technology as having the potential to meet the needs of our diverse population of students by (1) facilitating diverse teaching practices (Papert, 1980; Budin, 1991; Budin, 1997; Read, 1997; Sandholtz et al., 1997; McGee, 1999); (2) supporting individualized learning (Grey 1989; Mendrinos, 1997; Gore, 1997; Fisher-Stitt, 1994; Sandholtz et al., 1997); (3) fostering new methods of communication (Gore, 1997; Ryder & Hughes, 1997; Trentin, 1996; Margolies, 1991) and (4) providing powerful tools to transform teaching into vivid, student-centered interactive knowledge environments (Resta, 1993; Fisher-Stitt; 1994, Jonassen, 1996; Maletic; 1996, Sandholtz et al., 1997).

Current trends in education reflect the shift away from traditional, linear, highly structured "assembly line" pedagogy toward more active, student-centered, problem-based constructivist pedagogy (Budin, 1997). Constructivists argue that learning is an active process, in which students actively construct knowledge from their experiences in the world. The pedagogy suggests that students don't get ideas, they make ideas.

Instructional technology has been widely discussed as supporting constructivist-teaching practices (Budin, 1997). Such researchers advise moving away from the notion of teachers as the leader, delivering instructions toward the concept of the teacher as a facilitator and coach, and using "flexible strategies for learning" (Budin, 1991, p. 16).

Mendrinos (1997) advocates interactive multimedia technology as supporting individualized learning structures. Widely discussed is the ability of CAI to support the diversity of learners and addressing the needs of multiple populations at the same time. Multimedia technology works to personalize the students' experience by allowing students to progress at their own pace, providing immediate feedback and personalized instruction.

Instructional technology is fostering new methods of communication (Gore, 1997). Riel (1996) views the Internet and other mediated technologies as dynamic active places that promote meaningful discovery. The Internet is a powerful resource that encourages students to share ideas and acquire information. Computer-mediated communication serves as a great equalizer, allowing student's access to anyone, no matter the racial, economic, or geographical distance. Online students are able to form communities as they learn from, share, and consult with one another in a purely digital realm.

Instructional technology and multimedia technologies provide powerful tools to transform teaching into vivid, student-centered, interactive knowledge environments. Further, Baltra (1987) suggests that computers are suitable for the development of "communicative fluency by integrating the four communicative abilities--listening, reading, speaking and writing" (p. 8). Repeatable and patient, CD-ROMs can be viewed at any time and can be adapted to the learning needs of each student. Therefore, interactive video-based CD-ROMS can be used as powerful tools in creating a contextually rich instructional environment for learning. Thus it becomes clear that instruction incorporating technology has the potential to support students in various types of learning that include problem solving, communication, and knowledge construction. Accordingly, these new methods, when thoughtfully applied in the dance education curriculum, may be capable of adding a new dimension to the teaching and learning of dance.

Overview of the Study

This research study covers the research, development, and testing of the Discover Dance CD-ROM from 1996 to 2000. The study critically analyzes the results of the field test and examines the process of development and design. Case study methodology was used to determine the effects of the Discover Dance CD-ROM on fifth graders' ability to make dances, perform dances, and inquire in the dance domain.

Participants for this research study were 15 fifth-grade students from an elementary school in Columbus, Ohio. The students were instructed in dance using the Discover Dance CD-ROM and studio activities for a total of twenty hours, two hours a day for two weeks. Data was collected from multiple sources including student journals, interviews, focus groups, and dance making. All classes and student interviews were videotaped and selectively transcribed to provide a data record. A non-participant observer was employed to provide a broad representation of the workshop and to corroborate my research notes, observations and evaluations.

Research Questions

The following questions served as a foundation that helped guide my analysis. Can a CD-ROM be created that will:

- support the National Standards for Dance Education?
- provide a resource for dance education rich in multiculturalism and the principles of Motif Writing and Laban Movement Analysis?
- enhance the students' ability to inquire about dance, make dance, and share dances?

Methodology

The review of literature for this study indicated a need for further research to address the issues impacting the use of technology in dance education. The current study investigates the design, development and testing of the Discover Dance CD-ROM and made an attempt to determine the effects of the Discover Dance CD-ROM on fifth graders' learning in dance. Qualitative methods were used to collect and analyze data. Attempts were made to identify themes related to participants' experiences and other factors contributing to the integration of dance learning with the Discover Dance CD-ROM.

In the realm of dance education, Riley (1987) rejects traditional quantitative research methods when studying children's dance, because dance [a diverse phenomenon] impacts children's affective, cognitive, and physical domains. Conservative quantitative approaches, Riley believes, have detrimental influence on the phenomenon. He advocates natural and responsive qualitative approaches to studying children's dance, because they are flexible, emergent, and recognize the context-bound meanings in dance. As the researcher, software developer, and instructor in the current study, I matched the qualitative design with the research as well as the researched, since both are intertwined in the data collected and the process itself.

Participants/Subjects

Participants for this research study were 15 students from an elementary school in Columbus, Ohio. The break down of ethnic groups in the workshop was as follows: four African-American and three White/non-Hispanic boys, six white/non-Hispanic and two African-American girls. Columbus is the capitol of Ohio and has a population of 670,234. Students study dance from kindergarten through fifth grade with a full-time dance instructor. The school has a student population of 331 students, and a student-to-teacher ratio of 17 to 1.

Timeline/Outline

In preparation for the study, I spent three weeks at the school observing, talking to fifth-grade students, teachers, and their principal, viewing dance classes and performances, and collecting background information on the school community to build a profile on students. Initially, I had planned to conduct the study within the 1999-2000 school year but due to time constraints and the lack of available Macintosh computers and tech support, I decided to conduct my research at The Ohio State University (OSU) over the summer.

During the two-week workshop, students used the Discover Dance CD-ROM and physical dance exploration daily for two hours. The daily lesson content and student needs dictated whether classes began in the studio or the computer lab. Generally, class time was equally divided between the two locations. During the workshop, students worked independently and in small groups, improvising, creating choreographic studies, viewing dance movies, answering questions in the CD-ROM, creating annotated dances, and recording their experiences in dance journals.

Role of the Researcher

A qualitative researcher is a storyteller who becomes highly connected to her research participants to establish trust. Trust enables individual participants to feel comfortable and to tell their particular stories. A qualitative researcher becomes a part of the community she is studying. Aware that as the researcher/instructor I assumed a pivotal role in the workshop (guiding, observing, listening, and interacting with students), I was sensitive to the students' needs and interests and made them the highest priority.

Using the constructivist-learning model, I became a facilitator or a "coach" rather than the research project director. I was responsible for setting up inquiry projects, securing lab access, and creating the organizational structure for the students to do their work. Within the workshop, the pacing, tempo, and lesson content depended on student interest and abilities. A flexible student-centered inquiry process was useful, as it allowed me to step back and provide assistance to the students.

Design Considerations

The Ohio State University Department of Dance computer lab and a dance studio were used for the test sites. Although initially undesirable, as the OSU test site would entail removing the students from the context of their classroom and school, the OSU site offered several advantages. The OSU site afforded students access to large dance studios with high ceilings, lots of light, walls of mirrors and barres that were unavailable in their school. This contrast is striking because at their school, dance class is held in a cafeteria and students often complain of sticky floors, due to juice spills at lunchtime. Students commented that these studios were the "real thing," a place where dancing was the most respected and most highly esteemed experience. Students excitedly peeked in to see what was going on in "real" dance classes and rehearsals. Having professional facilities raised the significance of the research in the students' eyes, the value of which cannot be underestimated. The OSU facility also offered individual access to high-end Macintosh computers and Internet connectivity unavailable in most Elementary schools today.

Procedure for Data Collection

In the data collection, emphasis was placed on description and interpretation of the elements rather than measurement and predictions. This qualitative research takes into account the wider context in which CAI functions, connecting changes in the learning environment with intellectual experiences of workshop students.

A research strategy was used to examine the Discover Dance CD-ROM: how it operates, how it is influenced by various situations, and what its advantages and disadvantages are. Firstly, I became knowledgeable about the day-to-day activities and ongoing events in the school and with the students.

Secondly, my observation and inquiry became more directed and selective. I focused on selective questions and made inquiries to further familiarize myself with the students and about their methods of using the Discover Dance CD-ROM. This occurred during the two-week workshop.

Thirdly, I began looking for general principles underlying the Discover Dance CD-ROM. Here, I searched for patterns in the causal relationships and in the data analysis section and reported my findings in a broad explanatory context. This occurred upon the conclusion of the workshop.

I relied on multiple methods of data collection: observation, interview, dance making, and video to gather a broad picture of the issues surrounding the teaching and learning of dance using the Discover Dance CD-ROM.

Observation

Observation was selected as a main method for data collection in this research study, as observation techniques allow for the documentation of human behavior and events as they occur. During the profile building, descriptive observation was used to record the behavior of the students, teachers, and the overall school environment. Then based on my perceptions, hunches, and questions, more selective and focused observations were utilized during the workshop.

Observational data was gathered and recorded from all participants in the study. The students used personal dance journals, the non-participant observer used a notebook, and I used a personal dance diary to reflect and record my daily observations. In addition, the entire workshop was videotaped. Upon conclusion of the workshop, I reviewed all observation materials and developed coding sheets to structure the analysis.

Student Journals

As the Discover Dance CD-ROM was created with fifth-grade students in mind, I thought it appropriate that workshop students become stakeholders and active co-researchers in the data collection process. Janesick (1998) describes this method as "active learning," where "power is de-centered and the research process is demystified" (p. 71). With students as research stakeholders, I was able to encourage their feelings of empowerment and participation. Each student in the study was required to be (and honored to become) a co-researcher. In their journal, student researchers were asked to write about their ongoing dance experiences, discuss their own and other students' choreography, record in-class observation exercises, and discuss their opinions about this method of instruction.

As co-researchers, students enthusiastically took on this role, which was somewhere between a participant observer and active researcher. Students valued their journals and the private comments of the instructor, sometimes arriving 20 minutes early to read instructor comments.

Instructor/Researcher Diary

During this study, I kept an ongoing diary of events and experiences in the school. The diary included my verbal comments to the class, concerns, students' responses, anecdotal conversations with students, parents, teachers, and a record of what happened and when. Further, my diary became an invaluable resource, as it provided a place and time for critical reflection of my assumptions and perceptions during the investigation. This diary became an unexpected resource into the teaching-learning cycle of the workshop.

Non-Participant Observer

As the instructor and principal researcher in the study, I was immersed in the minute-to-minute teaching responsibilities regarding students' instruction. Consequently, I had rich personal data, but was unable to personally maintain an awareness of the "big picture" as it unfolded in the classroom. Therefore, a non-participant observer (NPO) was asked to watch and record activity in the classroom. NPO focused on the instructors' interaction with students, the students' interactions with one another, and students' employment of the technology, while noting changes in atmosphere in both the dance and the computer classroom environments.

Interviews

Interviewing was used in this research to reveal as much as possible of the students' understanding, reasoning, and viewpoint. Interviews were an important component, providing substantive data on the personal perspectives unique to the students being interviewed (Spradley, 1979; Janesick, 1991; Metzler, 1989). The interview structure offered students a chance to explain their answers and to elaborate further, which in turn brought new issues to the surface that had not been considered, predicted, or anticipated. Conscious that the manner and type of question I presented to the students would influence student answers, I employed two interview strategies: semi-structured individual and focus group interviews during the study.

Single-Subject Interviews

The first interview was semi-structured and occurred during the first three days of the workshop. In the interview, I asked descriptive questions to gather information about the students' experiences, their perspective on dance education, their interest and experience in technology, and their everyday lives at school. The second interview that occurred in the last three days of the workshop was more focused. I asked follow-up questions that are directly connected to my research question.

All interviews were videotape recorded and selectively

transcribed to establish a data record. Aware that videotape can intimidate and diminish frankness, I worked to build a warm, trusting relationship with the students. The students valued the interviews as personal one-to-one time with the instructor. All student's wanted to be interviewed. Unfortunately, this was not possible, due to the students other commitments.

Focus Groups

Semi-structured focus group interviews were also used in this research, as they can offer dynamic interactive relationships as students relate to one another. During the focus group process, students interacted with one another taking control, which in turn allowed me to step away from a position of leadership to listen and learn from the students.

In this study, I conducted two focus groups with the entire workshop group. Each took place in the computer lab and lasted approximately thirty minutes. The first focus group occurred at the beginning the workshop and the second focus group occurred at the end of the workshop. Focus groups were a highly effective means of letting me into fifth-grade student culture. Students were enthusiastic and jovial, sharing their thoughts and listening to their peers. As McBride (1998) states, "The language conventions, slang, jargon, and metaphors that characterize conversations... can reveal tacit assumptions, interpersonal relationships and status differentials" (p. 3).

Dance Making

As the focus of this research is the investigation of the Discover Dance CD-ROM as related to student dance making, the students' expressive body movements while dancing had great importance. To gather this type of data, I employed my skills and training as a Certified Movement Analyst (CMA), to analyze the students' physicality while in the process of dancing. Laban Movement Analysis (LMA) is used in a variety of research strategies, mainly concerning nonverbal communication or motor behavior. LMA as a research tool has seen limited use because it requires rigorous study and in-depth training to learn the system to attain accuracy of observations. LMA is not recommended as a stand-alone research method, but when used in tandem with other methods, it creates a solid foundation that is perfect for dance research (Brennan in Fraleigh & Hanstein et al., 1999).

During the research, I applied LMA frameworks and language to identify, analyze, and record the complex actions expressed through students' bodies. Specifically, I considered the details of how each student's body was engaged during computer use, improvisation exercises, and during the creative process. Upon the conclusion of the workshop, I developed coding sheets to record, compare, and analyze students' expressive physical process while dance making.

Methods of Data Analysis

Process of Data Analysis

In the process of data analysis, I developed coding systems to organize the accumulated data. This coding system has evolved during the data analysis process, as themes and patterns have emerged and developed from the data. To maintain the authenticity of my data interpretation, I have been cautious during the collection, analysis, speculation, and follow-up process to resist jumping to convenient interpretations.

Gathering data through multiple sources (observation, interview, and children's dance making activities) allowed for the triangulation of data. My experience, single-subject interview transcripts, non-participant observer notes, student journals, and the analysis of student process and product of dance making all ensure credibility. After my fieldnotes, journals, and interviews were transcribed and emergent themes identified, coded, and catalogued, I employed an analysis cycle. Using an analysis cycle modeled after Janesick (1998), I began by (1) looking for frequent patterns and empirical assertions in the data. (2) Then I organized exact participant quotations, descriptions, and observations of dancing, computer use, and situational vignettes to support my assertions. (3) Next, I returned to other research sources, journals, background information, and other research in the field (to draw insights from them). (4) I then added "interpretive commentary" as it related to patterns in the data. (5) I then included theoretical discussions relating data to the theories that guided the research study. (6) I then described my role in the research and (7) stated issues that arose during the research (pp. 64-65).

Specific Analysis Structures: Observation

Observation played an important role in this research. My observation diary, personal accounts from student journals, non-participant observers' notes, and daily videotapes were carefully examined for patterns and emergent themes. Specific analysis structures are as follows:

Instructor Diary

My observation diary provided a validity criterion and assisted in my sorting out shifts and changes in reasoning and methodological choice. The diary, while reflective in nature, secured a sequence of my thinking and decisions made during the research process.

Student Journals

Students' journals became a valuable resource, providing insight into students' understanding of their own experiences. These journals also offered a method to dialogue directly and privately with the students. Following each day's workshop, I collected and read each student's journal. Student journals were selectively transcribed to establish a data record.

Non-Participant Observer Notes

As I would be busy guiding and teaching students during the workshop, I chose to employ a non-participant observer (NPO) to assist me in gathering a broader picture of the workshop. The NPO was not required to use a particular coding sheet to record their observations. Rather, I encouraged observation in several areas. These included: (1) Transference: The dance making relationships between what is experienced through the technology and in the students; (2) Problem solving strategies: The type and kind of questions the kids ask. Where do the students get stuck? When they get stuck how do they resolve it? (3) Relationships and environment: Is there evidence of the class community changing? How? Evidence of students in showing signs of Boredom, Frustration, Enthusiasm, Excitement; (4) Learner/Teacher behaviors such as: evidence of kids helping or hindering kids to use the technology, or evidence of student autonomy in learning.

Individual Student and Focus Group Interviews

All interviews (individual student and focus group) were selectively transcribed to establish a data record and the relevant information was taken into the data pool.

Specific Assessment Structures

Research in assessment in the arts warns against oversimplification of assessment tasks. Rather, they propose assessment tasks that focus on the holistic aspects of artistic creation including performance, knowledge, understanding, interpretation, and judgement. In addition, complex tasks permit students to assume a more active role in defining their own learning goals and regulating their own learning. Students learn not because they wish to recount their studies on demand, but to comprehend a subject more fully and to seek new information. In this research, three specific assessment structures were implemented. These include (a) Student explorations, (b) "Out of Ohio Dances," and, (c) Fantastic Dance Documentation.

Student Free-Time Explorations

Students were given daily unstructured free-time when they could explore their own ideas in self-selected ways. This open-ended exploration could have included using the Discover Dance CD-ROM, writing in their journals, or dance making. Students were asked to record in their journals what they did during their free time. Student journal notes were corroborated with detailed description of student free-time explorations. The student explorations were documented in my journal, in the NPO's notes, as well as on video. At the conclusion of the workshop, these records were gathered and charted. Coding sheets were created to assist in the reflection of what the students did and how they used their time. As the CD-ROM developer, I was interested in matching content with student interest. My analysis focused on several themes:

- Which section of the CD-ROM was most desirable?
- Did choices reflect an interest in exploring unknown sections or reviewing known sections or activities?
- What activities or movies did they view?
- What methods were used to play/view them?
- When did they get stuck? How did they get unstuck?
- How much time did they spend in a particular spot?
- In what ways did they share their experiences with fellow students, with their teacher, and with the NPO?

"Out of Ohio Dances"

The second assessment activity is called "Out of Ohio Dances." In this activity, students employed a choreographer's cycle: to create, notate, record, reconstruct, perform, and analyze a dance. The assessment occurred over 3 workshop days. The point was two-fold: (1) A gauge of the students' abilities in symbol identification, movement invention, and memorization of individual choreography. (2) A visual, verbal, and written record of students' thinking when creating and describing their dance. Guiding questions included the following:

- How can we share our dances and choreography with other individuals?

- How can we document a dance?
- Why do we document dance?
- What do other people need to know about a dance?

Procedure. (1) Students created and documented a dance using Motif Writing and descriptive methods. (2) Students performed their dance. (3) Students wrote a short description of their dance reflecting personal importance submitting details on how it could be reconstructed. (4) Written documentation of their dances was collected. Later, a special courier then returned to the class and delivered dances from the students "Outside of Ohio" (their fellow classmates). (5) Students reconstructed and performed from the delivered dance scores. And (6) after each dance was performed, students wrote in their notebooks describing, interpreting, and evaluating each dance, after which, the class discussed them.

The "Out of Ohio Dances" assessment required the students to complete complex and authentic tasks. Assessment criteria included the following: Was the body fully engaged in the process of dance making and dance sharing? Were both students actively participating in the creative collaboration? Did choreography presented reflect innovative original ideas and an understanding of motif writing? When preparing the dance to be sent "Out of Ohio" did the students' writing include the following? (a) a description of the dance, what the dance is about, (b) why it is meaningful to you, (c) how it was created, (d) a title if there is one, (e) the important dance elements which define the dance, (f) an analysis of your dance. The collected data was analyzed and evaluated using scoring rubrics developed for the assessment task.

"Fantastic Dance"

The third assessment activity was called "Fantastic Dance." In this activity, students employed methods of analysis, description, and inquiry on a "Fantastic Dance." The assessment took approximately 20 minutes and occurred on the eighth day of the workshop. In this assessment, the students view a "Fantastic Dance" in the computer and answer questions about that dance on a dance database. The focus of the assessment was twofold: (1) to assess students' abilities to identify the Elements of Dance (Body, Effort, Space, Shape, and Relationship) to a short dance video and, (2) to assess students' ability to describe, interpret, and evaluate when asked to describe a dance.

Guiding questions included the following:

- How can we describe a dance?
- What concepts were students able to and unable to identify?

Procedure. On day 8 the students went to the "Fantastic Dance" section of the Discover Dance CD-ROM. The sequence was as follows: (1) students visited the "Fantastic Dance" section of the Discover Dance CD-ROM and looked at several Fantastic Dances; (2) the student chose one Fantastic Dance and answered the five inquiry questions relating to the BESSR dance analysis and the five description questions about the dance; (3) students recorded their comments and saved them on the computer's hard drive; (4) each student shared his/her observations with the class; (5) the class then viewed the "shared" dance on their own computers and added additional observations. The data collected from the assessment was analyzed and evaluated using scoring rubrics developed for the assessment task.

The following steps have been taken to ensure internal reliability. Integral to the study were multiple researchers. These included students as co-researchers, a non-participant observer, and the use of video recording to provide rich data collection and allow for data triangulation.

Data Analysis

Data from the study consisted of layered qualitative information to provide a vivid description of teaching dance education using the Discover Dance CD-ROM. In this discussion, I will analyze the CD-ROM based on stated goals, and analyze the data, substantiating the effects of the Discover Dance CD-ROM on students' dance inquiry, dance making, and dance sharing. All participant names have been changed.

CD-ROM Evaluated Against Multiple Criteria

As the literature indicates, the development and evaluation of technology in dance education is highly limited. This study looks at the research, development, and testing of the Discover Dance CD-ROM. Guiding this assessment of the technology were three main questions:

- Does it support the National Standards for Dance Education?
- Does it provide a resource for dance education rich in multiculturalism and the principles of Motif Writing and Laban Movement Analysis?
- Does it enhance the students' ability to inquire about dance, make dance, and share dances?

In the following section, I consider the second question, providing accounts of classroom observation, student focus group and individual interview comments, and Non-participant observer (NPO) notes and responses during the most recent field-testing with twenty-two dance educators at a National Conference in October 2000.

Broad Dance Knowledge

The researcher defined multiculturalism, Laban Movement Analysis, and Motif Writing as essential components in a student's comprehensive dance education. They were therefore central themes in the development of the Discover Dance CD-ROM.

In this discussion, I will present written comments, evaluations, and interviews as a gauge for assessing the Discover Dance CD-ROM's ability to deliver and instruct students in three key themes: Multiculturalism, Laban Movement Analysis, and Motif Writing.

Multicultural

When looking at multicultural learning, two key areas were identified as deficient in the Discover Dance CD-ROM: content and context. In my development of the CD-ROM, I felt I addressed the necessary content by providing a great deal of video and images of cultural dance forms. Going into this field test, I was confident that the CD did support multicultural learning. However, during this analysis I realized that the Discover Dance CD-ROM provided only a cursory glance at the issues of content and context in multicultural dance.

Dance teachers at conferences were often "wowed" by the multicultural content. One teacher wrote: "The CD-ROM would be a valuable tool to bring more of the dance world to my children." Another teacher wrote: "When completed, I will use the CD-ROM as a resource for bringing social and cultural dance forms to my students."

In examining these comments, I believe that the teachers were not addressing the quality of instructional resource that might encourage young dancers to explore dances of other cultures, but were focusing on convenience. The CD-ROM is thoughtfully organized and a handy instrument to deliver multicultural dance video clips which would enhance their teaching. Although I am unable to verify, it seems reasonable to interpret these teachers' comments, as equating the *recognition* of cultural dance forms with an *understanding* of cultural dance forms. This observation may reflect the broader field of dance education. The content standard as written, is difficult to attain and with the limited time assigned to dance education classes is seems questionable if the standard is met at all.

A possible benefit for the CD is the use of Web links that can empower the students with the tools to gather both content and context to support their learning multicultural dance education. The CD-ROM does promote a respect for other dance forms, which is directly related to comments made by students in the workshop. One example is Joseph who states, "In the CD I learned about different cultural dances like Chinese dance and African dance." This sentiment is further addressed by Heather who states, "I really like seeing all the dances from other countries." These student comments are in sharp contrast to their detailed comments regarding their experiences using LMA or Motif Writing. The students' simple commentary here relates to their cursory experience in multicultural dance.

The fact remains that in order to learn about a cultural dance, fully introducing the context is imperative. In this research it is clear that the CD-ROM's content is so brief that it does not allow for time to explore the context of a dance. It in fact presents the cultural dance form context-free. Multiculturalism, as an essential component in a student's comprehensive dance education as defined by the researcher, is not promoted in the Discover Dance CD-ROM. It is clear to this researcher that the Discover Dance CD-ROM, while presenting some resources for Multicultural inquiry and interesting movies, its scope is much too broad to influence true understanding in a cultural dance form. Greater depth is necessary, and this would require a single CD-ROM for an individualized dance form.

Laban Movement Analysis

In the research, development, and testing of the Discover Dance CD-ROM, Laban Movement Analysis was identified as being essential to comprehensive dance education. Prior to testing, the underlying assumption was that the innovative inclusion of LMA would support students' dance investigations and their ability to communicate their thinking in dance.

In their journals and interviews, the workshop students addressed LMA's relevance to dance analysis and creative process. The analysis of data from these journals, interviews, and observations presents two themes evidenced by students' dance making, dance sharing, and dance inquiry as related to their use of LMA in the Discover Dance CD-ROM. The students demonstrated that LMA (1) enhanced their movement investigations and expressive dance action and (2) provided a useful vocabulary for discussion, reflection, and analysis.

Enhanced movement investigations. After two weeks of using LMA vocabulary of Body, Effort, Shape, Space, Relationship (BESSR), the students were clearly building a foundation in a descriptive language used for dance. In their dance journals, students expressed that the LMA vocabulary had become a familiar tool easily applied to their discussion and self-reflection and did in fact change the way they observed movement and created their dances.

The students' final dances clearly demonstrate the investigation of new creative range and territory. In these dances students were exploring combined actions and complexity of actions not previously seen. The analysis revealed a significant expression of range of movement inventions. Furthermore, the use of BESSR concepts of body, space, and shape were highly represented. In conversation, many students directly related their investigations to the use of the BESSR framework in the Discover Dance CD-ROM. One student stated that the BESSR concept of space had influenced his dance expression. William wrote, "the CD-ROM has changed my space--how I use my space, the ways I use my space like levels, directions, and pathways, and the amount of space I use in my dancing. Before the workshop, I did not think of space at all, now I do." In this statement William not only confirms the significance of LMA informing his dance thinking, but he verifies that he has learned what space consists of (level, direction and pathway). This is not a simple task: even many university dance education students would not be able to identify their relationship to space and their use of space.

The LMA framework supported students' expressive physical dance action. Jennifer's dance "Mist" is a good example. In Mist, Jennifer reveals her knowledge of the LMA in her physical movement clarity. Presented below are three separate areas which demonstrate her thoughtful use of LMA in the process of creating and performing her dance Mist: (1) the expressive use of her whole body dancing as related to the length of time and spatial pathway she would travel in (walking, turning and running) *as* the mist, or (2) in the range of reach space (the distance described between her arms and head) used to signify that she was transformed and now was a person unable to see where she was going while lost *in* the mist, and (3) in her strong weight and quick time effort to demonstrate exuberant freedom (leaping and turning) when pushing forward to find her way out of the mist. While analyzing the students' choreography, it became evident that the structures found in LMA *did* provide a useful system for the students to think in allowing for invention and exploration in the creation of expressive individual dances.

A vocabulary for discussion, reflection and analysis. The data analysis showed that the students were highly accurate using the LMA vocabulary in the identification of the dominant features in the choreography of professionals and peers. They were able to apply this knowledge to dances which were performed live and which were viewed in the short movies on the CD-ROM. Students were significantly able to identify four (body, space, shape and relationship) of the five elements of dance. It should be noted that effort identification was somewhat difficult for the students to pinpoint. Effort identification requires investigation and practice and is inherently complex and challenging for novices as well as professionals.

As observed by the researcher and concurred by the NPO, the workshop students were able to apply this LMA vocabulary in class discussion among peers, while engaged in collaborative dance making and in interpretation and evaluative activities. The LMA framework was language-like and supported the student with the cognitive power of movement identification. One of the CD-ROM's great strengths was observed as the students' ability to control the playback of movies, which further encouraged the students' identification and descriptive analysis.

In the computer lab, Ryan realized that he was able to play the video clip at a variety of speeds and directions (forward, fast forward, backward, fast backward, and pause). Thrilled at this discovery, Ryan shared this information with the class. Soon, all students were exploring the playback function on the CD-ROM's movie clips. The video recording shows the students completely engaged with the controller bar on the playback feature. Several students began identifying the separate movement actions in a dance and locating the point of initiation of a new movement or body part action.

The NPO describes one such experience in the computer lab: "William and John view a Break Dancer. They play the break dancing guy movie in s l o w motion, going frame-by-frame isolating different body parts. Very methodical, one click and stop, they notice the changes, and another click is followed by pause. Moving very slowly, these boys are completely absorbed. William says about John, "He's so balanced, and so fast!" I walk over and ask William what he is doing and he shows me his analysis process and states, "I'll do it [the frame by frame analysis] again, because it's so fun!" The NPO continues, "they are really analyzing the frame by frame movement of the dance."

While using the CD-ROM, the students are able to practice and acquire the skills of movement identification and analysis. The Discover Dance CD-ROM is effective because the student can use it in practical ways: to go back, review, and view their work again; to choose what they wish to analyze and to write about; and to be able to create, record, and remember their dances. Clearly, the data reflects that the students were able to analyze, identify, remember, repeat, vary, and experiment, using the LMA vocabulary.

Furthermore, the workshop students corroborated these themes and addressed LMA's relevance to movement analysis and the creative investigation. Numerous students wrote of the variety of movements in the Elements of Dance section and how the section informed their choreographic choices. Heather wrote, "You can do so much with just the parts of your body, like wrists, hands, elbows, and knees and be very creative." Another student directly associated LMA in her creative process. Kathy wrote, "I now think of all the aspects of dance when I make a dance: body, space, effort, relationship, and shape."

Motif Writing

As stated in the review of literature, LMA and Motif Writing share the historical lineage of Rudolf Laban. Motif Writing is an integral component of Labanotation, created for identifying, investigating, and recording all forms of human movement from the simplest to the most complex. Motif Writing has been identified by this researcher as being essential to comprehensive dance education due to its flexible interpretation and capacity for developing students' skills of dance composition. The analysis of data revealed two themes as related to Motif Writing. The students demonstrated that Motif Writing (1) facilitates organization, preparation and planning dance compositions; (2) supports organized thinking in dance.

Organization, preparation and planning dance composition. During interviews and discussions, students identified the value of Motif Writing as allowing them to create, organize, and record their dances in writing; to translate dance movement; and to communicate with others about dance irrespective of place and time. Student organization and planning in association with Motif Writing was apparent in all aspects of the class. Many students addressed Motif Writing as a productive compositional tool. A good example occurred in an interview with William who stated, "Motif really helped me use my time effectively because now I can record my dances and read my scores to remember my dances. I don't waste time trying to remember what I did."

The advantages of Motif Writing were recognized in its capacity to enable the dancer to dance in his/her head before physically dancing in his/her body and vice versa. Motif Writing's structured organization and freedom of interpretation aroused the students' faculty to create their own movement inventions and to see more than one way of expressing their ideas. Furthermore, Motif Writing facilitated the investigation of timing, mathematical sequencing (i.e., cannon and accumulation), repetition, as well as the ability to visualize difficult concepts prior to their physical manifestation in the students' final choreography. Clearly, one advantage of Motif's symbol structure and visual representation of movement action is that the students could plan, describe, and organize their thinking. It was also apparent that Motif kept the workshop students grounded so that they could explore and think about their dance.

On several occasions during the workshop, students expressed difficulty collaborating and decision making without first solidifying the movement thinking into the structure of a Mini Dance or a Make a Dance printout. Paul and Joseph's collaborative dance making is a good example of the strength of Motif Writing maintaining a visual representation of the students' dance thinking.

The NPO's notes describe watching these two students in collaboration: "they seem to love the technology and the dancing equally." She continues, "each team is going through different processes. Paul and Joseph work out the movement before they choose the symbols. These boys do a lot of analyzing: "It's stillness at middle level...oh, that's a balance—oh, that's ok, try the low level, hmmm, that's hard to jump from a low level, yeah... that transition is hard. Paul and Joseph begin moving, creating their dance from the scores—the boys really seem to be talking it out, out loud."

Once in the dance studio, the students get to work reading their scores and creating their dances. Paul and Joseph are moving back and forth from the printed score. Having the Motif score seems to help them to make interpretive decisions and to work collaboratively. The "Mini Dance" guides and grounds them. It is a useful tool, affirming the team to remain focused on their task and to spend less time arguing.

Supports complex thinking strategies learning in dance. In the analysis of data, Motif Writing was identified as supporting the student's thinking processes. With ease and discernment, students were able to translate visual motif symbols into physical action on the first day. As the workshop progressed, the students were evaluated with highly proficient symbol to action transfer as is expressed in their Out of Ohio dance.

When observing the student in the process of dance making and dance sharing discussions, the students were becoming skillful at identifying what worked and what didn't, and where they needed to develop new movement material, to the point that they were maturing as dance thinkers.

The language and symbol identification both expanded the students' ability to analyze and describe a dance, but also worked to create meaningful movement choices. Motif writing builds cognitive associations between the written symbol, reading skill, and physical investigation. As students' dances grew in complexity and length, the dance scores and written notation symbols enhanced the students' ability to remember their dances. In preparation for our dance sharing performances, the students would rush to their dance scores for review so that they would not forget or omit anything while performing. Motif Writing became a manner of communicating and memorizing the students' thoughts and ideas about dance articulately and with rich detail.

Motif was the first aspect of the workshop that students shared with their parents. The students discussed the flexible interpretation of the symbols and the built-in relationship of understanding dance when expressed in reading and writing Motif symbols. They expressed their fulfillment in the command of the language and their ability to communicate and share their ideas with other individuals who had also learned the Motif Writing language. As Lilly addressed the inherent value in learning Motif, "It is important to learn motif symbols to make dances and to read dance scores." This is because the ability to identify, to read, and to write dance changes the way dance is understood.

The student application of Motif Writing was not limited to their thinking as related solely to a dance score but was understood physically in their improvisation and performance. An example of this is during a conversation with Kathy. She addressed the new clarity and intent in her movement due to Motif Writing as she stated, "I now think about what exact movements I'm making *as I dance*, because of the motif symbols."

Evident were the changes in the student thinking strategies. The CD-ROM made available multiple opportunities to support problem solving and inquiry activities, which the students found challenging and educational. When looking at the students' written journals, it became evident that the students went beyond problem solving to the implementation of Motif Writing as meaningful personal expression. It is further concluded that the use of technology as seen in the CD-ROM reinforced the students' verbal skills and writing abilities, while building associations between the written Motif symbol and creative process.

This evaluation presents three essential components in a student's comprehensive dance education as defined by the researcher, which were central themes in the development of the Discover Dance CD-ROM. Two of these three themes grant strong support in the CD-ROM, while one falls short. In this field test, the CD-ROM provides only a cursory informational overview of the intended component of multicultural dance education, while it provides convincing support of the components of Motif Writing and Laban Movement Analysis.

Summary of the Findings

In this research study, I learned that interactive multimedia in the

Discover Dance CD-ROM shapes what students learn and creates an environment for the students to organize, refine, and reflect on what they learn. The following is a summary of my findings.

The Discover Dance CD-ROM is an engaging and successful tool for fifth-grade students to learn about dance. The CD-ROM strongly supports four of the Content Standards as defined by the National Standards for Dance Education. In this analysis, four standards were identified as correlating directly to the CD-ROM: (1) the identification of the elements of dance; (2) choreographic processes; (3) communicate meaning; and (4) critical thinking skills. The remaining three National Dance Content Standards, (5) understanding cultural dance; (6) healthy living; and (7) making connections to dance and other disciplines, were identified as not correlating to the CD-ROM.

The researcher defined multiculturalism, Laban Movement Analysis, and Motif Writing as essential components in a student's comprehensive dance education. Two of these three themes were strongly supported in the CD-ROM. While the CD provides convincing support of the components of Motif Writing and Laban Movement Analysis, it provides only a cursory glance at the intended component of multicultural dance education.

When using the Discover Dance CD-ROM, students were "constantly engaged," "focused," and intent on learning. Individual and collaborative activities encouraged the student toward complex inquiry, goal setting and self-evaluation. Students' energy and enthusiasm was apparent at all phases of the workshop, extended beyond the workshop, and continued in their homes. Described as "packed to the max," the students characterized the CD-ROM as a valuable and useful resource for self-discovery, choreographic inspiration, understanding and clarifying difficult concepts, and for outlining and recording their thinking. Students also appreciated the CD-ROM for its large reserve of interesting dance movies and websites for active investigation and as a valued spot for self-reflection and productive dance thinking. One student comments that with the CD-ROM, "you can see more varieties of dances in the computer, and you can find more ideas." Vivid description of student dance making points directly to their construction of dance knowledge in the CD-ROM.

Students, evaluators and the NPO concurred on the range and breadth of dance content in the CD-ROM. Their descriptive comments and observations focused on the comprehensive LMA framework in the "Elements of Dance" section, and the interactive and layered use of Motif Writing throughout the CD-ROM.

The students expressed that Motif Writing was highly effective in enhancing their ability to organize, create, evaluate and reflect on their own and others' dances. One student articulately described the valuable Laban language and vocabulary for communicating, remembering and creating the meaning of his dance. "Motif helped me the most because you can make dances in your mind before you put them in your body."

Using the computer, the students were able to conceptualize, formulate and expand on their ideas. The students were *fluidly* able to transition from dancing to playing the CD-ROM to dancing again. As a result of the workshop activities and CD-ROM representation of all types of people dancing, the students identified their own role in the broad picture of dance.

Students exercised their knowledge in the LMA frameworks, Motif Writing and the other activities in the CD-ROM in their dance making, dance sharing, performance and reflective self-evaluation. Discussing the "Fantastic Dance" section of the CD-ROM, the NPO comments, "this activity ... show [s] that they are really getting this material, but then at a certain point it's just the tiniest bit beyond them, over their heads. Perhaps a perfect challenge!" While the material was rigorous and challenging, students ardently focused making connections to their choreography, creating dance scores and journal entries.

The interface, movies, interactive tasks, (even those created for students assessment) support a sense of learning as a game-like activity. Investigations and time to "mess around" on the computer were described by the students as inspiring and stimulating.

Self-navigation and student-directed controls were essential features necessary for the students to take charge of their own learning. As a result of the employment of multiple methods for viewing and interacting with the CD-ROM, students developed the skills for descriptive analysis.

The CD-ROM changed the way in which these students came to know about dance. Students described their experience using the CD-ROM as a journey and as an improvisation, where they could uncover, discover, consider, and follow their interests where they wanted when they wanted. Students were able to follow their interests, direct their investigation, and were able to learn what they felt they needed to learn.

This work in multimedia technology for dance education is still in its early stages. I hope others will begin to think critically about the integration of technology in dance education. Future research can draw from these results to help expand both the development of new media technologies and the integration of interactive CAI into teaching and learning in dance education.

REFERENCES

Baltra, A. (1987). Communicative fluency and the computer. *C.A.L.L. Digest, 3* (1).

Boyd, P. (1996). A case of a full-service school: A transformational dialectic of empowerment, collaboration and communication. Unpublished doctoral dissertation, University of Kansas.

Brennan, M. A. (1999). Every little movement has a meaning all its own: Movement analysis in dance research. In: S. Fraleigh & P. Hanstein (eds). *Researching dance: Evolving modes of inquiry* (pp. 283-308). Pittsburgh, PA: University of Pittsburgh Press.

Budin, H., & Meier, E. (1997). *School change through technology: The role of the facilitator.* Retrieved from http://www.coe.uh.edu/insite/elec_pub/HTML1998/td_budi.htm

Budin, H. R. (1991). Technology and the teacher's role. In Johnson & D. LaMont. (eds.). *Computers in the schools.* (pp. 15-26). Binghamton, NY: The Haworth Press, Inc.

Carlson, P. (1998). *Teacher-driven design of educational software.* Retrieved from http://www.coe.uh.edu/insite/elecpub/HTML1998/id_carl.htm

Fisher-Stitt, N. S. (1994). What can the computer do for me? Philosophical issues and practical considerations for the dance historian. *Proceedings of the Society of Dance History Scholars,* (p.257). Provo, UT: Brigham Young University.

Gore, M. C. (1997). Using teacher-made software to teach pattern recognition and Construction. Retrieved from http://www.coe.uh.edu/insite/elec_pub/HTML1997/yc_gore.htm

Grey, J. (1989). *Dance Instruction: Applied science through movement.* Champaign, IL: Human Kinetics.

Harrington, H. (1991). Normal style technology in teacher education: Technology and the education of teachers. In: Johnson & D. LaMont (eds.), *Computers in the schools.* (pp.49-57). Binghamton, NY: The Haworth Press, Inc.

Janesick, V. (1991). Ethnographic inquiry: Understanding culture and experience. In: E.C. Short (ed.), *Forms of curriculum inquiry.* (pp. 101-119). Albany: SUNY Press.

Janesick, V. (1994). The dance of qualitative research design: Metaphor, methodology, and meaning. In N. K. Denzin & Y. S. Kincon (eds.), *Handbook of qualitative research.* (pp. 209-219). Thousand Oaks, CA: Sage.

Janesick, V. (1998). *Stretching exercises for qualitative researchers.* Thousand Oaks, CA: Sage.

Jonassen, D. H. (1996). *Computers in the classroom: Mind tools for critical thinking.* Englewood Cliffs, NJ: Prentice Hall.

Maletic, V. (1996). Dance on CD: The medium preserves the message. *Ohio Dance.* (p. 14). Columbus, OH: Ohio Dance.

Margolies, R. (1991). The computer as social skills agent. *The Journal,* 70-71.

McGhee, D. (1999). Collaborative ventures as catalysts for systematic change in dance education delivery. Conference paper for the 1999 AAHPERD world congress.

Mendrinos, R. (1997). *Using educational technology with at-risk students.* Westport, CT: Greenwood Press.

Metzler, K. (1989). *Creative interviewing.* Englewood Cliffs, NJ: Prentice Hall.

Papert, S. (1980). *Mindstorms: Children, computers, and powerful ideas.* NY: Basic Books.

Read, D., & Cafolla, R. (1997). *Multimedia portfolios for preservice teachers: From Theory to Practice.* Retrieved from http://www.coe.uh.edu/insite/elec_pub/HTML1997/cp_read.htm

Resta, P. (Spring, 1993). Technology and changing views of the learning process. *Journal of Texas Public Education 1,* 67-77.

Riel, M. (1996). The Internet: A land to settle rather than an ocean to surf and a new "place" for school reform through community development. *T. I. E. News, 7*(2), 10-15.

Ryder, R. J., & Hughes, T. (1997). *Internet for educators.* Upper Saddle River, NJ: Prentice Hall, 53.

Sandholtz, J. H., Ringstaff, C., & Dwyer, D. C. (1997). *Teaching with technology: Creating student-centered classrooms.* New York: Teachers College Press.

Spradley, J. (1979). *The ethnographic interview.* New York: Holt, Reinhart & Winston.

Spradley, J. (1980). *Participant observation.* New York: Holt, Reinhart & Winston.

Stinson, S. (1985). Research as art: New directions for dance educators. Proceedings of the Third International Conference of Dance and the Child International (pp. 217-238). Auckland: Dance and the Child International.

Trentin, G. (1996). Internet: Does it really bring added value to education? *International Journal of Educational Telecommunications, 2*(2/3), 97-106.

U.S. Department of Education, Office of Educational Research and Improvement National Center for Educational Statistics. (1998). The NAEP 1997 Arts Report Card, NCES 1999-486, by H. R. Persky, B. A. Sandene, & J. M. Askew. Project officer: White, Sheida. Washington D. C. (Book and CD-ROM).

3

"LADIES AND GENTLEMEN: WHAT DO YOU SEE? WHAT DO YOU FEEL?" A STORY OF CONNECTED CURRICULUM IN A THIRD-GRADE DANCE EDUCATION SETTING

Karen E. Bond and Byron Richard

This article illuminates teaching and learning, as represented in a dance education action research project at a Pennsylvania charter school. An ethnically diverse third grade of 25 nine- and ten-year-olds participated in the study. In narrative style, the article synthesizes data gathered through observation, interviews, children's drawings and writings about dance, and the teacher's reflective journal to portray a collaborative process of curriculum development and participants' engagement in meaning-making. Research findings are then related to current issues in public school education and teacher professional development. The chapter concludes with a return to the voices of students and teacher, whose meanings extend previous curriculum research and resonate with possibilities for the future.

The project's origins were serendipitous and spontaneous. We were both new arrivals to Philadelphia, Karen coming to join Temple University's dance faculty from the University of Melbourne, Australia, and Byron arriving from The Perpich Center for Arts Education in Minnesota to begin a Ph.D. program. Byron had been Dance Education Coordinator at the Perpich Center for four years, providing professional support for K-12 teachers across the state. Soon after, we met Shane[1], a performing-arts specialist teacher, and seeds of collaboration were planted. To advance her professional development, and with permission of the school, Shane agreed to join us in an intensive inquiry into collaborative curriculum, a form of action research in which students and teachers share authority for class content (Bond, 2001; Bond and Deans, 1997).

---

[1] For anonymity, pseudonyms are employed for teacher and students.

Our curriculum journey took place in an environment shaped by educational reform. As a founding member of a four year old charter school, Shane's experience is at the forefront of recent systemic changes that include the creation of alternative models of schooling in the public sector, often in settings that incorporate arts teaching and learning (Riddell, 1997). Shane's school embraced a "multiple intelligences" approach in broad support of student achievement (Gardner, 1983).

Trained as a general elementary and mathematics teacher, Shane also has extensive teaching experience in the private studio context (tap and jazz), where she acquired her childhood dance education. Hired as a general classroom teacher initially, the charter school supported Shane's love of the arts; at the time of our study, she was in her second year as one of two performing arts specialists in the school. In the absence of a designated studio space for dance, her job involved delivering 'performing arts-on-a-cart' to 350 students over the course of the year.

At the time of our meeting, Shane had not yet conducted discrete dance classes at the charter school. Ironically, considering her extensive dance experience, "dance education" was the area where she felt least competent. Shane confided, "I have minimal knowledge of dance education... I am searching for answers to my never-ending questions as a teacher and dancer." One layer of meaning revealed in the study is Shane's ongoing struggle to reconcile her roles as artist/studio teacher and elementary arts educator.

New to dance education research, Byron was also stepping outside of his professional persona to take on the role of qualitative research apprentice. Specifically, he was invited to embrace the values of "experiential inquiry," a heuristic approach to research (Bond, 1991, 1994a, 1994b, 2001; Bond and Deans, 1997; Bond and Etwaroo, 2005) with roots in phenomenology (Moustakas, 1994; Spinelli, 1989; van Manen, 1997) and humanistic sociology (Denzin, 1998, 2001; Maffesoli, 1996). Denzin (1998) notes that experiential phenomena may be elucidated, as they are here, through immersive forms of fieldwork and analysis, and multi-voiced texts. Placing the study of experience in the foreground, experiential inquiry synthesizes multiple sources of qualitative data to illuminate personal, social, and "human" meanings in dance.

Methodologically, experiential curriculum inquiry is a form of action research, involving progressive cycles of planning, action, and reflection in the pursuit of desired educational change (Carr and Kemmis, 1986; Murray and Lawrence, 2000). It is also aligned with recent developments in narrative inquiry, autobiography, and other modes of self-study in teacher education and curriculum research (Clandinin and Connelly, 2000; Conle, 1999, 2003; Loughran and Russell, 2002; van den Berg, 2002).

Both Byron and Shane were engaged in a process of self-study designed to expand their professional identities from that of teacher to teacher-researcher. In this process, the lines between student(s), teacher(s), and researcher(s) became blurred, as all participants focused on the immediacy and progression of direct experience. Conle (2003) asserts the importance of the narrative "moment" in educational environments:

> Narrative curricula highlight the importance of the moment—the experience of the moment and what happens in encounters with people and things...But how often are teachers and students preoccupied with consequences, ignoring how the curriculum is experienced moment by moment? (p. 13)

Dance education sessions took place over five weeks during which Shane conducted nine 40-minute classes on Monday and Wednesday mornings. She was able to negotiate the use of a small gym (20 x 50 feet) for five of the sessions: a light, airy space with high windows along one long side looking out on the playground. The other four sessions were held in the familiar setting of the children's homeroom, where students were used to doing performing arts activities in aisles, corners and carefully contrived spaces. Sessions alternated between settings, with the first and last sessions held in the gym.

Experiential data sources include 15-minute conversational exchanges held immediately after each of the five gymnasium sessions (Byron and Shane); one in-depth 90-minute post-program interview (Byron and Shane); video-recordings of three classes (first, fifth, and last); on-site observational field notes (Byron and Karen); Shane's teaching journal and final report; follow-up conversations (Byron, Karen, and Shane); and students' reflective drawings and writings about their dance experiences. Children were invited to make captioned pencil drawings about "what we did today" during the last 5-10 minutes of each class, providing a progressive graphic and linguistic record of their immediate reflections on each session. Some wrote their own captions, while others dictated to an adult scribe. Captions were not compulsory, but most of the approximately 200 drawings collected have them.

Byron attended all open-space classes, writing qualitative observations and helping Shane to record drawing captions. After each observed session, Byron conducted a brief conversational interview with Shane (van Manen, 1997), practicing the phenomenological discipline of "bracketing" (pp. 175-6, 185), in which he endeavored to set aside his theoretical biases about dance teaching and learning to facilitate Shane's immediate reflections on her co-creative journey. During these fifteen-minute, tape-recorded exchanges, Byron asked Shane to recall what stood out for her, probing for vivid anecdotes that would illustrate her perceptions of the session. Over time, these exchanges became more hermeneutic as Shane began to identify and discuss emergent themes related to her life as a teacher and dancer.

Byron also wrote in-depth descriptions of video-recorded sessions. In these, he transcribed teacher and student utterances and described the movement content of class segments. He also noted his critical responses to particular content and interactions, thereby continuing the process of bracketing his preferences and expectations in an effort to understand Shane's experience of teaching.

Byron and Karen worked independently on descriptive content analysis of students' drawings and together on analysis and synthesis of the multi-modal data sources. We resonated with Richardson's (2000) metaphor of crystallization as we wrote and rewrote the layered data, selecting exemplary drawings to illustrate the felt life of a group of third-graders whose teacher becomes a champion of meaning making as a central focus of curriculum. The resulting story strives for what Denzin (2001) calls "descriptive realism," incorporating real-life dialogue, intimate voice, multiple perspectives, interior monologues, and scene-by-scene narration. We are indebted also to Polkinghorne's (1989) conception of narrative as ordered in time and revealing an intrinsic logic.

As introduced earlier, Shane began the study with the goal to explore a curriculum approach in which students' interests and interactions are integral to the development of content. Her pursuit of this innovation extended the children's prior understandings of performing arts education in the school, which had involved teacher-directed musical and theatrical skits, along with classroom activities incorporating kinesthetic interpretations of math problems and children's literature. The following story describes an unfolding journey in which a teacher widens her pedagogical perspective to meet children as collaborators whose intentions and values are as important as her own. The layers of meaning traced in the story include those held independently by Shane and by her students, and those negotiated as common interests and compromises. Out of respect for the students' individual expressiveness, their writings are not edited for spelling or grammar.

The journey has three phases: 1) The Beginning: "It's a Mystery" (Sessions 1 and 2), in which Shane confronts uncharted space and the (for her) frightening realities of her students' kinesthetic preferences; 2) "Road to the Wild Kingdom" (Sessions 3 to 5), in which participants develop a nature theme; and 3) "When We All Come Together" (Sessions 6 to 9), in which Shane and her students co-create a complex learning environment that integrates Shane's persistent interests in space, "story," and children's emotional and social development with her students' passionate engagement in dancing, linking/connecting, performing, watching, and interpreting each others' dance ideas.

The Journey

The Beginning: "It's a Mystery"

Shane has to plan the first session both without the benefit of the students' content ideas and for an unfamiliar teaching space. Adding to the challenge, she is being asked to "learn in public" (Weick, 1997), adapting to Byron's regular and Karen's intermittent presence as on-site observers. Karen provides only broad suggestions like "draw on your own experience," "share yourself," "you know these children...let them lead you," and "think about things you've done in the classroom and wished you had more space." Having observed Shane in her performing arts teaching role, Karen is confident that she has adequate professional and personal knowledge to take on the challenge of heuristic, experiential curriculum research. Even though Shane had agreed "without a second thought" to the collaboration, she admits to Byron about halfway through the series:

> The anxiety of the very beginning was immense. Not knowing really what I was doing...working in an unfamiliar environment, not knowing you or Karen...The first lesson was, "Oh no, this is not going to work... What am I doing?"

The journey commences in the school's small, basement gymnasium with a group of excited third-graders wondering why Miss M. is meeting them in the P.E. room. Hussein asks, "Are we going to do squats?" From the start, Shane invites children to take on leadership roles. She names five students who take turns leading a warm-up. Child-initiated warm-up vocabulary includes several kinds of leg stretches, a bridge, street funk moves, and push-ups.

Shane has drawn from Gilbert (1994) to plan this introductory session, which focuses on elements of space (personal/open/group; levels) and modes of locomotor and nonlocomotor movement cued from action cards. Throughout the class, she assesses conceptual learning in call-response style, shouting out questions like "What are the three areas of space?" and "What is traveling movement called?" Enthusiastic multiple voices respond to every question. It strikes us afresh that this form of "assessment-in-action" can be very engaging for young students.

Karen E. Bond and Byron Richard

Figure 1. Here's the radio doing the music and I was doing the monkey.

When Shane invites children to "explore your personal space," the group erupts into a "wiggly buzz"[2] of spins, falls, cartwheels, handstands, and street moves (popping and breaking). Shane looks on wide-eyed, delivering safety prompts. Two girls sing and dance a funk tune on top of Shane's selected music,[3] to which Philip does the monkey (Figure 1). Afterwards Travis tells the class, "I was doin' the wind." Shane's intense concern for safety in the open space takes over. She projects, "Find a *safe* spot, a personal space..." In the first of many pedagogical stretches, she proposes a bridge between her space content and students' observable penchant for spinning, asking, "Is your spin high, medium or low?" All want to do low spins and rolling. Shane relents, "Go ahead; get it out of your system" (Figure 2).

Students stay on the floor to draw about "what you did in here today." In spite of the wide comprehension demonstrated earlier in the call-response assessment, only Ophelia draws about the teacher's featured content of personal, open and "grop" space, showing an example of each. Fifteen students create a range of dynamic self-portraits showing handstands (four), spins (four), melting (three), splits (two), and having fun (two). Two boys portray images of empowerment: Pat's drawing caption tells us, "I want to fly like an eagle;" Seamus draws himself pulling an imaginary rope and declaring, "I can do it." Matt's is the only large group depiction, showing a mixed gender quintet "stomping our feet" (Figure 3). Two girls draw "Senor," a male Spanish teacher who assisted in the session. Shane's comments after the first session reveal discomfort with the increased size and intensity of students' movements in the open space as compared to the classroom: "Their movements are larger. They let loose a bit. It's hard for me. I need to back up and change my view that it's dangerous..." At the same time, Shane acknowledges the potential social-emotional benefits of a teaching approach that accommodates the range of individual choices:

> They seemed to enjoy themselves and have fun. I noticed their individual personalities come out. They can take their personali-ties to a new level. I hope it will carry over to recess time. At recess I see problems with interactions between the kids.

---

[2] From Karen's field notes for Session 1; both authors found "wiggly buzz" an apt descriptor for the overall energy quality of this and other sessions.

[3] Shane employs a variety of popular music during this series (1980s-2000), which she sees as a compromise with many children's preferred MTV genre.

Figure 2. It's me doing that spin on the ground.

Figure 3. This was when we were stomping our feet.

With a sense of uncertain optimism, Shane is eager to continue in spite of her summary reflection on Session 1: "Am I doing this right? It's a mystery right now."

In Session 2, Shane adapts the above content to the homeroom environment. She denies several students' requests to do handstands between the desks. Reflective drawings exhibit a plethora of kinesthetic experiences: flying, falling, "movemints," pushing, dancing, splits, "proforming," "presiting our movements on stage," leaping, skating, lunging, melting, rolling, running, twisting, crawling, slithering, and B-boy Travis's "It's a hop" (Figure 4).

"Road to the Wild Kingdom"

Sessions 3, 4, and 5 show Shane's efforts to develop a nature theme based on the students' kinesthetic interests. Observing a strong bodily response to the action card for "falling" during Session 2, Shane plans a class on the theme of autumn leaves. She employs "falling leaves" as a metaphor to advance her open space safety agenda, "to show them that they don't need to just fall to the ground and get hurt by slamming, that there are other ways to fall as leaves fall...our bodies can fall in different ways." She also lets go of a need to go in with specific learning outcomes in mind, instead allowing herself to be interested in "what would happen" when her students explore dancing with autumn leaves. Her perception of possibility broadens further to incorporate informal performance, using a popcorn strategy (students pop up to perform when the impulse strikes) and later inviting pairs to show. Most students raise their hands to perform.

After class, Shane comments on students' use of multiple senses of observing, touching, and moving; along with vocalizing (the wind) and simultaneous verbal description during leaf exploration. She reflects further that students demonstrated engaged learning without a highly structured teaching agenda:

> They understood that leaves fall in different ways and they could watch and imitate, as well as take it to a different level to make up their own movement...and then pair up with another person and try to do it together...I think they figured it out. So, maybe I can step back a little bit and do this...a little freer.

Students' dance drawings confirm that leaf exploration was a memorable experience, with 21 out of 23 showing some aspect of leaf engagement. Only one child depicts falling, Shane's kinesthetic impetus for the session. Others draw and describe people and/or leaves spinning (six), throwing (two), twisting (two), watching (two), as well as following, jumping, and soaring (one

Figure 4. It's a hop.

each) (Figure 5). As in the previous two sessions, most of the drawings are self-portraits, but duets are starting to appear, reflecting the introduction of partner work. B-boy Travis persists in highlighting his personal aesthetic, showing himself in a break-style back spin. Shane's safety concerns continue, especially for Andrew, who also does not represent the leaf theme in his drawing, instead depicting a handstand. After class she tells Byron,

> there are two children who might have to be removed. Their actual physical movements are not safe, they're going to harm someone...and I'm going to be responsible for it! Especially Andrew...his dives and slides and his speed....to me, a red flag.

Simone, another handstand enthusiast, draws herself with a tiny leaf floating above her feet, this session's best example of co-creative curriculum (Figure 6). Simone honors both her passion for handstands and the teacher's thematic content. (Note Simone's magic necklace, which appears to be immune to gravity.)

Session 4, a homeroom session, occurs during a school assessment week. Students spend the entire session drawing and writing about the previous class. Desiring a clearer understanding of children's perceptions, Shane asks children to: 1) Draw a picture of something that interested you in our last class. 2) Write and explain what and why. 3) Write about "If I were the teacher, what would I plan for the next class?"

Sixteen children draw and write about the leaf dance, six saying they want to do it again. For some, the leaf exploration was transformative. Vera and Scott write that they felt like "a new person" and others describe experiences of "flying thourw the aer" (Figure 7), floating, being a feather, and "like no one was around me." Seven write that they felt "happy" during the session. Andrew, one of the two "dangerous movers" who did not depict the leaf theme in his Session 3 drawing, reveals complex thinking and responsiveness to the teacher's theme rationale quoted earlier: "I feel good when I watch a leaf, how it falls, and follow it as best I can. What I want to do more of is watching a leaf fall but show a different way of how a leaf falls." Many make perceptive statements about wanting to do/learn more movements and dancing, including Wyatt, who wants to "do more running and exersiseing because it is good for your musuls."

Matt reveals his emotional stress experienced during the last class, about both performing and personal safety:

> I felt imbarest because I was in funt of the class and scared to go up. I thalt I was going to get hert because I wasn't looking. I didn't want to go up because I thoght I couldn't do it.

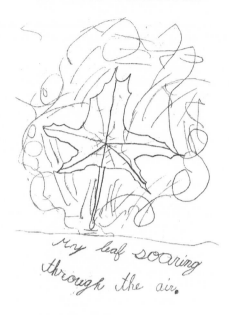

Figure 5. My leaf soaring through the air.

Figure 6. Help.

Figure 7. Flying thourw the aer.

Matt's reflection offers a deeper perspective on his individual affective experience, while also acknowledging the session theme. His self-portrait depicts a vulnerable-looking figure and also a leaf (Figure 8).

Shane's interpretation of the students' writings and drawings is succinct: "They want to work in groups, and they want to learn more movement." In fact, only two children mention wanting to work in groups, while six state specifically that they want to continue with leaf exploration. In addition to group work and movement exploration, Shane persists with her space curriculum in Session 5, conducting a structured warm-up focused on changing directions. She comments afterwards, "I wanted them to be able to use space better. So that was my component that I added." Only Sig, a boy whose drawings often include directional indicators (arrows and circular vectors), refers to spatial content in a drawing captioned, "I was moving in different directions." Several use the term "practicing" in drawing captions, showing a growing awareness of performance.

Shane retains a thematic focus for Session 5, going for breadth by extending to the general theme of nature: She tells the class, "Last time we worked with movement in leaves...I picked a theme for today. It's going to be nature." Voices chime, "Cool." She continues:

> You asked me to show you some new moves. I'm not going to show them to you. You're going to do them on your own. And you're going to work in groups...first, by yourself, you're going to pick out something in nature, and you're going to take a few moments and figure out how you can show what that theme, or object, or critter is.

Without anticipating it, Shane unleashes the full forces of nature when she invites children to extend away from the leaf theme. Much running, chasing, catching, pouncing and flapping are evident with an overall quality of dynamic enthusiasm. Students describe their nature explorations in class discussion: twister, animal, worm, crab, dog then frog, tree in the wind, bird arms, rolling rock, and junkyard dog. Students' drawings depict a number of solo and small group narrative dances around the theme of predator and prey. Among benign images of growing flowers, dolphins, water, vegetables, grass, trees, and birds, we see a "lion and a snake fighting like kids," "friends trying to jump on me, and then they get me," an "angry tornado knocking down trees," and "a wolf crawling" (daredevil Andrew, Figure 9). A trio of two girls and a boy create images of (girl) hamsters running away from and being caught and/or eaten by a (boy) snake, depending on the drawer's perspective. Seventeen children

Karen E. Bond and Byron Richard

Figure 8. Feeling scared.

Figure 9. That's me crawling as a wolf.

draw their interpretations of the nature theme. Deanna's self-portrait reveals her continuing fascination with the pure kinesthetic delight of spinning in space (Figure 10). We are struck by the range of energies and ideas, the "wiggly buzz" that is being accommodated in this co-creative dance education setting.

After the session, Shane reveals that, for her, safety concerns remain primary: "It was a struggle to keep them together and keep them focused...and my biggest fear is that I am responsible for their safety...at all times." Yet she acknowledges, "Most of them do prefer to be in the gym... I can see that the children are taking off with it." She describes qualities and changes in individual children with a sense of delight, admiring Vera's flow ("like it's all connected") and imagining a career for her in modern dance. She marvels at how kids who are low-functioning in the academic classroom setting are showing other sides of themselves; for example, Darren: "In the classroom he's a hermit, but downstairs, today he was up and smiling, raised his hand and spoke without hesitation."

As a whole Shane perceives in these third-graders a "desire to create." Looking back on her own childhood, she says quietly, "I don't remember if I ever really had a chance to create something from scratch, or work with someone and talk about it and figure out how to create something."

"When We All Come Together"

Though student drawings and captions indicate majority interest in the nature theme, Shane's plan for the next class (a homeroom session) steers away from the Wild Kingdom to safer terrain of body parts, space, and dance relationships. During Sessions 6 through 9, Shane and her students construct content based on these elements, accompanied by an increasing emphasis on performing, observing, and interpretation of meanings, which Shane calls "creating stories."

In Session 6, students explore gestures and body shapes, developing into partner and then group explorations of positive and negative space. Children notice the angles, lines, and empty spaces created as they explore different ways to shape and link with a partner. Jemma writes, "It was fun because we did it in partners." Shane encourages social flexibility in forming groups, later acknowledging that she is trying to extend the students' social realm beyond friendship cliques and "Siamese twins."

Reflective drawings include 21 depictions of dance relationships (four pairs, seven trios, nine quartets, one group

Figure 10. Little apple.

of five) using language like "connecting," "linking," "hooked together," "holding onto," and "dancing in a group" (Figure 11). Captions describe individual and group shapes, some detailing specific body parts and points of connection. Only Alyssa creates a solo self-portrait (her sixth), entitled "That's me when I was acting." The other drawing with a single figure is captioned in first person plural: "We played a game called Link."

After Session 6, Shane comments again on her deepening appreciation of students' unique nonverbal styles, comparing Vera's movement style to her own:

> She does a lot of spiraling. She'll circle around herself and then…around others…She just seems free about it. It's something I don't think I have too much of, and maybe that's why I find it intriguing. … If it's more of a bouncing, choppy, I'm fine…like a tap step. But when it comes to something modern, or more of a feeling . . . I guess my personality is sort of energetic and hers is…fluid.

In Session 7, Shane picks up on the students' linking metaphor, adding the element of tempo and "being more creative" to extend content. She directs students to "fit" their dancing to the music (an atypical classical selection), incorporating its dynamic qualities as they move through the open studio space finding, linking with partners, and freezing in linked shapes. Shane invites observers to verbalize what they see "going on" in these performative moments. Interpretive responses to one partner shape include superstar, model, and ballet. One small group performance at the end of the session inspires the following "stories:" "people locked in," "making something weird," and "I see squares, rectangles, and triangles." Shane is excited about these multiple interpretations:

> Some of them are getting it. Like, "I see an image. I get a meaning from it. I take something from that."…Whatever comes for each person who is making those connections is meaningful…a connection for whatever reason they decide.

Twenty-one students draw and write about linking with others (13 pairs, four trios, four complex configurations). A number of these convey specific cultural meanings (Figure 12). Alyssa's seventh self-portrait depicts a meticulous execution of a "bridge" shape, and Deanna's fifth shows her "trying to do a split."

On their way out of the gym, Shane asks each child to "give me a word." She recalls, "Fun came up quite a few times, and friendship and circle…also shapes, movement, free." She sees these word associations as a gestalt, and infers that students are experiencing significant social benefits in the open space setting:

Figure 11. Connecting and linking.

Figure 12. Connecting and linking plus…

"The social relation is a lot better than what it is in the classroom situation. The act of doing it, the physicalness of dance and movement gets them out of that little zone." A highlight of the session for Shane is observing two children from opposite ends of the academic scale working as partners: "At first it was not the best. But through each other's movement they overcame that...there was definitely energy, and there was a feeling involved and an intensity."

She feels this quality of social flexibility would be difficult to facilitate in the classroom setting. Shane observes that Matt, who felt "imbarest" to show his leaf dance two weeks earlier, is also making progress "moving, and taking initiative to move." Matt's drawing of a septet with linked arms and legs in assorted orientations is captioned, "When we all come together," our title for the third phase of Shane and her students' co-creative curriculum process (Figure 13).

Session 8 continues the connecting and linking theme in the homeroom setting. Partners do a "linking warm-up" incorporating arm swings, followed by spinning and skipping in a circle. The session culminates in small group performances that have the most formal quality to date. Groups have to enter from the corridor to perform. The number of drawings that feature linking drops to 14. Ten drawings show images of practicing, performing, and watching, some with performers entering the space through a door (Figure 14). Alyssa finally moves beyond self-portrait to depict herself and a linked partner "practicing."

A notable co-creative phenomenon of the linking series is the continuing exploration of themes from nature, as evidenced in drawings that include images of trees, flower, alligator, bird, ape, snake, and cheetah. Predatory images persist also, going beyond animals to include a roaring, square-toothed giant (the academically marginalized and often hermetic Darren) among a group of diminutive peers, a trio fixing a machine (Hussein), and Seamus getting his leg caught in a machine. Twelve children (nine boys and three girls) draw about their engagement in this sub-curriculum during one or more linking sessions. Donny, a low academic achiever, develops an extended narrative about an alligator under a bridge that spans all three sessions.

Everybody is Going to be a Leader Today

Following is a detailed description of Session 9, the last class of the series. This dynamic finale shows a high degree of engagement in dancing and dialogues among class members, and between class members and Shane, with neither teacher nor students abandoning their individual interests and values. This session demonstrates clearly Shane's growing capacity to "sit back

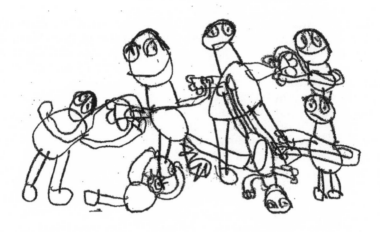

Figure 13. When we all come together.

Figure 14. When people came from out of the door.

and observe," to trust her students in the open space, and to interrogate meanings in her dance teaching.

The class begins with a teacher facilitated, student led warm-up. Shane appoints a succession of children to model upper and lower body actions in relation to spatial directions (a key focus for Shane throughout the series), "front, back, side-to-side." She instructs, "Leaders, you're going to have one minute, then I'm going to change you for someone else...." Students move closer to see the first leader, who begins to pump her arms up and down. Several start to bounce from their knees to the beat of the music. There seems to be a tacit understanding in the class that variations on the leader's movements, as well as completely different ones, are acceptable. Shane offers general content ideas on which leaders elaborate. She concludes the warm-up with praise: "really great job, awesome." The class applauds.

Kids form a circle and Shane asks, "What were some of the themes you saw in the warm up?" No one responds. She becomes more concrete, "What kinds of movements did you see?" This begins a three-minute wiggly buzz in which the group engages in movement description, accompanied by nonverbal behavior involving legs, arms, backs, hips, twisting, circling, and sliding. Shane probes for space concepts with questions like, "What shape is a spin? What direction did they go?" Many children contribute simultaneously.

The session moves on with the invitation, "Please face back to back." Many students understand, but Shane repeats this several times as she surveys the room to make sure everyone has a partner. Two mixed and ten same sex pairs are formed, along with one all-girl trio. Shane continues, "We did pantomime before and mirroring the leader," then explains, "This time we're not going to say, 'you're the leader'...just let it happen." She states that followers will need to have "what kind of vision?" Another wiggly buzz erupts as the group works to remember the word "peripheral." Shane instructs, "Go...move somewhere. And I want to see all kinds of directions, all kinds of lines, all kinds of shapes. Got it?"

During this nine-minute segment, Shane monitors the group, partners two different students, and manages the CD player. Students explore a variety of facings, though many persist with back-to-back. Some remain close to their partners, while others move at challenging tempos, leaving their partners behind. Shane extends the process: "One more time, back to back. Try to stay connected, but not connected. Did that make sense?" Some answer, "yeah." She attempts to move students beyond the physical linking theme that has taken hold over the previous three sessions, proposing further: "You're not linked on, but you're trying to stay with." Students move through space back-to-back, mostly walking. Some stay with the pulse of the Latin music. Some play with faster walks and runs, while others elaborate on stationary actions. They appear to be immersed, and it takes them awhile to respond to Shane's "freeze."

She advances the activity: "This time you can do it facing each other. But you are still not linking arms." Students take off with each other in different directions. A pair of boys drops to the floor to do crab walks. The all-girl trio tries out a variety of actions, with two of the girls appearing to vie for leadership and one moving little and with hesitation. One leaves the trio to talk with Shane. The two others stop and watch her.

Shane introduces the next spatial challenge: "Let me give you three key words: high, low, and (students guess "medium") medium or middle. And you are not to move your feet. Okay? Let's see how we do it." Immediately students begin shadowing and mirroring with their partners. One pair of boys travels across the room, while others mostly follow the instruction to stay in place. Some try moving at lower levels. Some are moving to a musical beat. Shane watches the socially challenged trio of girls and approaches to take hesitant Saleana as a partner. She selects three pairs to show their work simultaneously. She praises and applauds them, which the class echoes.

After class, Shane describes the partner activity as working "on how you feel when you dance with someone . . . looking at them, as opposed to the way you feel when you can't . . . see someone." Whether or not the experience engaged students' feeling in the tactile sense, or emotionally, they adapt to the inherent opportunities for leading and following, sometimes abandoning the back-to-back orientation, yet often persisting with this.

To introduce the final section of the class, Shane stands in the center of the room and, stretching her arms, bisects the space into a two-sided performing area. She divides the group in two, saying,

> We've been linking and creating stories, correct? We're still going to create stories, but we're not going to link. This side of the room, you dance around, dance around, dance around, freeze. That group (pointing across the room) creates the story.

Groups are to take turns with this development. Shane selects a 1970s popular tune *YMCA* (Village People) for musical accompaniment. Some kids start singing the song, and both sides of the room start moving.

Shane cues the first group to "make some kind of pose" when the music stops. They come together quickly, carefully constructing a group shape without physical contact. Dancers become quieter as the shape congeals. Viewers watch intently, moving forward to stand on the dividing line, their eyes on their classmates in the other group. This moment has a feeling of focus, excitement, and curiosity for both movers and observers. Shane calls for viewers' interpretations. One says, laughing, "It's too hard." Tara offers, "Um, I see...there were kids playing an airplane together, they were doing rock and roll." Shane reminds the performing group, "You're frozen." Ellie interprets through the lens of popular media, "Um...some were...one was Elvis, one was Britney Spears, one was Jessica Simpson, the other one was a rock star, and the other was an alien computer."

Observers and dancers reverse roles. This time the observing group steps up to the dividing line immediately. All the dancing group needs is to hear the music stop and they scramble to find their places in a group shape. Shane exclaims, "Hey...I see something that you can find. Ladies and gentlemen, what do you see, what do you feel?" This impassioned invitation has poignancy in light of these post-series interview reflections on her studio dance education:

> I value my childhood experience...technically...Looking back I could say, we did a wonderful dance, we won a gold medal... Okay, what, how did I grow personally? How did I grow socially? We weren't asked "do these steps fit here?" or "can we do the step?" ...It was just lacking something... the connections. My parents kind of made those connections for me, but they didn't have to. I could have done it on my own at five or six. ...And I think this is where I'm trying to make some kind of change in my own teaching.

Back in the class, children respond immediately to Shane's invitation to meaning-making. Language flows excitedly from one young viewer:

> Um, maybe Alyssa is some sort of clown or mime, and Vera is dying, and...and...and Seamus and Travis are watching beautiful butterflies, and Natasha is looking like she's getting ready to fill up a hole or something, and El is looking like she's like reading a book or thinking of something...and Andrew is a video tape of a whale...

Tara adds, "I think that El, Saleana, Natasha and Andrew are...a truck." She continues, "and then...Vera is water because she's dressed in blue and Deanna is a tree that fell over." Shane runs to the CD player and begins the music again. After a brief exploration (time is running out), students run together on the freeze cue and assemble their group shape. Peer interpretations of the final group dance include: rock star, actors, and sleeping.

Shane winds up with a series of quick questions: "How do you feel being involved in this?...Did you see what they saw?" A collective voice responds, "No." "Were ideas the same for performers and audience...or different?" Many voices toll, "Different." "What did you think you were doing when you were posing?" One student responds loudly, "I was supposed to be a mime frozen." Shane finishes with a pedagogical affirmation of the multiple meanings evoked in this dynamic finale: "You were supposed to be a mime frozen, but they didn't get that did they, they had their own interpretations." Children draw for the remainder of the session.

Reflections on the Grand Finale

Student drawings and captions, as well as the session video, illuminate students' culminating dance experiences, showing points of agreement and divergence from Shane's themes of leadership, space, and story. It is clear that the partner experience had impact on students today. Twelve drawings show two figures, with all but one exhibiting a connection to class content in depictions of back-to-back and other facings. However, the only drawing that conveys a leadership theme is Saleana's, depicting her partnership with "Ms. M." Instead, a high degree of inter-subjective relationship is evident in these expressive images of partner synchrony. Even though two weeks have passed since the class focused on nature themes, three boys represent themselves and their partners as animals, Figure 15 depicting a duet of synchronous seals.

A notable feature of the drawings as a whole is the high incidence of references to and images of dancing and moving "for its own sake." Twelve depict a variety of dynamic dance movement images with captions referring to dancing, dancing to the music, the dancing people, and "pose." Ellie draws her "partner game" with Natasha and their balloon dialogue tell us, "I like to dance" and "Me, too!" The popular child-driven sub-curriculum of spinning and handstands is still present in this last session. Matt reflects, "I got dizzy." There are numerous examples of children in rotational expressiveness in the session video.

Unlike Session 1, with its 21 self-portraits, only eight of 25 Session 9 drawings show solo figures. Of these, two depict someone other than the drawer. The others show and describe individual movement experiences. In her preferred garb of long skirt and chunky shoes modern dancer Vera shows herself smiling and saying, "Me making "Y" for Y.M.C.A.!" (Figure 16). Donny depicts himself "Melting" (Figure 17). Two clear examples of co-creative curriculum in this final session come from our riskful movers B-Boy Travis and Andrew. Travis is the only student who refers directly to Shane's story theme in his self-portrait of a characteristic break move. As for Andrew, he retains his aesthetic

Figure 15. Acting like seals.

Figure 16. Me making "Y" for Y.M.C.A.!

preference for "slamming," but transforms it to a mode of expression that won't worry his teacher. His final drawing tells us,"That's me *pretending* to bump on a wall" (authors' emphasis).

Shane's after-class reflections focus on the leadership theme she chose to highlight in this final session, revealing her enduring interest in children's social-emotional development. Today she talks about students' movement preferences and abilities, relating these to their social abilities in other school contexts. She refers to the innovation of spinning that Darren brought to leading Patrice, describing this as a breakthrough for Darren as a leader:

> I think he got frustrated, like, "I want to do more." So, you saw him take the ball in his own hands...He was very creative with his spinning...I saw him...look over his shoulder like, are you doing this with me ... So it's good for him to have the chance to be the leader and to be creative and have someone follow him.

In terms of her own leadership role, Shane cites her spontaneous pairing with Saleana as an experience that unified her artistic and teaching skills:

> As the artist, I was showing my love for dance. At the same time, I was educating her in different movements. So it was a collaboration...It was neat to see...with someone she respects and enjoys working with, she can develop her own creative process and body movements. So that was a blend.

One Month Later

This section highlights Shane's reflections in an in-depth interview conducted one month after the final session. She struggles to understand how she teaches and leads, and the implications of this inquiry for her dance teaching in public and private settings. Recalling the final session, Shane asserts that part of the challenge for students when they offer interpretations of their peers' dance expressions is to be assertive: "Can I be clear about it or not? Can I stand strong on this, look at this from my perspective?" She shares her own ambivalence with leadership as the member of a school faculty:

> It's something that I need to work on in myself, so it's good that they're getting it at a younger age. It's very hard, even as an educator...to come to a table when you stand so strong on something, and be able to collaborate to come to an agreement...

On the other hand, Shane's experience of leadership as a dance studio instructor has been one of absolute power. She is used to

Figure 17. Melting.

students repeating her actions, sometimes with an uncanny sense of accuracy:

> A lot of times it's...me being the leader, and the students being the followers...I can basically do anything...and they're going to model it. When we had parent day...someone said to me, "they do exactly what you do...they're even moving their hips like you."... If I laugh they kind of laugh...

The tension Shane senses between her past experiences and the kind of dance education she would like to provide her students in both public school and studio settings is beginning to shift her approach:

> I try not to let myself be always the leader. I'm doing that more and more...just, go, and see what happens. Try to give them a sense of independence. It's your body, you can move it. You can figure out how to move it.

Shane has taken risks to practice this point of view. The spinning phenomenon, which appeared unexpectedly in Session 1, frightened her for what she saw as its injury potential. In a relatively short time, however, she grew comfortable with the dynamic content generated by students in these classes. At one point, she compares this emergent dance activity with material she would teach from a technical point of view in her studio: "I see them doing dance steps that would be taught in another setting... without being taught..."

Influenced by her expanded sense of students' capacities to co-direct their learning in the charter school setting, Shane has introduced innovations to her private studio teaching with children she had previously considered too young. Innovations include peer coaching and independent dance-making:

> I've been trying more and more to say to students, "pair up and show each other how you're doing a specific step." I'm trying to step back and say, "It's time for you to be the teacher. You put two steps together and then show the class and we'll do it after you."

Shane's insight, however, does not resolve the conflict between her sense of self as an educator and her identity as an artist:

> When I entered college I was entering as an educator, and I left the artist at home...Now, I can see some kind of balance between the two, but I don't think it's a happy medium yet. I want to back up from being the academic educator and let myself

develop the more artistic side.

Shane seems to be in a predicament in her teaching life. Reflecting on the creativity she observed in Session 9 when Darren was leading Patrice, she comments, "I just feel like I need to let them do it." Yet, her goal to develop a collaborative approach to dance curriculum sits uncomfortably with her desire to fulfill the current arts education agenda that seeks to validate dance education on the grounds that it improves student performance in academic subject areas. Perched on the horns of this dilemma, these comments are tentative, almost apologetic:

> Maybe I don't have to give as much direction. I can let them go, ha ha, and in time it will just naturally take place. I think in a studio setting, I want turning to be... perfect, and I'm not looking for that perfection in this. I'm looking for what the body naturally does. So the child naturally wants to turn. It's a good feeling.

Shane's growing appreciation for children's "natural bodies" as a basis for dance currculum was influenced strongly by the large number of children who wrote and made drawings about their perceptions of happiness, pleasure, creativity, and freedom in relation to the session on autumn leaves.

The problems, breakthroughs, and insights Shane describes interest us greatly as we research and work with children and teachers in dance/arts education. Shane's concluding reflection on her students' capacity for inter-subjective learning describes some of the possibility we hold for teachers and learners of any age: "They can watch after someone and...feel the energy and feel the freedom and the spirit."

Discussion

As we complete our narrative of "connected curriculum" in third grade dance education, the language of data-based decision-making is in the air of public education. A recent column in *Educational Leadership* (Holloway, 2003) suggests that "evidence of student learning can be a powerful tool to guide professional development and teacher collaboration" (p. 85). Though our reliance on student responses to guide curriculum appears to resonate with this language, we differ with the exclusively diagnostic mission suggested by Holloway, who urges the use of "student achievement data" aligned with curricular standards to reveal deficits in student knowledge. Instead, the present study relates teacher/student development to immediate experience in the classroom. In this approach to teacher development, "events find their meaning in subjective encounters where knowledge is constructed and reconstructed in every unique situation" (Slattery, 2003, p. 662); in Conle's (2003) narrative moment.

Though it would seem essential for educational policy makers to understand teachers' meaning-making in pedagogical situations, van den Berg (2002) asserts that "little or nothing is typically said about the existential meanings of teachers," which are often "at odds with the rational linear management of processes of school development" (p. 612). He stresses the importance of a cultural-individual perspective on teacher professional development, one grounded in how teachers attribute meaning to their lives and work.

Even though teachers' meanings are seldom considered in policy decisions, students have even less say in shaping educational policy, let alone the daily life of the classroom (Bond and Stinson, 2000/2001). This study contributes to the small body of literature in dance education that does focus on students' meanings as a relevant basis of theory and practice (Anttila, 2003; Bond, 1994a, 1994b, 2001; Bond and Deans, 1997; Bond and Stinson, 2000/01; Macara and Nieminen, 2003; Marques, 1998; Purcell-Cone, 2002; Shapiro, 1998; Stinson, 1993, 1997, 1998). Underpinned by traditions of phenomenological, feminist, and critical pedagogy, this genre of dance education research grounds education in "the being of children and youth" (Vandenberg, 2002, p. 321). Vandenberg traces the application of phenomenology to educational theorizing from Herbart through Freire, Dewey, and Maxine Greene. Freire's concept of "co-intentional education" (Vandenberg, 2002, p. 321) is particularly relevant to the curriculum research examined here for its emphasis on teachers connecting with students' own vocabularies and meanings as a basis for curriculum.

In this article, we have chosen to highlight expressions and negotiations of pedagogical and aesthetic meanings rather than the production of dance art from a discipline-based point of view (Eisner, 1988). Though Shane made a place for discipline concerns and activities in her class, especially spatial skills, and there were artistic exemplars among student dances, our priority has been to illuminate the inter-subjective construction of meanings in a social educational setting. Shane promoted exchange with and between students in a number of ways, such as her ongoing call and response assessment of conceptual understanding and invitations to describe movement experiences, their own and others'. Collected drawings with captions allowed another form of access to experiences—including social and emotional issues—of individual students, and analysis of emergent group phenomena. Shane's strategic invitation in Session 4 for students to express their dance interests and desires resulted in exchanges when Shane acknowledged students' feedback and allowed it to influence curriculum.

At the same time, Shane honored her sense of responsibility for substantive learning, and was selective in her reading of student feedback. She responded to the students' penchant for falling and spinning, offering the leaf activity during Session 3, integrating it with her own agenda of safety instruction. Then, even though the majority of students responded unequivocally to the leaf activity in writing and drawings, Shane decided to generalize from leaves to a theme of "nature." She also picked up the suggestions of two students who asked for more emphasis on group dancing. This responsiveness to a minority voice yielded significant social benefits. During the nature session, when student movement interests exceeded Shane's tolerance for movement dynamic and risk in the open space, she again redirected the class, compromising with the majority student fascination with nature.

Shane increasingly critiqued her experiences of dance education and matched her insights to gradually more sophisticated observations of students and dance situations in her class. She gravitated to social meanings; for example, the shifting capacities of the low academic and socially challenged students. The right of students to independently perceive and express meanings in dance became a pedagogical priority over the nine sessions, activated in part by Shane's memories of her childhood dance education in which personal meaning-making was not encouraged. Parallel to her desire for student empowerment ran a concern about the potential for student injury and her ability to control and direct class activities in effective ways. As teacher/researchers involved in professional development for classroom and studio teachers, we found Shane's struggle provocative. We both experienced internal monologues that went something like this: "If a trained teacher who has danced since childhood experiences such uncertainties, what must it be like for general classroom teachers with no formal dance background?"

Implications for Teacher Education, Professional Development and Classroom Practice

Though Shane had intuited the potential value of dance education for her diverse class of students, she had not been able to make connections between her experiences as a dancer and studio dance instructor and her role as an elementary educator. In this heuristic, experiential inquiry, Shane was asked to be in a direct pedagogical relationship with her students without any mandated reference to an external organizing theory or standard of dance education. She was asked to trust an unfolding, exploratory process, to interpret and shape her responses to student expressions of meaning.

Shane's development as a dance educator in an action research framework has implications for teacher preparation and professional development. Her experience counters conventional teacher education pedagogy based on the acquisition of teaching theory and its subsequent application through clinical practice (Lee and Yarger, 1996; Shulman, 1986; Tripp, 1993). The locally situated meanings that Shane discovers are accessible to her through systematic analysis and reflection. Through the action research process, she seeks student feedback and makes increasingly detailed observations of student responses. She engages with video data and student drawings, and takes part in regular conversations about her experience of teaching. Instead of coming to judgments about her teaching on the basis of external standards, over time Shane pursues a number of emergent questions, including what she and her students are making of the learning process she guides.

Experienced as a studio dance teacher, yet new to dance in public education, Shane bridges the categories of expert and novice teacher. Within the expert/novice paradigm, teachers work to acquire more informed practices by emulating the strategies of more experienced colleagues (Cruikshank and Haefele, 2001). Though she sought to improve her teaching, Shane's efforts to conduct collaborative inquiry in her dance classroom subverted the distinctions of expert and novice. To the extent possible, this inquiry removed explicit influences of experts and supported Shane in a pragmatic inquiry about her own values and experience, and the experiences of her students.

Shane's activities intersect with current teaching reform initiatives. Holloway (2003) cited above underscores fundamental expectations of teachers engaged in professional development. Reforming teachers can be asked to critique their practices (Carr and Kemmis, 1986) and to collect, document, and interpret student work for purposes of making formative and summative assessments (Kafka, 2003), often with the intention of meeting the unique needs of individual learners (Tomlinson, 1995). Shane's development implicitly engages and extends these activities of reforming teachers.

Examining Student Work

The phrase "looking at student work" has been used to describe contexts for teachers to build understanding of student experiences and classroom work. Typically these contexts involve convening teacher groups to engage in deliberate discussion about examples of student work. The goal is to "interrupt or slow down teachers' usual responses to student work and to stimulate an open-minded but focused examination of what that work can tell teachers about student understanding and teaching practice" (Kafka, 2003, p. 188).

These efforts often employ group processes that seek to limit the intrusion of interpretations and evaluations that are not based on the evidence at hand, and to encourage description instead. In the present study, Shane was similarly invited to engage with student learning directly through a descriptive process. This inquiry differs from current models for examining student work, however, by including evidence of the teacher's inter-subjective response and the teacher/student collaborative process of making work.

While current research on examining student work does not provide detail about the shifts in teaching practice that occur (p. 186), this study reveals Shane's growing understanding of the meanings of her teaching and of her students' dancing. To allow this level of detail, the study provided many opportunities for Shane to state, critique, revise and elaborate on her understanding of classroom experiences.

Differentiated Learning

Currently, the No Child Left Behind Act (2001) drives the efforts of many schools and teachers to collect and interpret data on student achievement, often in the form of standardized test scores. The act penalizes schools whose disaggregated scores on achievement tests [Sec. 1111(b)(3)(C)(xiii)] fail to meet minimum standards of academic progress in math and reading from year to year. The act has sparked new interest in raising student test scores, and in some cases, in how to respond to the variety of student learning styles and dispositions.

"Differentiated instruction" deconstructs the notion that all children can learn the same things in the same ways and suggests that teachers respond to differences among students by making modifications among one or more of these educational elements: subject content, classroom processes, learning product, and classroom environment (Tomlinson, 1994, 1995, 2002). Differentiated classrooms are described as places where student differences are studied as a basis for planning, assessment is ongoing and diagnostic, multiple forms of intelligence are supported, and excellence is defined by individual growth from a starting point.

Guided by a pursuit of meanings that have intrinsic value for students, Shane's thoughtful reflection on linguistic and visual evidence helped her to support students in making choices about their dancing that were satisfying to both individuals and the group as a whole. She augmented the scope of differentiation in her classroom by facilitating cohesive group aesthetic experiences that often accommodated and extended individual styles of learning.

What about teacher differentiation? Rather than valorizing the accumulation of an increasing repertoire of tools, techniques, and instructional approaches to meet the potentially endless variety of student learning styles, temperaments, and affinities, Shane's experience reveals the possibility of authentic, in the moment, teacher leadership in pursuit of collaborative meaning-making. Without negating the value of skill development, she comes to place a higher priority on discovering and responding to emergent meanings in her classroom.

Class Size

Recent research indicates the benefits of small class size for reducing persistent achievement gaps between social groups (Achilles, Finn and Gerber, 2002). Earlier and concurrent research also shows that although staff-to-student ratio is important, quality of teacher attention is also significant for students to experience the benefit of small class size (Cohen, Raudenbush, and Ball, 2002; Maxwell, 1996). The size of Shane's class in this study was 23 students, at the large end of the class size continuum at primary level. We conjecture that the affirmation of students' and teacher's personal style active in the study may have been a moderating influence on the importance of small class size, and that the responsibility for teaching and learning could be diffused similarly in many learning environments, leveraging the teacher to student ratio considerably.

Teacher Inquiry

This project was designed to meet Shane's professional development goals, as well as those of the co-authors—a university professor and a Ph.D. student. Shane's experiences and her interactions with her co-researchers point toward the potential value and versatility of collaborative, disciplined inquiry into the meanings of educational relationships and situations. Further, our study illuminates the potential of experiential curriculum inquiry for deep and sustainable teacher education, thereby contrasting observations made by some educational research authorities that research either doesn't answer teachers' questions, or worse, has been used to disempower them (Willis, 1994, p. 6).

Similar attitudes toward research may prevail in teacher education generally. Ducharme and Ducharme (1996) suggest that the reception of research, by teacher education institutions and teachers, is often complicated by the difficulty of reducing education to the application of theory into replicable practice. Studies about the use of teacher education research indicate that the literature is ignored by the very practitioners and institutions it was designed to benefit (p. 1031).

In considering why this may be so, Berliner (2002) describes the extraordinary difficulties of conducting research in educational settings, especially for those who are interested only in results that have the generalizability and predictive power of the natural sciences. He argues that such thinking fails to recognize the nature of educational inquiry, specifically that findings of educational research often add up to different conclusions for different practitioners, in different contexts and historical periods. Noting the lag between the production of educational research and its application, Eisner (1992) asserts that schools provide teachers with few opportunities to apply what they know, and if they do succeed in making an application of their knowledge, the school environment provides little feedback on their work (p. 592).

This inquiry contributes to the growing discourse on the role of self-study in pre-service and in-service teacher education (Buck, 2003; Hansen, 2001; Loughran and Russell, 2002; Martusewicz, 2001; Ottey, 1996). Hansen suggests, "to judge from its long tradition, the most important factor in the practice of teaching is the person who occupies the role of teacher" (p. 20). Ottey (1996) argues that training which stresses the development of personal voice will have the greatest impact on teachers (p. 40).

Buck (2003) employed a case study approach to research primary teachers' meanings of dance. Nine New Zealand classroom teachers with diverse dance experience went through a professional development activity in which the researcher interviewed each teacher, observed in classes and engaged them individually or in small groups in a shared dance-making activity. The study found that teachers' meanings of dance were often grounded in cultural stereotypes related to training, performance, and "high art" aesthetic values. Like Shane, these teachers wanted to look beyond themselves and their students for content.

Buck's study concluded that many obstacles to teaching dance disappear when meanings emerge from within the classroom instead of being imposed from external expectations and theories. This finding is congruent with those of our intensive study of a single teacher in a collaborative curriculum context. Shane seeks to understand local relationships and student construction of knowledge, developing and applying discoveries based on classroom feedback. Her struggles to obtain and use self-reliant understandings of dance teaching and learning in her classroom underscore Berliner's (2002) admonition that:

> We should never lose sight of the fact that children and teachers in classrooms are conscious, sentient, and purposive human beings, so no scientific explanation of human behavior could

ever be complete. In fact, no unpoetic description of the human condition can ever be complete (p. 20).

Back to the Future: Synthesis and Postscript

Returning to the conscious, sentient, and purposive environment of third-grade dance education, students' reflective drawings and captions provide a multi-modal perspective on curriculum as a process of meaning-making. Drawings reveal a complex assortment of meanings with accumulations and layerings around natural themes, interactions with other students, and popular cultural phenomena. Children's connection to nature and animals has been illuminated in other early childhood dance settings (Bond, 1994a, 2001; Bond and Deans, 1997; Purcell Cone, 2002). Intrapersonal meanings are also represented, suggesting that reflective drawing may be a useful tool for identifying individual differences and motivators. Some intrapersonal meanings were persistent and transformative, revealing children's affinity for what Bond and Stinson (2000/01) have called "superordinary" experiences in dance.

Even though only one drawing produced in the final session reflected Shane's major theme of "story" (Figure 18), her students' high engagement in writing and verbal interaction is a feature of the series, and their drawings have an overall quality of natural realism in which children depict "what happened" in the dance classes. Further, similar to Purcell Cone's (2002) study of first-graders' creation of dances inspired by a story, these third-graders both talked and sang during dance classes. The Appendix provides a categorized list of children's vocabulary (words and phrases) gathered from video transcripts and drawing captions.

Regarding the influence of gender roles on students' participation, there was a general absence of gender antagonism, although some notable polarizations were noted; for example the trio composed of a predatory boy snake chasing two girl hamsters. Boys persisted more than girls in the pursuit of themes from nature during the linking and connecting series. The collective kinesthetic affinity for spinning, explored both directly and symbolically (in the leaf session), seemed to create an early bond between the sexes in this group. Although not dominant, mixed gender pairings and groupings were evident and depicted in the drawings. One of our favorites is Jesse's portrayal of his back-to-back duet with a superordinarily long-haired Tara from the final session (Figure 19). Overall, the drawings provide a concrete source of data on the students' awareness of gender, with depictions ranging from strong images of genderedness (e.g. Figures 4 and 6) to neutral (e.g. Figures 3 and 14). Another favorite from the collection as a whole is Vera's tender illustration of herself "performing" the maternal

Figure 18. My story.

Figure 19. Back to back.

caring role (Figure 20).

Students' engagement in kinesthetic social experiences developed progressively over the series, reaching a level of what Bond refers to as aesthetic community. She described this phenomenon first in relation to nonverbal children with dual sensory impairments (1991, 1994b), and since then in several Australian early childhood dance contexts (Bond, 1994a, 2001). The common denominator in all these studies is commitment to student-influenced, collaborative curriculum. Characteristics of aesthetic community observed in Shane's class include accommodation of individual differences, emergence of a collective style of movement, whole body engagement of individuals with heightened group affect, creation of new forms, and participants' adaptability in shifting between roles of performer and observer.

Bond (1991, 1994b) found that affirmation of personal style is central to the development of aesthetic community, along with relaxation of classroom status hierarchies. Shane's acceptance of children's dynamic movement preferences is salient, along with her encouragement of leadership and individual interpretations of performances. Development of group style was observed in the gradual transformation from solo, parallel dancing to more frequent instances of spirited group dancing. As the final session shows, the class has created a fluid inter-subjective relationship in which children alternate easily between focused self-presentation and committed observation and interpretation of each other's dances.

In an informal conversation 18 months after the field research, Shane stated, "I see students differently." Unfortunately, a change of principals had resulted in a less arts-friendly environment at the charter school. Shane has changed schools and opened her own dance studio. Recently, in an email, she commented further on what she learned about teaching through our research collaboration. She writes:

> I see now that all children create their own educational path. I can creatively weave the required information in and through student led curriculum...allow students to have a voice in their educational destiny. Constant reflection makes a better teacher. Careful observations make the teacher more in tune with students. Now with that said, I look at my students with a new lens, a lens that is more flexible, child centered and evolving at all times.

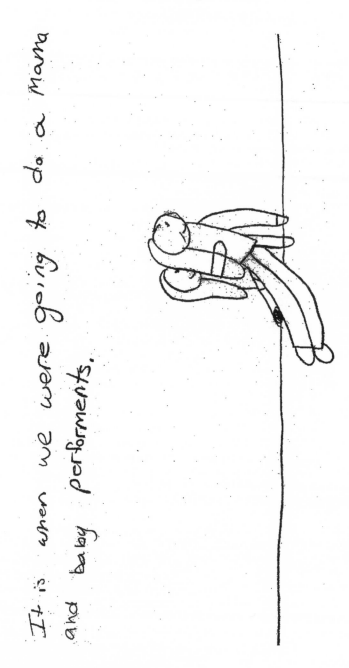

Figure 20. A mama and baby performents.

REFERENCES

Achilles, C. M., Finn, J. D., & Gerber, S. B. (2000). Small classes do reduce the test-score achievement gap. Paper presented to the Annual Meeting of the Council of Great City Schools, Los Angeles. Retrieved from http://searcheric.org/

Anttila, E. (2003). *A Dream Journey to the Unknown: Searching for Dialogue in Dance Education.* Helsinki, Finland: Theatre Academy.

Berliner, D.C. (2002). Educational research: The hardest science of all. *Educational Researcher, 31,* 8: 18-20.

Bond, K. E. (1991). Dance for children with dual sensory impairments. Unpublished Ph.D. thesis, La Trobe University, Bundoora, Victoria, Australia.

Bond, K.E. (1994a). How 'wild things' tamed gender distinctions. *Journal of Physical Education Recreation and Dance, 65,* 2: 28-33.

Bond, K.E. (1994b). Personal style as a mediator of engagement in dance: Watching Terpsichore rise. *Dance Research Journal, 26,* 1: 15-26.

Bond, K.D. (2001). "I'm not an eagle, I'm a chicken!" Young children's experiences of creative dance. *Early Childhood Connections, 7,* 4: 41-51.

Bond, K. E., & Deans, J. (1997). Eagles, reptiles and beyond: A co-creative journey in dance. *Childhood Education. International Focus Issue,* 366-371.

Bond, K. E., & Stinson, S. W. (2001). "I feel like I'm going to take off!": Young people's experiences of the superordinary in dance. *Dance Research Journal, 32,* 2:52-87.

Buck, R. (2003). Teachers and dance in the classroom: "So do I need my tutu?" Ph.D. Thesis, Otago University, Dunedin, New Zealand.

Carr, W., & Kemmis, S. (1986). *Becoming critical: Education, knowledge and action research.* Philadelphia: Falmer Press.

Clandinin, J., & Connelly, F.M. (2000). *Narrative inquiry: Experience and story in qualitative research.* New York: Jossey-Bass.

Cochran-Smith, M., & Lytle. S.L. (2001). Beyond certainty: Taking an inquiry stance on practice. In A. Liebermann (ed.) *Teachers caught in the action: Professional development that matters.* (pp. 45-58). New York: Teachers College Press.

Cohen, D.K., Raudenbush, S.W., & Ball, S.W. (2002). Resources instruction, and research. In R. Boruch and F. Mosteller (eds.) *Evidence matters: Randomized trials in educational research.* (pp. 80-119). Washington, D.C.: The Brookings Institution.

Conle, C. (1999). Why narrative? Which narrative? Our struggle with time and place in teacher education. *Curriculum Inquiry, 29,* 1:7-33.

Conle, C. (2003). An anatomy of narrative curricula. *Educational Researcher, 32,* 3: 3-15.

Cruickshank, D.R., & Haefele, D. (2001). Good Teachers, Plural. *Educational Leadership, 58,* 5: 26-30.

Denzin, N. (1998). *The landscape of qualitative research: Theories and issues.* Thousand Oaks, CA: Sage.

Denzin, N. (2001). *Interpretive interactionism, 2nd Ed.* Thousand Oaks, CA: Sage.

Ducharme & Ducharme, M. K. (1996). Needed research in teacher education. In J. Sikula (ed.), *Handbook of research on teacher education. 2nd ed.* New York: Simon and Schuster Macmillan.

Eisner, E.W. (1988). *The role of discipline-based art education in America's schools.* Los Angeles, CA: Getty Center for Education in the Arts.

Eisner, E.W. (1992). The misunderstood role of the arts in human development. *Phi Beta Kappan*, April, 592.

Gilbert, A. G. (1994). *Creative dance for all ages: A conceptual approach.* Reston, VA: American Alliance for Health, Physical Education, Recreation and Dance.

Hansen, D. (2001). *Exploring the moral heart of teaching: Toward a teacher's creed.* New York: Teachers College Press.

Holloway, J. H. (2003). Linking professional development to student learning. *Educational Leadership, 61*, 3:85-6.

Kafka, J. (2003). Looking at student work for teacher learning, teacher community, and school reform. *Phi Delta Kappan. 85*, 3: 185-192.

Lee, O., & Yarger, S. J. (1996). Modes of inquiry in research on teacher education. In J, Sikula (ed) *Handbook of research on teacher education. 2d. ed.* New York: Simon and Schuster Macmillan.

Loughran, J., & Russell, T. (eds.) (2002). *Improving teacher education practices through self-study.* New York: RoutledgeFalmer.

Macara, A., & Nieminen, P. (2003). Children's representations of dancers and dancing: Children in Portugal and in Finland express themselves about dance. Di_logos Possiveis: Proceedings of the 9th Dance and the Child International Conference. Salvador, Bahia, Brazil.

Maffesoli, Michel (1996). *The contemplation of the world: Figures of community style.* Tr. Susan Emanuel. Minneapolis: University of Minnesota Press.

Martusewicz, R.A. (2001). *Seeking passage: Post-structuralism, pedagogy, ethics.* New York: Teachers College Press.

Maxwell, J. (1996). *Using qualitative research to develop causal explanations.* Cambridge, MA: Harvard Project on Schooling and Children.

Moustakas, C. (1994). *Phenomenological research methods.* Thousand Oaks, CA: Sage Publications, Inc.

Murray, L., & Lawrence, B. (2000). *Practitioner-based enquiry: Principles for postgraduate research.* London: Falmer Press.

No Child Left Behind Act of 2001, Pub. L. No. 107-110. Retrieved from http://www.ed.gov/policy/elsec/leg/esea02/107-110.pdf

Ottey, S.D. (1996). Critical pedagogical theory and the dance educator. *Arts Education Policy Review, 98*, 5:31-40.

Purcell Cone, T. (2002). Off the page: Children's creative dance as a response to children's literature. Unpublished Ph.D. dissertation. Temple University, Philadelphia, PA.

Richardson, L. (2000). Writing as a method of inquiry. In N. Denzin and Y. Lincoln (eds.), *Handbook of qualitative research*. Thousand Oaks, CA: Sage Publications, Inc.

Riddell, J. B. (1997). The political climate and arts education. *Arts Education Policy Review, 98,* 5:2-8.

Shapiro, S. (ed.) (1998). *Dance, power and difference: Critical and feminist perspectives on dance education.* Champaign, Illinois: Human Kinetics Publishers, Inc.

Shulman, L. (1986). Those who understand: Knowledge growth in teaching. *Educational Researcher, 15,* 4-14.

Slattery, P. (2003). Hermeneutics, subjectivity, and aesthetics: Internationalizing the interpretive process in U.S. curriculum research. In W. Pinar (ed.) *International Handbook of Curriculum Research.* (pp. 651-665). Mahwah, New Jersey: Lawrence Erlbaum Associates.

Sparshott, F. (1988). *Off the ground: First steps towards a philosophical consideration of dance.* Princeton: Princeton University Press.

Spinelli, E. (1989). *The interpreted world: An introduction to phenomenological psychology.* Newbury Park, CA: Sage Publications, Inc.

Stinson, S.W. (1993). A place called dance in school: Reflecting on what students say. *Impulse: The International Journal of Dance Science, Medicine, and Education. 1,* 2:90-114.

Stinson, S. (1997). A question of fun: Adolescent engagement in dance education. *Dance Research Journal. 29,* 2: 49-69.

Stinson, S. (1998). A feminist pedagogy for children's dance. In S. Shapiro (ed.), *Dance, power and difference.* Champaign: Human Kinetics.

Stinson, S., Van Dyke, J., & Blumenfeld-Jones, D. (1990). Voices of young women dance students: An interpretive study of meaning in dance. *Dance Research Journal. 22,* 2:13-22.

Tomlinson, C.A., Tomchin, P., Callahan, C., Adams, C., Pizzat-Tinnin, C., Cunningham, C., Moore, B., Lutz, B., Roberson, C., Eiss, N., Landrum, M., Hunsaker, S., and Imbeau, M. (1994). Practices of preservice teachers related to gifted and other academically diverse learners. *Gifted Child Quarterly 38,* 3:106-14.

Tomlinson, C.A. (1995). "All kids can learn": Masking diversity in middleschool. *The Clearing House.* November 1.

Tomlinson, C.A. (2002, September 1). Different learners different lessons: Squeezing students into a one-size-fits-all curriculum has left many behind. *Instructor 112.*

Tripp, D. (1993). *Critical Incidents in teaching: Developing professional judgement.* New York: Routledge.

van den Berg, R. (2002). Teachers' meanings regarding educational practice. *Review of Educational Research, 72*, 4:577-625.

Vandenberg, D. (2002). The transcendental phases of learning. *Educational Philosophy and Theory, 34*, 3:321-343.

van Manen, M. (1997). *Researching lived experience: Human science for an action sensitive pedagogy*. London, Ontario, Canada: The Althouse Press.

Weick, K. (1997). The teaching experience as learning in public. In R. Andre and P.J. Frost (eds), *Researchers hooked on teaching: Noted scholars discuss the synergies of teaching and research*. Thousand Oaks: Sage Publications.

Willis, S. (1994). Putting research to use. *ASCD Update*. August, 6.

APPENDIX

Children's Descriptions of Experiences in 3rd Grade Dance Education:

Actions and Movement Qualities

A bridge	Bending	Cartwheel	Connecting
Cralling	Cricleing	Chasing	Dizzy
Dragging	Excersiseing	Exorsizeis	Falling
Fighting	Flapping	Flying	Folow
Freezing	Galop	Growing	Handstand
Holding on	Hooking onto	Hops and shrinks	Jog
Jumping	Leaping	Linking	Melting
Movement	Move mints	Opening	Pose
Power	Pulling	Pushing	Ripples
Rolling	Running	Shape	Skating
Skip	Slithiring	Soaring	Spinning
Splets & stratles	Splits	Stomping	Strainth
Stretching	Tackling	Throwing	Turning
Twisting	Walking	Wrapping around	

'Practesing and Performents'

Acting	Charades	Dancing with the audience
Go up	In funt of the class	Onstage
Out of the door	Pose	Practicing
Presiting	Proforming	The play
Upfront	Watching	

Space

Around	Back and forth	Different directions
Down	Far apart	Forward and back
Going out	Grop space	Ground
In a circle	Medium	Next to
One side, other side	On the floor	Open space
Out of the door	Outside	Over
Peripheral	Personal space	Rectangles
Squares	Through the air	Triangles

Under a bridge   Up   Up front

Social Experience

Back to back	Chasing
Connecting	Following
Grop space	Hooking onto
It's when we…	It was fun
Linking together	Me and my friends
Me and my group	Most all of the kids
My friends	Parnerts

"They were telling stories about our dancing and pose"

Trying to connect	We are acting like…
We are pretending	When we all come together

Nature and Animals

Air	Alligators	Angry tornado
Apes	Bird	Butterflies
Cheetah	Clouds	Comets
Crab	Dolphins	Eagle
Feather	Flowers	Frog
Grass	Hamsters	Junk yard dog
Leaves	Lion	Monkey
Moon	Mountain	Panda
Rolling rock	Seals	Snake/s
Sparks	Sun	Tomato
Trees	Twister	Water
Whale	Wind	Wolf
Worm		

Human-made Phenomena

Airplane	Book	
Computer	Machine	
Rope	Truck	
Video-tape		
Cultural/media imagery		
Alien Computer	A mime frozen	A rapper deal
Ballet	Basketball	Britney Spears
Charlie's Angels	Chicky Licky	Clown
Cool dudes	Disco pose	Electric Slide

Elvis	Hawaii dancing	Jazz
Jessica Simpson	Like an Egyptian	Mama and baby
Model	Shake your Booty	Square dancing
Tango	The Monkey	"Peace!"
Rocken rollen	Rock and roll	Rock star
Sailor dance	Superstar	

Self-statements and Transformations

Free
I felt imbarest.
I felt like a whole new person
I felt lonely.
I felt silly.

I feel like I am flying in the sky.
I am flotting in the air.

I feel more energy coming in my body.
My leg was getting caught in a machine.
Pretending to bump on a wall

I feel like laughing.
I felt happy.
I felt like I was invesable.
I felt shy.
I feel like a feather when I do this.
I feel like a new person.
I feel like no one is around me.
I feel like a wind-up toy.

4

THE ETUDES PROJECT: INSPIRING INNOVATIONS FOR DANCE EDUCATION

Diane B. McGhee

Thanks to American Dance Legacy Institute founders Carolyn Adams and Julie Adams Strandberg, the invention of the Repertory Etude™ has become an unparalleled gift to the field of dance. In the 1990's, the sisters concluded that study of master repertory was central to dance literacy and that the legacy of dying American modern dances should be maintained. Etudes introduced the idea that kinesthetic aspects of dance masterworks could be available to everybody for ongoing access and performance, thereby perpetuating legacy. Teacher professional development and public school dance programs were seen as vehicles for disseminating the dream. One year after birth of the first Repertory Etude™ by Donald McKayle (Rainbow Repertory Etude, 1997), an effort was made to fuse Etude dance and masterwork studies with comprehensive standards-based teaching and learning. The initiative became known as The Etudes Project. This report describes the dynamic collaboration that shaped the design and process of this new model for dance education. It considers how the innovations and implications advance dance literacy. Repertory Etudes™ are a new source for accessing magnificent dance creations, deepening historical connections, and influencing emerging student art. The Etudes Project is generating unprecedented resources for the field where none had previously existed.

The 1990s were dramatic times of turbulence and promise for the field of dance and dance education. Philosophical debates sparked as educational dance transformed its identity from a misunderstood subdivision of physical education to a core academic subject centered in the arts (Bonbright, 1999). The change caused the dance field to painfully examine the neglect of its own cultural and artistic literacy base. For some time, dancers had been left trying to train the next generation without adequate resources or repertory access (Adams and Strandberg, 2000). Pressures to expand teacher-licensing programs in dance were compounded by simultaneous needs in education to implement standards, develop comprehensive dance curricula at all levels, and delineate assessment strategies. These plural forces influenced and foreshadowed the launch of The Etudes Project. The urgency and risk of moving dance through unchartered waters were imminent. As Project founders aggressively sought solutions to improve the state of affairs for dance, artists, educators, and students were invited to the conversation. Inspiration and new ideas emerged from the collaboration. This is the story of a seven-year journey from The Etudes Project's inception to beginning investigations, from field-testing methods and ideas to considering results and implications for the future of dance. The quest is on going. This reflective paper marks a mere pause in the continuing work of The Etudes Project.

Signs of the Times: Justification for the Etudes Project

Frail Memories

The art of dance lives in the moment- it is present (we see it or do it) and then it is gone. Technology helps us sustain particular effects of original dances but the language is no longer authentic. Technology often becomes a presenter of information about a dance or a media translation of a dance. Other startling complications arise because of the instantaneous, non-lasting presence of dance. Creating analogies to experiences in other arts disciplines may illuminate these complexities.

Consider Pablo Picasso as he completed his painting, *Portrait of Ambroise Vollard*. Imagine that with the last brushstroke, the work suddenly evaporated. For those persons privileged to view the portrait in its final stages, they may try to relate the painting's remarkable qualities to others through words. The viewers could discuss Picasso's revolutionary departure from the style of earlier masters and illusionary dismantling of three-dimensional forms. Some may be haunted by the memory of the work and attempt to reproduce its likeness. Would reproductions be true and accurate to the original? Inspired by a great dance performance, what methods do dancers use to keep a memory lingering?

What if a poem created by Maya Angelou disappeared off the page as soon as the words were read? How could one ever enjoy the poem again? What memories would be left of word, rhyme or passionate idea? How important are written symbolic representations of ideas derived from the mind and oral language? What about dance can be accurately transferred using alternate means of communication?

What if a budding pianist could never hear or play the European classic works of Chopin, Bach, or Beethoven? What historical information and meaning would be lost? What if links to most music masterpieces were nonexistent? How would this change the field of music? How does missing historical information affect the field of dance and student learning?

We cannot turn on a radio and enjoy a variety of dance as we can in music. It is impossible for families to stroll through an important collection of authentic dance as with an exhibit at a local art museum. How then does a dancer perpetuate the legacy of his craft and memory of his work? Which dance masterpieces become the hallmarks of time and culture?

Other than in entrenched traditions (as with ethnic dance or well established genres such as ballet), dancers have been generally unable to pass on their legacy beyond a generation or two. For a dance called into performance at a later date, a classic legal issue emerges: Who owns copyright to the intellectual property? If a choreographer holds copyright "close to the vest," what are the chances the work will ever be perpetuated? What happens to twentieth-century American modern dances when the creators are gone? How does the art form grow without constantly reinventing the wheel of ideas, technical style, and creative craft? If American citizens cannot call up their own cultural dance masterpieces, does it mean that the role of dance in American culture was/is nonexistent? Lack of dance works in the public domain, copyright laws preventing public access, and dying legacy have been almost insurmountable obstacles for perpetuating the founding ideas in American modern dance.

Of course a dancer examines questions of legacy on a daily basis. A choreographer may ask her dancers, "What do we remember from yesterday's session?" Working in the language of the dance she says, "Show me!" Rehearsals insure technical competence of a work in performance. Practice protects nuances from being discarded. It is hoped the choreographer's intent will remain alive and pure. Let us surmise that the work of a particular choreographer is complete and deemed extraordinary or successful by audiences, peers, and critics. Now the choreographer grapples with how she and the dancers will remember the piece until its next performance. The next performance could be tomorrow, in a week, next year, or twenty years away. She uses practice to keep the dance alive in the bodies of her dancers. However, what if the dancers choose to leave the choreographer's company, or the choreographer passes away, or dancers' memories become dulled or less accurate with time? What happens to the work? If the dance cannot be recalled, does this mean it is not worth remembering or dancing again?

In our present state of affairs, some of our early modern dance has been lost forever. Other works of early twentieth-century masters are endangered. Attempts to keep the memories alive have mostly come "too little, too late". At best, many great dances will be reduced to historical text descriptions. "The prospect of dance simultaneously losing its past and its future has been a source of great concern" (Adams and Strandberg, 2000).

It is because of these impending losses that a few professional organizations scrambled to address such horrific happenstance. In 1993 one group, Dance/USA established the National Institute to Preserve America's Dance (NIPAD) (Dance/USA, n.d.). Upon recognition of dance's imperiled legacy, Pew Charitable Trusts and the National Endowment for the Arts became primary supporters of NIPAD preservation efforts. Now just ten years later, much funding support for dance preservation has dried up or has been redirected to other priorities. This ended NIPAD initiatives. Although heroic attempts were made to archive well known works, usually using videography and Labanotation formats, videos and scores seem mainly confined to the shelves of a few select libraries. Therefore, this author believes the true meaning of public access to dance repertory had not been fully addressed.

Established at Brown University in 1991 and continuing to this day, the American Dance Legacy Institute (ADLI) gathers, documents, and preserves archival and repertory materials of American modern dance artists (American Dance Legacy Institute, n.d.). Dancing sisters Carolyn Adams and Julie Strandberg founded the American Dance Legacy Institute. Carolyn is curator of ADLI, a former principal dancer with the Paul Taylor Dance Company, and a faculty member at the Juilliard School. Julie is Executive Director of ADLI and Director of Dance at Brown. Together, they identified problems in preservation and access and suggested responses (American Dance Legacy Institute, n.d.). Other questions then emerged: What works should be saved? What happens too less popular works that are nonetheless landmarks in history? How does the field invite and perpetuate access to great dance works of art? How are signature qualities of dance masters identified? What are the quintessential elements of a particular modern dance?

Similarly, each of us in dance should be asking: "How do we identify a Graham dance from a Limon work, a Nagrin piece from a Parsons, a Sokolow work from a McKayle?" And, what cultural and historical dance information should every American citizen know? How do dancers bring understandings of master works into common knowledge? What implications do these questions have for what and how we teach? Within the mission and goals of the American Dance Legacy Institute, Carolyn and Julie were destined to discover a tool that would give a boost to frail dance memories. Their invention became known as a Repertory Etude™.

What Do We Teach?

Without access to repertory of dance masterworks, teachers in schools and studios seem destined to practice the art of self-perpetuation. What then are the implications for dance education, teacher training, and school curricula? An egocentric focus of a well-meaning teacher may sacrifice rich, relevant, and comprehensive learning at the expense of students. Karen Bradley (2001) comments on the unilateral perspective perpetuated in some dance classrooms:

> Where dance exists, programming is tied to the talents and desires of "we few, we happy few, we band" of dance educators. Oversight of curriculum is not a concept in most places. Because dance has been, in this nation at least, a field built on the cult of personality... (Bradley, 2001, p. 32)

In colleges and universities where nationally accredited dance education programs lead graduates to teacher licensure, standards and accountability for pre-service programs are appropriately monitored for quality. We have the National Association of Schools of Dance (NASD) and the National Council for Accreditation of Teacher Education (NCATE) to thank for their work in this area. Accountability insures that a dance department will offer breadth, depth, and multiple perspectives in programs of study with dance centered in the arts. Accreditation insures a healthy intellectual and physical environment for student learning. Where this accountability is absent, quality of pre-service dance teacher programs remains questionable. Many reasons for poor or failed efforts in dance teacher certification programs of the early years have been described by Nancy Brooks Schmitz (1992, pp. 29-30). Yet, program certified or not, today there remains a general void of repertory studies of great American masterworks in pre-professional and teacher pre-service training.

What then constitutes the nature of what we teach? Just as works of Henry David Thoreau, Ernest Hemingway, Langston Hughes, or Tennessee Williams are central to the study of American literature, master repertory in American dance should be central to our subject matter knowledge in dance. It is not enough to read about a dance. Comprehension and understanding come from working within the language of the body. It is imperative that colleges and universities be accountable for addressing these critical issues within dance departments and teacher training programs. If we expect the youngest of students to meet dance standards and develop dance literacy, where are the curricula, models, and resources to help teachers in delivery of such?

Frank Abraham's states a parallel issue in music education

reform:

> If the national standards for music education are to have impact
> on practice in general education, teacher education programs
> must respond. Preservice music teachers must themselves meet
> the benchmarks set in the standards...
>   The future success of education in the nation's public
> schools depends to a great extent on how quickly and effectively
> universities can adapt their curricula to the national standards.
> Colleges and universities must reconsider their teacher
> preparation programs in light of the skills and competences that
> the standards articulate (Abrahams, 2000, p. 2).

In greater detail we dancers must ask ourselves: How can we
adequately prepare teachers to deliver standards if resources and
repertory access are almost nonexistent? Without these, what does
a university curriculum actually prepare students to know and do?
How does a teacher or student learn intellectually about a work,
know it kinesthetically, enter into its choreographic process, and
understand its intent beyond entertainment value? How do our
historical works provide points of reference for associated
meanings?

We cannot continue to work under illusion or false assumption
that we are adequately preparing our teachers and pre-professional
dancers. Shall we be content to busy ourselves with interpreting
our interpretation of interpretive dance? We must consider what
we can do to foster best practice and strategically plan and execute
solutions that lead us with competence and confidence into the
future. To meet these demands requires college faculty and dance
organizations to embrace new challenges in professional
development, preservation and access to master repertory, and
educational resource development. These efforts will lead to
improved quality of dance education curricula.

As critical as these issues are today, lack of professional
development and networking opportunities coupled with
inadequate dance education resources were recognized and
specifically addressed in 1993 with the founding of the Southeast
Center for Dance Education (SECDE) at Columbia College in
South Carolina. The Center (now the South Carolina Center for
Dance Education) was established and guided by a unique public-
private partnership that included the South Carolina Department of
Education, South Carolina Arts Commission, Arts in Basic
Curriculum (ABC) Project, Columbia College, Coker College,
Winthrop University, and the Coca-Cola Foundation (SECDE,
1997). To support effective delivery of dance education, partners
offered solutions to the difficult issues facing dance and made
them central to the Center's mission and goals. The large state

agencies and higher education infrastructures moved dance education powerfully ahead in ways that could not have been possible by small stranded communities of dancers alone.

With help from the ABC Project, the Center identified public schools with model dance programs centered in the arts. Through grants, Center partners offered attractive funding incentives that spurred others to emulate the models and to grow viable, quality, arts-centered dance education programs. Grants encouraged schools to develop action plans leading to systemic change and arts education reform. The Center fostered dialogue and interaction among dance specialists, dance artists, classroom teachers, higher education faculty, and colleagues across the arts disciplines. SECDE was a keystone for dance advocacy and disseminated information on improving practice in teaching and learning dance. It established a dance resource library providing free access for teachers and artists across the state. SECDE worked with schools and districts to develop dance curricula facilitating achievement of national and state standards in dance. Leadership training initiatives were fostered through the Arts in Basic Curriculum Project. Graduate courses and professional development institutes in dance education were delivered through Columbia College.

Some of the grand forces driving arts education in South Carolina included: federal legislation (i.e., Goals 2000: Educate America Act of 1994), federal and state agency funding to implement standards-based education initiatives (e.g., National Standards for the Arts, 1994), new research studies in the arts (e.g., Champions of Change: The Impact of Arts on Learning, 1999), new developments in arts education assessment (e.g., the NAEP Arts Education Assessment Project, National Assessment Governing Board, 1997), dissemination of arts advocacy information (e.g., through Arts Education Partnership and Americans for the Arts), public and private partnerships, and partnerships of state agencies with higher education to initiate or improve teacher pre-service certification programs in the arts. To meet teacher demands for resources and professional development, the Dance Education Center frequently collaborated on discipline-based curriculum work with faculty at the University of North Carolina–Charlotte, the Southeast Center for Education in the Arts at the University of Tennessee–Chattanooga, the Alabama Institute for Education in the Arts, and others.

As a former public school dance educator, community dance artist, Director of the Southeast Center for Dance Education (from 1996-99), and college professor, I knew first-hand the frustrations of delivering quality dance curricula and training to people who needed it most. Early Center initiatives recognized the importance of working across levels, kindergarten through college, to provide a seamless education for student learning. It was believed that sharing ideas and applying methods of inquiry in authentic settings would set in motion improved learning and teaching in dance. It was widely known that dance educators often worked in isolation without benefits from professional or collegial discourse. Interestingly, within a small geographic triangle, Columbia College and Winthrop University in South Carolina, and the University of North Carolina–Charlotte had each established relationships between their dance education certification programs and local public schools. Field experiences and internship courses were fertile ground for trying new ideas in dance education under the mentorship of college faculty. This connection helped to move dance beyond mere physical activity to its rightful place as an academic field with unique knowledge and skills centered in the arts. Still missing was critical content that could only be accessed through the learning of master repertory.

Need for Inclusive Dialogue

SECDE helped the South Carolina dance community realize the value and power of collaboration. Yet, the voices of artists and their contributions seemed to be missing from the dance education conversation loop. SECDE was aware that quite often dance residency artists were not acknowledged for the important artistic work and ecological changes they brought to a school community.

Artists and educators knew that meaningful opportunities were needed for sharing artistic practices and learning dance repertory. To serve the tiny struggling artist and educator populations, SECDE desired to build a more cohesive community dedicated to the teaching, learning, and practicing of dance. The time had come to make the dialogue inclusive of artists and educators. The professional association for dance at the state level supported this idea.

Artists and educators needed significant professional development with each other. Although one-session workshops at conferences and dance festivals were valuable for networking and introductory understandings, SECDE formulated multi-day institutes and graduate coursework for in-depth learning.

Other dancers and educators across the nation were battling with defining artist and teacher roles in the training and education of young people. In his article, Finding the Thread of an Interrupted Conversation: the Arts, Education, and Community, Arnold Aprill (n.d.) remarked about the changing paradigm taking place across the country. Positive connections were observed in the working relationships between artists and education communities.

The big shift that has occurred in these situations is not just a shift in opinion about the value of the arts as content areas to be covered or skills to be acquired, but more important, a fundamental shift in relationships between the education communities and the arts communities within networks of shared work (Aprill, n.d., pp.1-2).

For ADLI and SECDE, serendipity was about to enter the picture. Their work was about to converge with amazing consequences.

Proposal for a Productive Relationship

In February 1999, Carolyn Adams and this author met for the first time at a statewide dance conference at Coker College in South Carolina. Booked as presenters for separate back-to-back dance sessions, Carolyn and I listened to each other's ideas with increasing interest. We were immediately aware that artistic preservation, repertory access, comprehensive dance education, and professional development for teachers and artists were issues that were intimately connected. For the remainder of the weekend, we drew inspiration from emerging ideas and stimulation from the fact that ADLI and SECDE were vehicles uniquely positioned to pilot a new conceptual design for dance teaching and learning. We believed aspects of great dance works could remain alive and vital through creation of a repertory literature base for dance education.

Coincidence played a role in connecting us again. Carolyn and I were destined to meet in Charleston, South Carolina the following June. Within the same week, we shared presentation sessions at Dance/USA's Education Peer Council meetings and the Spoleto Festival's Teachers' Institute. Julie Adams Strandberg joined her sister for presentations on these occasions. To continue the conversation, I invited Carolyn and Julie to attend SECDE's new Making Connections: Technology, Education, and Dance professional development institute two weeks later in Columbia. At the week-long institute, dance educators, classroom teachers, school administrators, and artists were guided through dance curricula units of study that included learning in aesthetic perception, art-making, student dances and performance masterworks, history and culture, and aesthetic valuing. Computers, special software programs, and digital technology aided delivery of dance content.

Among the sessions, Carolyn, Julie, and I perceived how SECDE and ADLI might effectively address the national dance issues at hand. The idea of an "Etudes Project" emerged. We believed it was necessary to place American modern dance repertory at the center of professional development experiences introduced through "Repertory Etude™" study. What is a Repertory Etude™?

...a dance repertory etude is a piece of choreography or a segment of a larger work that contains quintessential elements of that dance. Seminal choreographic works contain their own distinct signatures, with specific motifs, gestures, and uses of weight and space. An etude may be extracted from the larger work and utilized not only to hone specific skills in technique and nuance but also to convey the essence of the choreographer's style and intent (Adams and Strandberg, 2000, p.21).

For comprehensive understanding of a singular work, the Etudes Project would include examination of the original dance within cultural and historical contexts, application of aesthetic understandings, study of the master artist and his unique process of art making.

Just one summer before, Donald McKayle captured the attention of dance artists by creating a Repertory Etude™ of his signature work *Rainbow 'Round My Shoulder* for ADLI (Rainbow Etude™, 1997). The Etude concept crystallized for Donald as he worked with students at the New York State Summer School of the Arts (NYSSSA) School of Dance in Saratoga Springs. It was not a coincidence that Carolyn and Julie were Artistic and Associate Artistic Directors of the School. During the next academic year, Mr. McKayle developed the Etude with his own students at the University of California, Irvine. Donald brought the finished product back to the NYSSSA School of Dance in 1998. There he taught his Etude to students and teachers in attendance. The concept of an Etude and the charitable act of Mr. McKayle making his work accessible for ongoing study and performance was revolutionary and inspired other dance artists to step forward and follow similar example with their own dances. Lorry May for Anna Sokolow, Mary Anne Newhall for the late Eve Gentry, Danny Grossman, and David Parsons followed suit.

SECDE and ADLI directors devised a plan for teachers to learn more about American dance repertory, preservation, and access. The teachers were to arrive in August at the NYSSSA School of Dance where Repertory Etudes™ development was moving into full swing. Later, SECDE would charge teachers with taking this learning back to their respective classrooms in the South. Funding support was secured for the teachers to participate in the groundbreaking work. SECDE, US Airways travel donations, and public school professional development funds made these ventures possible.

During this time, a dance curricula conceptual design model for teaching and learning emerged. The first ADLI and SECDE conversational exchanges articulated the necessity for shared participation and involvement of students, teachers, and artists in a continuous learning cycle that was child-centered. This author envisioned a symbiotic system of dance learning and curricula development as proposed in Figure 1. It is believed this same system can easily be applied to other arts disciplines. The model is comprised of spherical learning layers that lead from simple to sophisticated levels of understanding.

Figure 1 shows learning that starts with a child's immersion into standards. Mid and advanced learners move sequentially through standards-based content and experiences. Students desiring further training may progress to levels as pre-professional dancers and/or pre-service dance educators. With increased competency, some may later gain eventual recognition as dance master artists or master teachers. The proposed master categories are intended to be inclusive of other dance careers as well: historians, critics, choreographers, researchers, etc. In the model, learning becomes a synchronous and perpetual process that builds content over a lifetime.

Another dimension is added to the progression. Learning is not restricted to the individual learning spheres, but rather, each layer communicates, complements and interacts with learning at other levels. Feedback from learned experiences inform and influence other levels of work. The generation of new learning theories and dance art is evolved from actual practice in authentic work settings (classrooms and studios). Members of learning and career categories never work in isolation or exclusion of others. Of course, contributions by other stakeholders (classroom teachers, dance studio teachers, community leaders, school administrators, parents, etc.) to student learning are recognized. The symbiotic system invites full participation by all parties. This premise assures:

- participants are equally connected to the conversation.
- multiple perspectives are offered to learners.
- contributions of each participant are valued.
- learning is child-centered.
- learning continues at each level of a dancer's career.
- increasing competence of dance knowledge and skills.
- associations are made across artistic and teaching practices.
- theory and practice continue to evolve and inform each other.
- theory and practice inform and influence needs in art-making, cultural and artistic preservation, repertory access, and development of new educational resources.
- Other stakeholders in the learning process: Classroom teachers, dance studio teachers, community leaders, school administrators, parents, etc.

Learning at every stage becomes interrelated and is intended to

Diane B. McGhee

Figure 1

SYMBIOTIC SYSTEM OF
DANCE LEARNING AND CURRICULA DEVELOPMENT

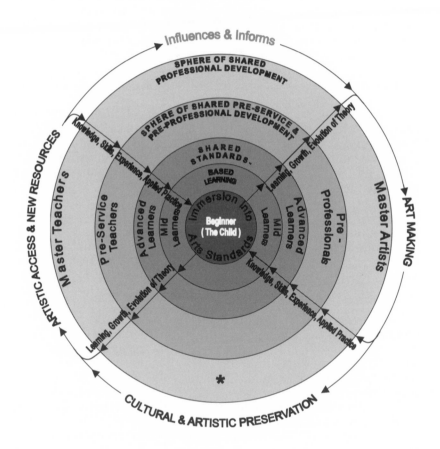

Conceptual Design: D. McGhee 2004
Graphics: M. Parsons 2004

influence and inform work of the discipline at large. Ideally, students gain competence in knowledge and skills while teachers and artists improve teaching and artistic practice. The total action research process results in the production of dance resources and new art simultaneous with preservation and access to dance masterworks. In turn, the educational and artistic resources are reinvested into teacher and artist practices as they work with students. Discipline, knowledge, and skills are therefore ever expanding as more art-making, artistic preservation, repertory access, and material resources are generated for dance. Although this was the original vision of The Etudes Project, it had yet to be determined if this model would work in real classrooms and studios.

Beginning Investigations at the NYSSSA School of Dance

As plans progressed, partnership members of SECDE and ADLI provided related funding support for The Etudes Project. The New York Department of Education through NYSSSA, the Harlem Dance Foundation, and the National Endowment for the Arts (NEA) provided additional support. These collaborations helped to generate further enthusiasm.

Artists at Work

Groundwork for The Etudes Project had been laid just a few years earlier at the NYSSSA School of Dance when Carolyn and Julie fostered a special dialogue between early modern dance artists and students at the school. The assembled group of aging artists represented a unique dance collective that had its origins in the 1930's. Known as the New Dance Group (NDG), these artists created landmarks in American modern dance history. The gathering sparked intergenerational connections. The high school students were astounded by the powerful stories the aging artists had to offer. ADLI knew the historical significance of the body of dance works represented by these artists and therefore applied for NEA grant funding to help document and archive the original works. The quest of young dancers to explore NDG kinesthetic material provided a catalyst for developing repertory studies. Thus, the first Repertory Etude experiments began with works of the New Dance Group.

The New Dance Group was formed in 1932, prospering as a professional company and school through the 1940s, 1950s, and beyond. The founding women studied at the Wigman School with teacher Hanya Holm. Most members of the NDG were from working class and first generation immigrant families. Economic hard-times, social injustices, and world chaos deeply affected the hearts and minds of the dancers. The dancers organized to communicate their experiences and expressions. Their first rule became: "that one must dance on subjects which concerned them personally, and in a clear, almost simplistic manner: one necessary to reach a mass audience" (Burns and Korff, 1993; Newhall, 1995).

Students from all ethnic and social classes were welcomed to their studios. Removing barriers of elitism, dance classes were made affordable to all. At the New Dance Group, marginalized factions of American society found a common forum for their voices (Graff, 1990; Newhall, 1995). The dancers were able to confront issues of religious, racial, and other biases head-on. During the mid-fifties the New Dance Group became a popular meeting place for black dancers, and connections there helped young African American artists find work (Dunning 1996; Haskins, 1990; Thorpe, 1989).

Recreational and social dance opportunities were offered to the community through the NDG. Formal classes offered study in a range of modern techniques and ethnic forms. The standard sequence of classes included one hour of technique, one hour of improvisation, followed by group discussions of social issues of the day (Burns and Korff, 1993). The purpose of these discussions was to inspire creativity- all were expected to create. Members were "motivated by the concept that dance has a contribution to make to everyone at every level" (Delman, 1993). As a result, dance works of this group give insight to our diverse American heritage, its evolving culture, current thought, and hopes for the future.

Although the New Dance Group members are a long list of distinguished and noteworthy dancers and choreographers, ADLI's developing *New Dance Group Anthology* (American Dance Legacy Institute, 2003) eventually focused on the pioneer work of: Donald McKayle, Anna Sokolow, Eve Gentry, Jean León Destiné, Sophie Maslow, Pearl Primus, Mary Anthony, and Daniel Nagrin. The plan was to develop dance education learning modules, tested in classrooms, featuring each artist and a corresponding signature work. Beginning modules were to form the foundational backbone for evolving dance studies. This author presents a schematic diagram of the plan in Figure 2. The first eight vertebrae in the content spine represent NDG artists included in the *Anthology*. Simultaneous with the New Dance Group developing studies, other artists voiced concerns about trying to save and disseminate their personal works. Several began working diligently to develop Repertory Etudes™ under the auspices of the American Dance Legacy Institute. Some of these early efforts are also recorded on the content spine.

Figure 2

EVOLVING DANCE CONTENT SPINE
A Resource Collection of
Repertory Etudes™, Documentaries,
and Curricular Materials

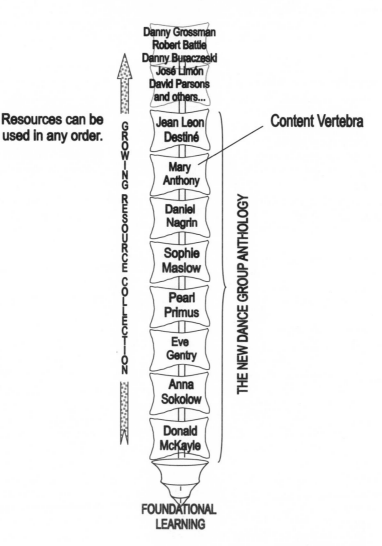

Conceptual Design: D. McGhee 2004
Graphics: M. Parsons 2004

The Charge for Teachers

In July 1998, selected high school students from across the state of New York again converged in Saratoga Springs to participate in the extraordinary NYSSSA School of Dance. Sponsored by the New York Education Department, the teaching facilities were located at the well-equipped National Museum of Dance. In August, the students were joined by a team of nine dance educators from three Southern states (North Carolina, South Carolina, and Georgia). They arrived to take part in professional development classes, conversations with artists, and teacher seminars. SECDE Director Diane McGhee had identified these educators as leaders for developing educational resource materials centered on Repertory Etudes™.

> The chosen group (of southern teachers) represented the diverse population of learners where reliable dance programs existed. It was necessary for work to be authenticated with students and that it address educational standards for dance. Representatives came from schools with extreme variations in financial means and racial composition... The purpose of this array was to give depth and broad purpose to the new educational materials in the initial stages of development (McGhee and Sofras, 2003, Acknowledgements).

Three teachers were higher education faculty from dance departments with dance teacher certification programs: Columbia College, Winthrop University, and the University of North Carolina, Charlotte. These faculty were connected to networks of public school dance educators (numbering approximately 200) in the combined states. One high school teacher hailed from each of the participating states, representing dance programs with regular and gifted education. One middle school teacher came from the urban Charlotte-Mecklenburg School District of North Carolina. Two middle school teachers representing large dance programs in South Carolina—metropolitan Richland County in Columbia and rural Beaufort County—completed the team.

Project accountability relied on these qualified dance educators who previously:

1) demonstrated school, district, or state leadership abilities in various capacities,
2) emulated standards-based learning practices in the art of dance within an established curriculum,
3) were identified for incorporating best practices in dance education,
4) earned school community support through principal

endorsements backed by district professional development monies for this Project,
5) committed to disseminating information learned from Project participation, and,
6) demonstrated willingness to lead further professional development efforts for other educators within their home school or district.

Teachers were given primary access to learning repertory from the creators and began collecting data. Educators listened to the "voice of the artist" in the teaching and sharing of artistic process. This provided educators with opportunities to consider teaching approach, dance style, and evolution of choreographic ideas, along with meanings assigned by choreographer, dancer, and viewer. Teachers were interested in how NYSSSA School of Dance students inquired, learned, and processed the new information. Teachers immersed themselves in technique and repertory classes with junior and high school students.

While in New York, the teachers felt it was critical to observe dance preservation and Repertory Etude™ creation first hand. This information gave the teachers another frame in which to view a dance. Preservation of an Etude involved filming and editing, drawing Labanotation scores (created by Mary Cory of the University of California, Irvine), plus other production aspects. This meant teachers were present when selected etudes were being created and documented. Teachers observed and asked: What did choreographers, historians, notators, and film editors identify as important about a work? For teachers, each step and decision informed the later writing of the new dance lesson studies for the *New Dance Group Anthology* (ADLI, 2003).

Repertory learning for teachers started with the Rainbow Repertory Etude™ (1997). Mr. McKayle and former company member Clay Taliaferro provided direction. The etude was based on Mr. McKayle's 1959 work, *Rainbow 'Round My Shoulder* (Donald McKayle Documentary, 1999). In the heart wrenching original dance, chain gang workers scorched by the sun, recall memories of freedom and consider what lengths they would go to retrieve it. "In every phrase he (McKayle) pictured the stifled and strangled being in man and his desire for freedom." (Sorrel, 1962, p.91) The original work is popular and relevant to audiences today. It is in the current repertory of the Alvin Ailey American Dance Theatre. Teachers knew their public school students would connect to the feelings of desperation, the power of the movement, and the yearning for psychological and physical freedom found in the dance.

During the same summer, two more dances were in the process of being archived. One was the late Eve Gentry's 1938 solo,

Tenant of the Street (Eve Gentry Documentary, n.d.) as taught by Mary Ann Newhall. Studying the dance invited examination of basic survival and the nature of human dignity. In the dance, viewers (and dancers) empathetically feel the pain and isolation of a homeless woman.

Anna Sokolow, extremely ill when The Etudes Project began, bestowed her infamous *Rooms* (Rooms Repertory Etude™, 1999) to the collection. Taught and staged by Anna's protégé Lorry May, the minimalist work highlighted the stark loneliness of people living in city tenements. Thinking of students in their home classrooms, teachers saw immediate connections to adolescents in search of love and belonging.

The richness of the dances were unfolding as a length of red carpet before the teachers. Content previously sequestered for more than half a century was becoming available. And with the unveiling of new content, teachers working with Repertory Etudes™ reshaped their thoughts on the meaning of a comprehensive and sequential dance curriculum. Repertory Etudes™ offered fresh points of view for teaching dance history.

The first three dance studies in the *Anthology* (ADLI, 2003) provided contrast in modern dance style, choreographic form, and subject matter. It was the subject matter that transcended meaning across generations and would eventually give reason and relevancy for engaging contemporary youth in the learning of dances. Members of the New Dance Group believed creating and performing were fulfilling to the soul and communicated deep feelings to others. The subjects that touched the hearts of the original artists, touched the hearts of the teachers in the seminars, and would in turn give meaning to dances created by the youngsters in their classrooms. It seemed that the spirit of The Etudes Project was following the spirit of the New Dance Group.

NDG choreographies were an effective means for communicating specific thoughts, needs, desires, beliefs, and opinions of the time. Sometimes the emotional, physical, and intellectual themes seem to parallel standard learning and psychological theories of today. As an example, some dances align with steps in Abraham Maslow's dynamic Hierarchy of Needs. Using just the first three *Anthology* (ADLI, 2003) dance studies, we begin to see the associations: Gentry's *Tenant* (Eve Gentry Documentary, n.d.) is an example of a woman caring for "physiological" and "safety" needs; Sokolow's *Rooms* (Rooms Repertory Etude™, 1999) demonstrates the city dwellers needs for "love and belonging"; in McKayle's *Rainbow* (Donald McKayle Documentary, 1999), prisoners have lost "self-esteem" and show their secret desires for independence and freedom. Perhaps for New Dance Group members, making dances were pathways toward "knowledge and self-actualization."

The dances of the early years were also statements on the plight of the human within society. This was played out in such dances as *Strike, Uprising,* and *War Trilogy.* For NDG choreographers, it was not enough to consider only the traumas of these desperate personal and social situations. It was the artists' intent to open doors of hope and understanding, provoke thought and modify stereotypes, and perhaps mobilize citizens to enact changes for the betterment of their fellow man. It seemed natural that young students today would recognize similar desires within themselves.

Together

At the conclusion of the NYSSSA School of Dance, students, artists, educators, videographers, notators, musicians, and administrators were drenched in perspiration and inspiration. The collaborations to preserve and give living legacy to dying indigenous American modern dance works invited new camaraderie and respect for each other. Creating and documenting etude work had turned out to be an education in itself. Ms. Adams and Ms. Strandberg encouraged students and teachers to take the work home and share repertory ideas in as many ways possible-and they did! Students returned to towns across New York. Artists returned to their homes across the country where they would continue to reflect and refine their work. Teachers returned to the South to meet their next and biggest challenge.

Field Tests in Southern Schools

As a result of learning experiences in Saratoga, questions emerged. What would teachers share with their students in the classroom? What would be selected to include in dance curricula? Would the Repertory Etudes™ perpetuate the kinesthetic legacy of dance? Teachers chose a variety of ways to deliver the new content and inspire the learners. The educators had been asked to experiment with methods and practices that would serve as guideposts for future learning and teaching. Each practitioner concentrated on using one or more Repertory Etudes™ throughout the next school year. Working with youngsters within their well-established programs, teachers connected content to existing school dance curricula. Every aspect of the work addressed district, state, and national standards for dance. Participants became part of a grand action research project as they experimented, documented, analyzed and synthesized information, applied ideas, predicted outcomes, and shared their results with others.

The long-term purpose of the work was to assist other

educators in the teaching and learning of dance by developing
resources where none had previously existed. The immediate goal
was to assemble best ideas and practices into a series of dance
education lesson studies centered on New Dance Group artists and
their signature works. Prior to this time, public school dance
educators had long searched for kinesthetic connections to
masterworks. They valued the study of varied choreographic
processes that could be used with youngsters and that would result
in the creation of quality personal art. Learning Repertory
Etudes™ gave the teachers a huge leap forward in this journey.
Research continued for the next two years.

   The SECDE Director had asked educators to track what was
being taught in classrooms and to document the learning progress
of students. During this time, an overwhelming amount of
documentation was generated at each school site. I therefore
enlisted the help of Associate Professor of Dance and Dance
Education at UNC–Charlotte, Pamela Sofras, to assist in reviewing
teacher and student work in the project. Professor Sofras had been
involved in discussions and workshops from the beginning of The
Etudes Project. Over the years, she had trained a large percentage
of dance educators in the state of North Carolina and was therefore
experienced in observing dance education practices and programs.
Pamela monitored project work in North Carolina schools; I did
the same in South Carolina and with the participating school in
Georgia.

   In sharing our observations, together we discovered something
quite remarkable. It seemed New Dance Group members were
truly the first dance educators to have a clear set of discipline
standards centered in the arts! Across all classrooms, we saw the
New Dance Group as a natural guiding light for teachers and
students. As stated by McGhee and Sofras (2003, Vol. I, The New
Dance Group—A History), developing lesson studies were
beginning:

> ...to follow in the spirit of the New Dance Group by "assisting in
> the development of the literature, history, and technique of these
> works and to promote general appreciation of the cultural
> significance and value of the art of dancing" (Articles of
> Incorporation of New Dance Group, 1944, as cited in Burns and
> Korff, 1993).

As with the New Dance Group, current students trained in
modern technique and studied historical forms of expression to
illuminate truths and inform dance making. Again, students
followed the first rule of the NDG, "that one must dance on
subjects which concerned them personally...". Far more than a
lesson in history, students in this project were discovering their

personal dance voices as they reached deeply into the legends within their own bodies. As a result, dance classes displayed an array of introspective and powerful dances created by the youngsters.

The process work of each participating teacher was aligning closely with Content Standard #3 of the I (Consortium of National Arts Education Associations, 1994). Therefore, we specifically used that standard to focus the further development of lesson studies. With etudes experiences and the guidance of good teachers, students were becoming better-informed creators and communicators in the medium of dance. We hoped to direct a meaningful future for dance education by using building stones of the past to create a road of literacy.

From the observations and documentation of work in classrooms, researchers found there were two basic approaches to acquiring this understanding. When students began the process by learning a Repertory Etude™ first, this became known as Etude Entry. Teachers used this as a starting point for a lesson when students were in need of a technical and motivating challenge. The teacher was considered the best judge of student readiness for attempting skills required of a particular etude.

When students learned about a masterwork through guided study of creative process, historical background, cultural contexts, aesthetics and later the Repertory Etude™ itself, this became known as Pre-Etude Entry. Donald McKayle and Pamela Sofras coined this particular phrase during a national phone conference involving teachers, artists, and researchers in the project. Some artists and teachers felt very strongly that the students should create their own Pre-Etude dances and studies before going on to the technical work.

Figure 3 is a visual aid to viewing these two approaches to teaching and learning content. Entering via the Etude at the center, the learning path proceeds outward, building understanding of knowledge and skills related to the original dance. Pre-Etude entry begins with broad understandings of the masterwork, artist, and artistic process then proceeds inward toward culmination with the Repertory Etude™. The particular approach may be selected based on learners' skills, ages, intelligences, prior knowledge, and experiences. Time for completion of the process would be determined by student abilities, class needs, and goals of a school's dance curriculum.

Figure 4 can help us complete the original analogy of evolving dance content to a growing spine of knowledge (refer back to Figure 2). There we visualized the *NDG Anthology* (ADLI, 2003) and evolving preservation work as a series of vertebrae. Each

Figure 3
<u>ENTRY POINTS FOR THE LEARNER</u>

Etude Entry

Pre-Etude Entry

Learning path starts within the Repertory Etude and proceeds outward adding knowledge and skills related to the original masterwork.

Learning path begins with knowledge and skills related to the original master work and proceeds inward culminating with the Repertory Etude .

Figure 4
<u>CROSS SECTION OF A COMPLETE</u>
<u>ETUDES PROJECT VERTEBRA</u>

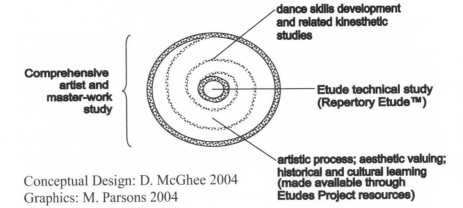

Conceptual Design: D. McGhee 2004
Graphics: M. Parsons 2004

vertebra was an individual artist module representing that artist's signature dance elements and featured masterwork.

Figure 4 reveals the deeper process to understanding an artist's particular work. Figure 4 illustrates a vertebra cross section of the knowledge and skills needed by learners to arrive at full understanding. Every artist module then becomes a miniature comprehensive study in dance. The marrow (center) of a bone represents the core of learning in and through the body such as the technical training provided by a Repertory Etude™. Surrounding the center is substantive learning in values, aesthetics, art-making process, history and culture, and interrelated associations to other subjects. All is integral to the core study of a selected artist and his signature work. Additional kinesthetic dance studies and experiences happen in tandem throughout the learning process of a work, as indicated by the visual spiral. To name a few, these kinesthetic studies might include practice of movement elements, dance motifs, or effort-shape concepts.

A particular teaching methodology was not endorsed in the developing lesson studies. Certified dance educators had already been trained in best practice through their teacher licensing programs. The selected teacher practitioners of The Etudes Project had many years of experience in their well-established public school dance programs. As experts, they were left to determine practices suitable for their respective student groups.

As etude studies were introduced into classrooms across three states, a set of essential questions repeatedly emerged: what is a masterpiece, who is the New Dance Group, and how can we make dances informed by our own heritage? The questions indicated that certain understandings in dance were necessary prior to working on The Etude Project material. Consistently, all teachers began NDG lessons with a review or introduction of foundational concepts related to these questions. Therefore, each of these essential questions and areas of inquiry developed into its own set of lesson studies. The trilogy of foundational concepts eventually became Volume I of *Roots & Branches: Exploring an Evolving Dance Legacy* (McGhee and Sofras, 2003) within the *New Dance Group Anthology* (ADLI, 2003).

The next developing lesson studies were simply presented in the order in which they had been learned by the teachers. Volume II became Donald McKayle's Rainbow Repertory Etude™ Lesson (McGhee and Sofras, 2003). Volume III became Anna Sokolow's Rooms Repertory Etude™ Lesson (McGhee and Sofras, 2003) and Volume IV was Eve Gentry's Tenant of the Street Repertory Etude™ Lesson (McGhee and Sofras, 2003). No attempt was made to sequence the volumes in a particular order. Teachers felt it was important for this option to be fluid. With flexibility, thematic or concept associations could easily be made within dance, among arts disciplines, or across the entire academic curriculum. For example, a teacher might introduce the work of New Dance Group artist McKayle during black history month. Perhaps character studies in theatre could be appropriately linked to personality studies in Sokolow's *Rooms* (Rooms Repertory Etude™, 1999). In social studies, the ills of homelessness and poverty could be examined through the lens of Eve Gentry's *Tenant* (Eve Gentry Images & Reflections Documentary™, n.d.). American history would find many interesting stories related to 1930s politics and New Dance Group member attitudes. Specific to dance, extensive comparisons could be made among the dances and choreographic styles of NDG artists.

Throughout the development of the lesson studies, evaluation of student work occurred in areas of creating, performing, and responding. These categories had been delineated by NAEP for validating learning in the arts (National Assessment Governing Board, 1997, p.7). Classroom teachers, higher education faculty, and the SECDE Director looked at improving student achievement in dance. Rubrics were developed to measure accomplishment of standards-based learning objectives in the NAEP categories for each lesson set. Although the following examples are taken out of lesson context, they give a sense of rubric statements used in the devised measurements.

Category: Creative and Perceptual Skills
Sample Rubric Statements - A student will:
- demonstrate stillness as a compositional device.
- choose feelings, images, and movement ideas that convey associations to the masterwork studied.
- accurately document, organize, and present research influencing personal compositions.
- choose movement vocabulary appropriate to the assignment.
- demonstrate growing sophistication in the art-making process.
- follow a choreography assignment through to completion.
- choose effort qualities appropriate for conveying select concepts/ideas/issues.
- use movement motifs in a variety of compositional forms.

Category: Performance and Technical or Expressive Skills
Sample Rubric Statements - A student will:
- execute a movement skillfully.
- remember a chosen sequence accurately.
- perform effort qualities with clarity.
- use clear movement transitions to enhance understanding of the theme.

- retain strong focus throughout the work.
- accurately reproduce selected movement.
- select music or sound accompaniment to enhance the theme or main idea of the dance.
- communicate the intended meaning of a work.

Category: Response and Intellectual or Reflective Skills
Sample Rubric Statements - A student will:
- discuss and defend movement choices.
- make critical observations of one's own work.
- make critical observations of work created by others.
- provide proof of cultural or historical associations within or across dances.
- write about editing choices used in the dance making process.
- note similarities and differences in individual dance phrases.
- compare and contrast personal work to that of select NDG choreography.

Learning was considered successful when individual students met or exceeded expectations.

Within a lesson study, various forms of evaluation were used. In addition to dance rubrics, quality of student performance was measured in writing assignments (i.e. journal reflections, reports, research) using standards in English/Language Arts (National Council of Teachers of English, 1996). Portfolio review, video, or digital photography documentation provided other means of assessment. Pamela Sofras and I checked documentation of work and collaboratively reviewed classroom assessments.

Throughout the entire process, participating teachers and their students could direct inquiries to me, Pamela Sofras, ADLI directors, Mary Daley (organizer for NYSSSA) at the New York Department of Education, higher education faculty, each other, and the artists. Dialogue continued at professional conferences, through email, phone conferences, and within an ADLI website chat room. Some schools hired New Dance Group artists to work with their students and provide professional development for other district dance educators. School workshops and residencies permitted artists to see first-hand the fruits of Etude learning and to get a sense for how the work was received by youngsters.

As an observer in the schools, I often witnessed effects of The Etudes Project beyond the dance classrooms. I heard the excitement of parents as they watched their children perform "the Rainbow dance". Some teachers spoke of the dances as inspiration for youngsters learning more about American history. I saw language arts writing assignments and reports featuring NDG artists posted in the hallways or on classroom doors. Some papers were part of student research projects on the life of an artist, the cultural significance of a particular dance, or revealed a youngster's view of the world as informed by NDG teachings. As a dance educator for more than 30 years, I experienced an exhilarating "rush" when I encountered these gems. I couldn't help thinking how far we had come in the new discipline of dance education.

Results

The development of Repertory Etudes™ continues to this day under the leadership and guidance of Carolyn Adams and Julie Strandberg of the American Dance Legacy Institute. They invite and contract artist participation, attend to details of documenting and preserving an artist's work, and consult with the artist during creation of a new Repertory Etude™. ADLI documents an etude in a variety of formats including but not limited to: Labanotation scores, oral and written histories, and video. ADLI artists are available to provide workshops and teach repertory. Remarkable developments have been made in the area of creating Repertory Etude™ teaching/coaching videos. By the end of summer 2003, Etude modules had been completed or begun for each artist featured in the *New Dance Group Anthology*: Donald McKayle, Anna Sokolow, Eve Gentry, Pearl Primus, Sophie Maslow, Daniel Nagrin, Mary Anthony, and Jean Leon Destiné (ADLI, 2003). The Anthology refers to the cumulative resources now available, including:

- Repertory Etudes™ packages with performance, instructional and coaching videotapes, music CD, Labanotation score, costume and lighting suggestions for performance, and resource guide.
- Images & Reflections™ Documentaries with complete performance of a work and comments by choreographers and dancers.
- Research-based curricular materials- Dancing Rebels containing artist biographies and an annotated bibliography, and *Roots & Branches: Exploring An Evolving Dance Legacy*, Volumes I through IV containing standards-based education lesson studies for dance and interdisciplinary teaching and learning.

At the time of this writing, other artist modules were in process: Robert Battle, Danny Buraczeski, Danny Grossman, José Limón, and David Parsons.

Roots & Branches:Educational Lesson Studies for Dance Teaching and Learning

Following the good work of teachers in the schools, Pamela Sofras and I were able to discern the common learning threads across dance classroom lessons. We considered designs for effectively presenting dance content through the new educational volumes. The final lesson designs include the following components: overview of an artist's masterwork and introduction to the Repertory Etude™, student objectives for the lesson, lists of materials needed for delivery, introduction of vocabulary, explanations of planning and preparation needed by teachers, background information on subjects or concepts within the lesson, biographical information on the artist, the sequence of teaching activities, instructional strategies, related assessments, lesson extensions, interdisciplinary connections, correlated national standards, student readings, and a glossary.

Each lesson study is filled with ideas tried by teachers with students in public schools. Lessons include guides for helping students plan for research, convert observations to authentic movement with personal voice, view and inquire into a masterwork, create a personal etude, consider processes of dance preservation, write about dance, and so much more. Each volume contains handouts for students, such as: the time line of a choreographer's life and works, games for introducing or reviewing dance titles, and newsletters with biographical information on the featured dance artist.

Along with viewing extraordinary student artistic work, Pamela and I were impressed with the verbal and written expressions demonstrated in the learning process. We included a selection of these in text boxes throughout the *Roots & Branches* resources (McGhee and Sofras, 2003). We felt these expressions could help readers hear the voices of artists, teachers, and young people engaged in the project.

For instance, we did not want to lose the intensity of Lorry May's artistic voice as she coached students in Sokolow's *Rooms* Etude:

> Anna (Sokolow) says: 'Actions are what you feel!' What does this mean? (Vol. III)

We wanted to hear the intimacy of teacher Jeanna Cromer Nitsche speaking to her middle school class:

> Other dances are produced for an audience. The dance you are making is just for you. (Vol. I).

We wanted to share the enthusiasm of students making new dance discoveries:

> The shapes I envision when I hear the word "isolation" are
> concave and angular. The movement quality itself could range
> from very weak and heavily weighted to sharp percussive
> movement. (Vol. III)
>
> > 12th grade student, Davidson Fine Arts H.S.,
> > Augusta, GA

Watching students follow in the footsteps of the masters, we
marveled as youngsters found ideas for new personal dances:

> How do you know if you love someone?
>
> My cousin is a drug addict and she has four children. I wanted to
> make a dance about what I see when I look at the kids. (Vol. I)
>
> > 8th grade student, Hopkins Middle School
> > Columbia, SC

Photo D. McGhee

And, we were overcome with emotion as young people saw their
world in a new way:

> This dance will show everybody what homelessness is all about.
> This dance can help people by showing that homeless people are
> just like you and me. (Vol. IV)
>
> > 7th grade student, Wilson Middle School
> > Charlotte, NC

Teachers who participated in The Etudes Project eagerly shared
their new knowledge and skills with other teachers, parents, school

administrators, and fellow professionals at district sites and state meetings. Project organizers shared information about process and progress at the national level. From across the spectrum of educators and artists came the plea for "more etudes"!

Surprises in Higher Education

Although Directors of The Etudes Project had not planned to study the effect of etudes on teaching and the curriculum at college and university levels, Julie Strandberg at Brown University had been using Repertory Etudes™ in her classes as they were developed. She was excited by the implications for students in her own program. As college faculty from the Carolinas took resources and professional development experiences away from the NYSSSA School of Dance, they committed to use Repertory Etudes™ in their respective dance programs. I observed a variety of implementation processes and astonishing success for meeting particular curricula needs for each institution. I believe the implications for reforming the teaching and learning of dance are profound. Below is a synopsis of major efforts and ideas as noted from observations at the following institutions.

Columbia College in Columbia, South Carolina. Professor Martha Brim used two approaches. First, she successfully integrated information on the New Dance Group and its choreographers into a college introductory interdisciplinary Liberal Arts course. Then in the dance major program, she was inspired to focus on the *Rooms* Etude (Rooms Repertory Etude™, 1999) created by Lorry May for Anna Sokolow.

With the dance majors, Martha explored how to use an etude as inspiration for personal choreographic work. A small idea for a composition course eventually grew into content that filled an entire semester. Students appreciated Sokolow's concern for the human condition and her understandings of internal motivators for dance action. Studies developed by college students in the composition course were based on individual case and character studies of real people in the immediate community. Movement was derived from character words that were transformed into gestures. These were built into sensory phrases that moved into and through space. "Stream of consciousness" writing accompanied student artistic processes. Written entries explored motivations for movement stemming from an individual's deep desires, fears, or fantasies. The student dances were eventually combined into a full work with monologues. The completed dance was performed on campus. College students then created a "People Etude" from that original work and took it on tour to schoolchildren in the schools. A lecture demonstration was developed to describe student artistic

Diane B. McGhee

processes and to talk about Sokolow's work as inspiration for their own dances.

Winthrop University in Rock Hill, South Carolina. In 1998, under tutelage of artists associated with the American Dance Legacy Institute, Associate Professor Sandra Neels became a designated coach for the *Rainbow* Etude (Rainbow Repertory Etude™, 1997). Within the dance major program, she offered the etude as a repertory piece to enhance the performance capabilities and technical vocabulary of her students. The piece was then performed in the annual college dance concert. In collaboration with another university department, music students learned the score and sang accompaniment for the dancers in concert.

At a dance education and technology national conference held at Winthrop in 2000, eleven dancers from four area colleges performed the *Rainbow* Etude together (Rainbow Repertory Etude™, 1997). Dancers had learned the etude separately yet simultaneously within their respective college classes from resource materials provided by ADLI. Prior to the collaborative performance, Ms. Neels gave a two-hour coaching session. Students were astounded they could perform the dance together in unison without extensive prior rehearsals.

University of North Carolina, Charlotte. Professor Pamela Sofras chose to explore etudes content in a dance pedagogy class for pre-service dance teachers in the dance certification program. These same students had earlier performed Rainbow and now tried the ADLI resource materials in pedagogy. Students were encouraged to create lessons for young public school students based on these materials. In student teaching experiences for seventh and eighth graders, college students created pre-etude lessons to introduce work of the masters. Lessons were primarily designed around movement problems motivated by work themes or ideas introduced by the chain gang songs. These pre-etude lessons were tried in the schools with each college student meeting for four class periods of 45 minutes each. The college students shared results of their experiences with peers within the pedagogy class.

Later the college students performed the etude for high school students who requested to learn the dance. Four college students spent two months working with high school classes one time per week. College students found it helpful to practice deconstruction of an etude for teaching.

In another outgrowth, *Rainbow* (Rainbow Repertory Etude™, 1997) was introduced into two classes of seventh and eighth grade boys. The boys were grabbed by the powerful message of the movement and the athletic prowess of the University of California, Irvine student dancing the etude on videotape. At that point,

UNCC student teachers developed a research unit of study on "men in dance". Both classes performed sections of the *Rainbow* Etude (Rainbow Repertory Etude™, 1997) to parents and the public. The young boys received a standing ovation.

Summary, Conclusion, and Implications

With thanks to the American Dance Legacy Institute founders, the invention of the Repertory Etude™ is an unparalleled gift to the field of dance. It was given at a time when most twentieth century American masterworks were becoming endangered or were on the verge of extinction. At first considered controversial and revolutionary, over a few years' time the work became legitimized. Development of Repertory Etudes™ caused artists to realize that issues of dance preservation, access, education, and legacy were inextricably linked. For the memory of a dance to live beyond the immediate moment, something of an artist's work had to be available for ongoing access and performance. New Dance Group artists influenced the entire field by personally passing the legacy of early modern dance to others through Repertory Etudes™. Since those humble beginnings a few years ago, contemporary choreographers are stepping forward to create their own etudes under the auspices of the American Dance Legacy Institute.

The act of creating an etude invites an artist to reflect on elements, signature style, and personal choreographic voice. It gives the artist the right to choose what and how an artist's work shall be remembered. It highlights the importance of documenting a work from the moment of inception to ensure accurate perpetuation. The Repertory Etudes™ are not only keys for accessing precious dances, they are also technical and stylistic studies that enhance training of the body. It is in authentic dance language that kinesthetic legacy is transmitted through an etude.

Educational project directors were aware that when students focus only on technical aspects of a work, learning has potential to become dull and shallow. Both Croce (1977) and Gibbons (1992) address the problems of eroding repertory and the missing spirit of reconstructed dances as affecting stylistic features, genre, and performance quality. Strict repetition of a dance can cause students to lose interest. Without interest or commitment from the performer, the real meaning in a dance work can be lost.

The etudes learning process brings a personal connection of the original work to the student performer. It allows the participant to see beyond the immediate moment of technical training by rejuvenating the choreographer's true intention of the dance through comprehensive understandings of the total work. The educational lesson studies bring these understandings to light, capturing and then sharing the kinesthetic, cultural, and artistic legacies. The meaningful connections are made indelible in the body and brain of young students when the emotional and intellectual connections to the work are imbedded into the study process.

Reaching beyond the world of the performing elite, Repertory Etudes™ and the educational lesson studies have begun an avalanche of innovations in dance. For the first time in the history of the field, American dance legacy has the potential to be shared across all populations of people in the authentic language of the art form. Public school dance education programs are making this happen. Classrooms across the United States are becoming the vehicles for accessing the great dance works that every American should recognize. The Etudes Project has potential to improve the cultural and artistic literacy of every child. Furthermore, the lesson studies deliver content to students in a way that is accountable and standards-based for our educational system.

We found New Dance Group choreographic subjects and themes to be engaging to the hearts, minds, and bodies of young people today. When the dance themes made connections to youngsters' psychological and growth needs, then the historical dances became relevant to the new generation in a deep and exciting way. When dance is taught as an artform, it must draw on the mind to problem-solve, create, and communicate. Focusing on Content Standard #3 of the *National Standards for Dance Education: Understanding dance as a way to create and communicate meaning*, lesson studies emphasized these competencies. The Etudes Project lessons have opened doors for students to create unique personal expressions, perform new dances and historical art, and respond to and communicate ideas informed by American history and cultural study.

Throughout the years of The Etudes Project, dedicated dance teachers working in various levels of the public educational system participated in professional development and furthered the action research of the project. Teachers helped design, develop, and implement lessons around etudes content, artists, and their corresponding masterworks. From work with students, the teachers' inspiration, knowledge, and effort produced beautiful heart-touching lessons. The results of field-tested lessons were reviewed, edited, and finally compiled into educational volumes known as *Roots & Branches* (McGhee and Sofras, 2003). Together, teachers and artists made signature twentieth century dances and educational resources available where none had previously existed. The new dance education resources are believed to be the first to:

- offer comprehensive standards-based content with accountability informed by NAEP guidelines,

- apply a process for specifically addressing Content Standard #3,
- provide entry points for all abilities of learners (through pre-etudes and etudes),
- join kinesthetic legacy with dance literacy,
- include and access great works critical to aesthetic understandings in dance,
- look at dance as a source for sharing cultural information about our unique American heritage, specifically contributions of the New Dance Group, and
- include Repertory Etudes™ in a process that creates a living learning text and literature foundation for dance.

(McGhee and Sofras, 2003, Vol. I: To Teachers)

The goal of disseminating resources to the field is finally coming to fruition. The American Dance Legacy Institute Repertory Etudes™ packets (with videos, music CDs, costume and lighting designs, and Labanotation scores), Images & Reflections™ Documentaries, *Dancing Rebels* (artist biographies and annotated bibliography), and *Roots & Branches: Exploring an Evolving Dance Legacy* lesson studies make up the spine of dance learning modules. More resources are becoming available with each passing year.

The Etudes Project has caused higher education faculty to rethink curriculum content of teacher pre-service programs and pre-professional training. The profession is beginning to view inclusion of American historical repertory as essential to the study and literacy of our discipline. New observations and inroads are being made as more colleges and universities are challenged by the outcomes of The Etudes Project.

The dance department of the State University of New York, College at Brockport is in the stage of rethinking college course offerings and student performances as informed by etudes. The department is examining etudes as potential repertory for young dancers entering the program. Discussions have also centered on infusing the content into dance history courses, inclusion in children's dance classes, and impact on pedagogy at the undergraduate and graduate levels. Some graduate students are using etudes with success in introductory dance classes for the general college population. Brockport's Assistant Professor Juanita Suarez has said,

> To inform higher education curriculum we need a literate view of man and his work. Etudes do this. The process (of creating etudes and related resources) is research driven. Information is concrete and legitimate because it is coming directly from the source. It also gives another level of training for the dancer. (J.

Suarez, personal communication, February 2, 2004)

She also has considered the influences of etudes on her work with professional dance company, Latina Dance Project:

> It raises issues in the development and documentation of new work and gives further awareness to the sense of historical place. (J. Suarez, personal communication, February 2, 2004)

The Etudes Project Directors are eager to see the impact of these first experiments and resources on future teaching and learning with youngsters, pre-professional dancers, pre-service dance educators, dance curriculum at all levels, preservation and archival work, and new artistic creations.

The process of documenting and preserving dance work, creating Repertory Etudes™, researching and compiling lesson studies content, and creating new dances informed by new information is valuable in its own right. The process has brought artists and educators into a symbiotic system of communication and learning—one that has potential for modeling how we develop new knowledge and resources in dance. The intention of such a system is to make dance learning intellectually healthy and full-bodied rather than one-sided or self-perpetuating. The interactive learning model, outlined earlier, diminishes elitist hierarchies and replaces them with the basic moral principles of mutual respect and work for the common good. Many rewards are then generated back to students, artists, teachers, and the dance discipline at large. Choreographer Danny Grossman expresses his personal satisfaction on sharing his art with young learners:

> When I perform my art I am trying to give a gift to the audience. When I see students performing my art they are giving a gift back to me.
> (McGhee and Sofras, 2003, Vol. I: Acknowledgements)

Pamela Sofras elaborates on a grander scale:

> Each generation of dancers was moving farther and farther away from the source of traditional modern dance. Etudes help preserve dances for the generations ahead. (As teachers) It's rare we can give students complete works of dance. This provides an interim step while giving them access to the professional field. We all gain movement vocabulary yet we have the freedom to evolve the elements into personal creative expressions. Previously, this was not the way we learned dance. Now we are able to experience the movement and experience the work and therefore we have legacy. (P. Sofras, personal communication,

February 15, 2004)

On March 17, 2000, the dance world and those involved in The Etudes Project mourned the loss of New Dance Group member Anna Sokolow. In the obituary written by Jack Anderson of the *New York Times*, he recognized Ms. Sokolow's vital contribution to modern dance (Anderson, 2000). Today, the Rooms Repertory Etude™ (ADLI, 1999) is a lasting tribute to Anna as young dancers embody the quintessential elements of her *Rooms* piece and allow it to inspire new dances on alienation. Fortunately, all of us will benefit from Ms. Sokolow's commitment to The Etudes Project and Lorry May's teaching. In the true NDG spirit, Anna was convinced that early modern dance was worth saving and sharing, and should inspire others to make art.

When the Project began eight years ago, it was difficult to convince funders that etudes were realistic and valid learning tools for dance. Organizing project start up had required extraordinary time and energy as there had been no precedent. The first time round, Directors had to clear a path while creating the road map. Often the pace of development was interrupted for Directors to address funding and organizational priorities to keep the Project going. Nevertheless, participants at every level now consider The Etudes Project a monumental accomplishment of collective work and an idea that revolutionizes dance learning for the future. Through The Etudes Project, artists and educators established a profound respect for the meaning of collaboration.

Carolyn Adams has made extraordinary contributions to the dance world through her work with the Paul Taylor Company, NYSSSA School of Dance, the Harlem Dance Foundation, American Dance Legacy Project, and teaching at The Julliard School. Yet, as many would agree, she feels The Etudes Project is a special accomplishment:

> This is my finest achievement to the field. Starting with the concept of the dance etude, taking on a set of values and goals and going about achieving them is the contribution. Looking at The Etudes Project twenty years from now, dancers won't understand the concept of non-access. It will become an invisible resource. New questions will arise: What is the gift of the hour and who will be looking at this?
> (C. Adams, personal communication, February 14, 2004)

REFERENCES

Abrahams, F. (2000). National standards for music education and college preserve music teacher education: A new balance. *Arts Education*

Policy Review,102 (1), 5. Retrieved Jan. 12, 2004 from Academic search premiere.

Adams, C., & Strandberg, J. (2000). Access, education, and preservation through the prism of American dance. *Arts Education Policy Review, 102* (1): 19-25.

American Dance Legacy Institute (n.d.). About. Retrieved November 12, 2003 from http://www.adli.us/about.html

American Dance Legacy Institute (n.d.). Anthology. Retrieved November 12, 2003 from http://www.adli.us/anthology.html

American Dance Legacy Institute (2003). *New dance group anthology.* Providence, RI: Author.

Anderson, J. (2000, March 30). Anna Sokolow, a modern choreographer known for studies in alienation, dies at 90. *The New York Times*, p. B14.

Aprill, A. (n.d.). Community arts network. Retrieved January 23, 2004 from http://communityartsnet/readingroom/archive/intro-education.php

Bonbright, J. (1999). Dance education 1999: Status, challenges, and recommendations. *Arts Education Policy Review, 101* (1), 33. Retrieved January 12, 2004 from Academic search premiere.

Bradley, K. (2001). Dance education research: What train are we on? *Arts Education Policy Review, 103* (1), 31-35.

Burns, M., & Korff, W. (1993). The New Dance Group History. *The New Dance Group Gala Concert Journal.* New York: American Dance Guild.

Consortium of National Arts Education Associations. (1994). *National standards for arts education: What every young American should know and be able to do.* Reston, VA: Music Educators National Conference.

Croce, A. (1977). *Afterimages.* New York: Alfred A. Knopf.

Dance/USA (n.d.) National initiative to preserve America's dance. Retrieved December 29, 2003 from http://www.danceusa.org/ problems_publications/nipad.htm

Delman, J. (1993). The New Dance Group. *The New Dance Group Gala Concert Program.* New York: American Dance Guild.

Donald McKayle Images & Reflections™ Documentary. (1999). Providence, RI: American Dance Legacy Institute. Interviews with archival footage of original cast performing entire work, *Rainbow 'Round My Shoulder*, on a 1959 CBS Camera 3 live television broadcast.

Dunning, J. (1996). *Alvin Ailey.* New York: Addison-Wesley Publishing Company, Inc.

Eve Gentry Images & Reflections™ Documentary. (n.d.). Providence, RI: American Dance Legacy Institute. Interviews with artists who worked with Eve and a performance of her 1936 signature work, *Tenant of the Street.*

Fiske, E. (Ed.). (1999) *Champions of change.* Washington, D.C.: Arts Education Partnership and the President's Committee on the Arts and

Humanities.
Friedes, D., Newhall, M., & Shepard, K. (2003). Dancing rebels. Providence, RI: American Dance Legacy Institute. (draft).
Gibbons, B. (1992). A prismatic approach to the analysis of style in dance. In L. Overby & J. Humphrey (eds.). *Dance: Current selected research,volume 3* (pp. 119-144). New York: AMS Press, Inc.
Graff, E. (1990). *Stepping left: Dance and politics in New York City, 1928-1942.* North Carolina: Duke University Press, 1990.
Hubbard, K. (1992). Donald McKayle: Dance is Movement that Lights the Soul. African American Genius in Modern Dance. Durham: American Dance Festival.
Haskins, J. (1990). *Black dance in America: A history through its people.* New York: Harper Collins Publishers.
Maslow, A. (1970). *Motivation and personality.* New York: Harper & Row.
McGhee, D., & Sofras, P. (eds.). (2003). *Roots & branches: Exploring an evolving dance legacy, Volume I: The walk-up to masterworks.* Brockport, NY: American Dance Legacy Institute.
McGhee, D., & Sofras, P. (eds.). (2003). *Roots & branches: Exploring an evolving dance legacy, Volume II: Donald McKayle's rainbow Repertory Etude™ lesson.* Brockport, NY: American Dance Legacy Institute.
McGhee, D., & Sofras, P. (Eds.). (2003). *Roots & branches: Exploring an evolving dance legacy, Volume III: Anna Sokolow's rooms Repertory Etude™ lesson.* Brockport, NY: American Dance Legacy Institute.
McGhee, D., & Sofras, P. (Eds.). (2003). *Roots & branches: Exploring an evolving dance legacy, Volume IV: Eve Gentry's tenant of the street Repertory Etude™ lesson.* Brockport, NY: American Dance Legacy Institute.
Murfee, E. (1995). *Eloquent evidence: Arts at the core of learning.* Washington, D.C.: The President's Committee on the Arts and Humanities and the National Association of State Arts Agencies with the National Endowment for the Arts.
National Assessment Governing Board (1997). NAEP arts education consensus project: 1997 arts education assessment framework. Washington, D.C.: National Assessment Governing Board.
National Council of Teachers of English and the International Reading Association (1996). *Standards for the English language arts.* Author.
Newhall, M. (1995). Strange Heroes: The Role of the New Dance Group in American Political Dance.Scholarly paper.
Rainbow Repertory Etude™ (1997). Providence, RI: American Dance Legacy Institute. Choreography by Donald McKayle.
Rooms Repertory Etude™ (1999). Providence, RI: American Dance Legacy Institute. Based on Anna Sokolow's masterpiece, *Rooms,* arranged by Lorry May.
Sussman, W. (1984). *Culture as history: The transformation of American*

society in the Twentieth century. New York: Pantheon Books.

Schmitz, N. (1992). Influences affecting k-8 dance education in the United States. In L. Overby & J. Humphrey (eds.). *Dance: Current selected research, volume 3.* (pp. 27-38). New York: AMS Press, Inc.

Seidel, K. (2001). Many issues, few answers – The role of research in k-12 arts education. *Arts Education Policy Review, 103* (2), 19-22.

Sorrel, W. (1962). *Dance Observer, 29,* 19.

SouthEast Center for Dance Education (n.d.) Home. Retrieved December 7, 1997 from http://www.colacoll.edu/secde/home.html

Thorpe, E. (1989). *Black dance.* The Overlook Press: Woodstock, NY.

Warren, L. (1998). *Anna Sokolow: The rebellious spirit.* United Kingdom: Harwood Academic Publishers.

5

BODY THINKING BEYOND DANCE

Michele Root-Bernstein and Robert Root-Bernstein

Scientists, philosophers and educators are growing increasingly interested in somatic cognition, or body thinking. We present a general approach to creativity in which body thinking, one of thirteen thinking tools used across the arts and sciences, links body disciplines such as dance to many non-body disciplines that rely upon body thinking for creative insight and achievement. Some of these also use dance technique and notation to enhance research. This suggests a need to exercise body thinking through dance—not just in elementary and secondary settings, but in higher education as well. Examples of purposeful training in body thinking in non-dance college classrooms are presented. Despite its imaginative importance, however, body thinking is most often ignored at the college level outside of dance. By insisting on the relevance of body thinking to all disciplines and by building bridges to courses in the sciences, humanities, and arts, dance educators can fill a void in the teaching of somatic knowledge. We advocate a tools-for-thinking approach to the dance-integrated classroom that fosters process-oriented collaboration in which both dance and non-dance disciplines are equal partners. In sum, our transdisciplinary model argues strongly for the inclusion of dance within the core curriculum at every level.

The Body-Mind Nexus

A composition teacher asks her community college students to get up from their desks and use their bodies to build a "group machine" that mimics essay form and function. An entomologist schedules a graduate seminar in the gym, blindfolds participants, and has them navigate open space by echo-location. A physicist teams up with a choreographer to create a dance for science students that explores the physical properties of superconductivity. What is going on here? All these instances share a common purpose: to exercise body thinking beyond dance. In each instance

173

the verbal and mathematical languages of the classroom receive supplementation from somatic experience, that is, knowledge of the world apprehended, considered, and expressed through the body. With the exception of the choreographer, none of the professors, none of the students, are professional dancers yet they turn to exercises, improvisations and expressive forms usually considered the province of dance in order to expand understanding in their own discipline. There is a growing recognition that somatic knowledge, intuitive and non-verbal as it may be, should no longer be ignored in educational settings. Dance, as an art and as a science, stands ready to benefit.

Support for the importance of somatic knowledge comes in part from the scientific community. In the last half-century, psychologists and neuroscientists have begun exploring in depth the nature of proprioception[1] and motor cognition and their role in other processes of mind (Gardner, 1983; Seitz, 2000). Despite acceptance, for 300 years and more, of the Cartesian dichotomy between mind and body, many researchers find it increasingly probable that the mind is embodied. Antonio Damasio (1994), for one, has argued that emotion, felt experience of body, sits at the core of our capacity to reason—not to the side. Others argue that there is a logic to motor activity just as compelling as ratiocination. "I move," writes psychologist Jay Seitz (1993), "therefore I am" (p. 50). Seitz (1992; 2000) draws on a wide array of psychological and neurological research to argue that the sequencing capabilities involved in motor tasks may in fact support and structure verbal, logical, visual, and musical capacities hitherto considered separate, brain-only, intellection. Much of this ongoing research and scholarly speculation has yet to be confirmed. But it does suggest that what we call intelligence depends upon the integration and synthesis of brain/body function. To that end we can look forward to increased neurological understanding of somatic knowledge. Bodily-kinesthetic thinking and knowing, long ignored and resistant to analysis, may finally get its scientific due.

Increasing numbers of researchers outside science have also explored the role of somatic knowledge—however inexactly understood in its particulars—in their various professional settings. In the first half of the twentieth century, the art historian and critic Herbert Read (1956) argued that much of art had developmental origins in human motor behavior. Citing Emile Jacques Dalcroze, founder of eurythmics, and the psychologist Rudolf Arnheim, Read acknowledged a kinesthetic basis for the rhythm and harmony found in the visual images produced by artists. (1956, p. 126 n15 and passim). Arnheim (1969) himself investigated the role of

---

[1] Proprioception refers to our sixth sense or awareness of body balance, muscular tension and motor activity.

gesture in producing abstract perceptual experiences of motion. Together with the perceptual images formed by our other senses, these kinesthetic images formed the experiential basis for thinking and for spoken language (p. 229 and passim). Picking up where Arnheim left off, the philosopher Mark Johnson claims that the mind's embodiment indeed shapes our entire experience of the physical world—and sets the stage for metaphorical thinking that is "very much a matter of…perceptual mechanisms, patterns of discrimination, motor programs, and various bodily skills" (1987, p. 137). Other scholars, such as Mark Turner (1996) and Jude Todd (2001) similarly investigate the role of somatic awareness in areas as diverse as storytelling and moral choice making.

Aside from psychologists, literary scholars and philosophers, educators too have explored somatic awareness. In the schooling of the three to six year old, Maria Montessori (1984/1949) made a case more than fifty years ago that movement of the whole body and especially of the hand was absolutely necessary to the acquisition of language and of general knowledge. Thought and action, Montessori argued, are integrated—a principle reiterated more recently by research (as cited in Hanna, 1979, p. 75) demonstrating that the earliest linguistic articulations of children (and of adults forming pidgin languages) focus upon moving objects and bodily actions. In the wake of Jean Piaget, who also argued that the very young develop cognitive capacity through sensori-motor activity, psychologists have extolled the efficacy of "enactive representation" (John-Steiner, 1985, p. 5).

Educator Jeanne Bamberger (1991) discovered that that link between thought and movement lasts well beyond early childhood. In her Laboratory for Making Things, an inner-city school program in Cambridge, Mass., grade school children who failed to demonstrate symbolic (i.e., verbally or mathematically expressed) knowledge of physical objects like levers often displayed a keener hand knowledge of those objects than their teachers and those students who tested well. Somatic or hand knowledge alone was sufficient to build with levers, whereas symbolic knowledge alone was not. The challenge, in this situation, was for student and teacher alike to ground hand-acquired knowledge to formal languages of communication such as verbal description or mathematical formulas, to translate act into symbolic expression and symbolic expression into act.

One might also expect dancers and dance educators to consider the role of somatic thinking in dance, as indeed many have done. Among these, dance educators such Lynette Overby (1992) and Sandra Minton and Jeffrey Steffen (1992) have turned their attention to the assessment of body awareness or kinesthesis among dancers, concluding generally that seasoned, talented dancers performed significantly better than novice or untalented dancers on tasks involving the initiation, control, and replication of movement. Others involved in the study of dance, many of whom are cited by Judith Hanna in *To Dance is Human* (1979), have further argued that somatic awareness as it is manipulated in dance creates, as Hanna puts it, "a conceptual natural language with intrinsic and extrinsic meanings, a system of physical movements, and interrelated rules guiding performance…" (p. 5). Indeed, Hanna has written elsewhere (2001) and extensively on that natural language as the basis for our most fundamental, verbally independent thought (p. 40).

Given the wide range of investigations into somatic awareness across the sciences, social sciences, and arts, one thing is clear. At the nexus of bodily awareness, body "logic" and communicative power, there is a powerful way of knowing that dancers and increasingly others know about and consciously exploit.

The Body/Mind's 13 Thinking Tools

What is this nexus that connects the body to thinking and expressing? We believe it consists of a diverse and interlinked set of imaginative skills—what we call tools for thinking. By collecting what hundreds of brilliant, self-reflective minds have had to say about the way they think, we identified 13 intuitive mental tools common to problem-solving endeavors across the arts and sciences.[2] These tools are:

observing—honing all the senses to perceive acutely;
imaging—creating mental images using any or all senses;
abstracting—eliminating all but one essential characteristic of a complex thing;
recognizing patterns—perceiving similarities in structures or properties of different things;
forming patterns—creating or discovering new ways to organize things;
analogizing—discovering *functional* similarities between structurally different things;
body thinking—*reasoning* with muscles, muscle memory, gut feelings, and emotional states;
empathizing— "becoming the thing" one studies, be it animate or inanimate;
dimensional thinking—translating between two and three (or more) dimensions, for instance, between a blue print and an invention; to scale up or scale down; to alter perceptions of space and time;

---

[2] A full description of each tool and the similar ways in which each is used in a wide variety of disciplines can be found in our book, *Sparks of Genius* (1999).

modeling—creating a simplified or miniaturized analog of a complex thing in order to test or modify its properties;
playing—undertaking a goal-less activity for fun incidentally developing skill, knowledge, and intuition;
transforming—using any or all tools for thinking in a serial or integrated manner; for example, using analogies to image a new invention, creating a model, playing with it, tinkering with scale, and then translating the optimized invention into drawings; and
synthesizing—knowing in multiple ways simultaneously—bodily, intuitively and subjectively as well as mentally, explicitly, and objectively.

There may, of course, be more or less than 13 imaginative tools—we are not dogmatic on that issue—but these 13 appear frequently enough in the language of creative thinkers to warrant considering them as distinct, if also interconnected. Indeed, creative individuals across the arts and sciences make use of the whole range of thinking tools at one time or another in their imaginative and compositional processes. Depending on their personal talents, the problems they choose to tackle, and the disciplinary languages they use to communicate solutions, individuals may also exploit some tools more than others. A dancer, for instance, may cultivate her capacity for observing or empathizing or dimensional thinking; or he may concentrate on imaging, abstracting, and forming patterns.

Consider the importance of **observing** to choreographer George Balanchine. "It is necessary for the choreographer," he wrote, "to see things which other people do not notice, even though they are before their eyes, and to cultivate his visual sense" (Steinberg, 1980, p. 30). Doris Humphrey (1959) similarly defined the choreographer as "observant in general," a "keen observor of physical and emotional behavior" (pp. 20, 22). In the tranquility of study or studio, the dancer/choreographer begins **imaging** or recalling past experience as interior sensation. Balanchine called upon a "kaleidoscope" of movements swirling in his mind as "abstract memories of form" (Steinberg, 1980, p. 34). The dancer uses visual, aural, and haptic images, as well. Asking his company to soften a gesture, Alonzo King of Lines Contemporary Ballet in San Francisco says, "It should look like a reverberation" (as cited in Gladstone, 1998, pp. 26, 34).

Keen observing and multi-sensory imaging both provide a rich experience from which the dancer extracts essential images. "To create," Balanchine once observed, "means, first of all, to eliminate" (Sorell, 1992, p. 42). Choreographer Martha Graham concurred (Steinberg, 1980, p. 46). Indeed, she often compared **abstracting** to squeezing (and drinking!) the juice from an orange (Graham, 1991, p. 231; Taylor, 1987, p. 115). She explored and simplified the "juice" of a movement on its own terms until the original narrative or image was no longer clearly recognizable in the dance. "I don't want to be understandable; I just want to be felt," she once said (as cited in Kisselgoff, 1984, 51), imitating Picasso's famous statement about his abstractions, "I want to say the nude. I don't want to do a nude as a nude" (Ashton, 1972, pp. 10, 131).

Observed gestures and abstracted movements have little dance meaning in and of themselves but, as Balanchine put it, "they acquire value when they are coordinated in time and space" (Steinberg, 1980, p. 34)—in other words, when they are patterned. For Agnes de Mille (1991), this is the dancer-choreographer's primary creative act: the dancer searches for "the meanings behind gesture and expression—and then reassembles them, works them into a pattern, a design or purpose..." (p. 22). **Forming patterns** in dance means making connections between movements on the dance floor; it also means **recognizing patterns**, making connections between those movements and what Humphrey (1959) called "everyday designs" of form and movement in wind, cloud, landscape, cityscape, or crowds (p. 22). For Glen Tetley, elements of all sorts fall into patterns relevant to dance. "When I come to work on a ballet," he has said, "...scores I have loved, incidents, things suddenly make connections that I have never put a connection to before...There is a structure to all things" (as cited in Crisp and Clarke, p. 26).

Many such connections depend upon functional similarities (analogies), rather than resemblance of form or aspect (metaphors). De Mille (1962) was **analogizing** when she likened the dancing body to a percussive instrument (p. 31); so was Graham (1991) when she based *Diversion of Angels* upon a Kandinsky painting: "It...had a streak of red going from one end to the other," she later wrote. "I said, 'I will do that someday. I will make a dance like that'" (p. 98).

For most dancer-choreographers, preparatory, creative thinking takes place in advance, as choreographers Balanchine (Cornfield, 1998, p. 282), Graham (Root-Bernstein and Root-Bernstein, 2003, pp. 17–20) and Tharp (2003, p. 70) have indicated in interviews and memoirs, but actual dance steps more often than not materialize on the dance floor. "I could prepare, order, organize, structure, and edit my creativity in my head," writes Tharp, "but...[t]o generate [movement] ideas, I had to move" (p. 99). Indeed, because the dancer's medium of expression is the body itself, **thinking with body** becomes a paramount imaginative activity. "The person drawn to dance..." wrote Humphrey (1959), "thinks with his muscles" (p. 17). That is certainly the case whether he enacts movements and tensions, images or feels body sensation without moving, or infuses body feeling into costume or prop until they become, as one critic noted in Graham's case, "an extension of [the] body" (as cited in de Mille, 1991, pp. 210–211).

Like verbal language, such body thinking has structure. Body movement, wrote Graham, had a "lovely animal logic" (as cited in Horosko, 1991, 146). According to Linda Tarnay, this logic "is different from the way verbal ideas are connected. One movement leads to another the way the body responds kinesthetically. Movements also have a spatial logic of their own" (as cited in John-Steiner, 1985, p. 158). Indeed, by thinking dimensionally as well as bodily, the dancer exploits the level and size of gestures, and the force and speed of body movements, to carve a "design in time-space" (de Mille, 1952, p. 79). Writes de Mille (1962):

> Each gesture makes a path in time, and a path in space... of necessity, the gesture is expressed within the sphere and orbit of your body's reach, but the implications extend far beyond, and an outstretched hand establishes an atmosphere. (p. 31)

That atmosphere in turn creates an "emotionally charged space" (Noguchi, 1994, p. 80). No matter how non-narrative, non-representational the dance, the dancer can't help but infuse posture and movement with latent emotions. Feeling her self "a part of the cosmic world," (Brown, 1979, p. 22) she empathizes with the thing that must "appear to be pushing through a heavy mass, much like...water" (Horosko, 1991, p. 65) or must "rest on" (Graham, 1991, pp. 74–75) the tone of an oboe. In turn, the spectator can't help but respond with her own powers of kinesthetic empathy to the felt meanings embedded in gestural references and movement patterns.

By observing, imaging, abstracting, patterning and analogizing, the dancer makes sense of his or her world. Using body thinking, empathizing and dimensional thinking, one explores physical reaction and emotional response to that sense-making experience. In using the next three imaginative thinking tools—modeling, playing and transforming—the dancer acquires further means for inventing and composing.

Many a choreographer speaks of modeling dancers like clay in the hands (Sorell, 1992, pp. 41, 139; Nijinska, 1981, p. 316). They push, pull, and mold the dancers' bodies "to give dancers a sense of the physicality of a step" (Dunning, 1999, p. AR8). They are modeling their conception of the dance as a whole as well. The choreographer, says Christopher Wheeldon, has an idea, brings it to the dancers, sees if it works, fiddles with it, goes home and over wine or half asleep, figures out the dance "moment" (Marks, 2001, p. B1). Similarly, the choreographer who relies on finger movements, dance notation, or sophisticated computer programs such as COMPOSE (commercially known as Life Forms) models the dance away from the dance floor. When modeling also entails unrestrained improvising or **playing**, the dancer-choreographer courts the serendipity of chance discovery and insight. Tharp (2003) likes to spend time each day "daydreaming" dance movements, with no expectation that the improvisation will produce anything "good or great or even interesting" (p. 100). Careful not to defeat the playful aspect of improvisation, she makes no effort to think about or remember what she is doing, but videotapes these sessions for later review, happy if she discovers 30 seconds of new and remarkable movement in several hours of tape.

Whether the dancer-choreographer discovers dance steps by observing, modeling, or playing, he or she ultimately **transforms** between one thinking tool and another, between imagining an idea in many ways and expressing it in a singular, kinesthetic form. "First there is the concept," Graham wrote of choreographic creativity. "Then there is the dramatization of that concept which makes it apparent to others" (Steinberg, 1980, p. 40). In the composition of *Diversion of Angels*, Graham observed, imaged, abstracted, recognized and formed patterns, analogized, thought with body, empathized, and ultimately transformed her emotional reaction to Kandinsky's painting into dance (Root-Bernstein and Root-Bernstein, 2003).

Similarly, Oscar Schlemmer, painter–sculptor–dancer–choreographer, explored the artistic idea of geometrical man in drawing, painting, bas-relief, sculpture, costume, set design, and dance (Lehman and Richardson, 1986). In fact, Schlemmer conceived of and taught dance not as an end in itself, but as a way of exploring man's relationship to everything else. His was a **synthesizing** approach to dance, relying on the use of multiple imaginative tools to think and to express in varied ways. In a drawing called "Man in the Sphere of Ideas," he depicted a nude running through a profuse experience of body, earth, vegetation, ethics, psychology, science, art, space, time, mass, and mind (Root-Bernstein and Root-Bernstein, 1999, pp. 307–308). To one degree or another, all dancers and choreographers synthesize bodily what they imagine mindfully into a seamless whole that is dance. The ultimate result of such synthetic thinking is that one knows what one feels and feels what one knows.

The thirteen thinking tools described here form a nexus of skills that tie the body to thinking and expressing. Through the lens of dance we see embodied, figuratively and literally, the creative mind at work. Indeed, the thinking tools provide three distinct links between the dancer's creative world and that of individuals in other disciplines. One is through the common use of the thinking tools as a whole. Creative individuals across the arts and sciences observe, abstract, form patterns, model, and transform. The second link these imaginative tools forge between dance and other disciplines is through the body thinking that creative individuals in many fields find necessary to their work, and often incorporate into non-dance classrooms. And the third link is through the use of the body to express ideas imagined, whether those ideas originated bodily or not. A demonstration of the first link may be reviewed in our book, *Sparks of Genius* (1999). We discuss the last two of these links separately below.

Body Thinking Beyond Dance

Among all the thinking tools at the dancer-choreographer's disposal, at least one would seem absolutely essential—the body thinking that ranges from skilled physical behavior to imagining movements and feelings, from the projection of bodily sensitivities to intuitions emotional and physical that accompany the generation of ideas. No body thinking means no dancing, if only because dancers use body as the medium of their expression. Dancers are not the only ones to perform with and through body, however. Actors reenact the gait and gestures of characters; surgeons wield the scalpel by feel, even at the remove made possible by computerized telepresence surgery. In fields other than those characterized by bodily skill or performance, too, individuals think with and through their bodies, though they express themselves otherwise.

The role of body thinking in non-dance, non-performance disciplines has been recognized before, but not generally emphasized in studies of creative thinking. Educational philosopher John Dewey (1934) maintained that the skilled "motor sets of the body," which heightened perceptions of movements and movement patterns, were necessary to the skilled performance of surgery, sports, music, and painting as well as dance (pp. 97–98). Psychologist Eliot Dole, Hutchinson (1959) argued that body thinking was used by all persons—even those outside the realm of body performance—whose ideas first arose in kinesthetic form:

> By no means all insights express themselves in verbal form. The organism is capable of responding in many ways. What shall we say of ideas, which come through other means? To the pianist and sculptor, the instrumentalist, dancer, surgeon and manual artisan, they burst upon awareness in a kinesthetic form, feeling their way into varying types of muscular expression. Fingers "itch" to play, music "flows from the hands," ideas "flow" from the pen. Movement expresses the "idea" of the dancer or orchestra conductor, the almost sensuous desire to model plastic form becomes compulsive in sculpture. (p. 142)

Both Dewey and Hutchinson realized long ago that practitioners in every profession are likely to use body thinking to develop new ideas, to imagine and create. Take, for instance, non-performing artists. "One of the driving forces of sculpture," says Red Grooms, "is to actually become physically involved with the materials" (cited in Greenburg and Jordan, 1993, p. 39). Many sculptors and artisans have felt and expressed much the same thing and more—that feeling for the form and shape of substance becomes a whole body experience (Root-Bernstein and Root-Bernstein, 1999; Maloof, 1983, p. 56). Auguste Rodin described The Thinker, his most famous public sculpture, as a man cogitating with knitted brow and "every muscle of his arms, back and legs..." (cited in Root-Bernstein and Root-Bernstein, 1999, p. 169). Henry Moore enacted the posture of his sculpture to feel the stresses and strains within his own body. Sculptor Louise Nevelson went one step further and actually studied eurythmics—expressive, spontaneous movement to music—in order to "solve plastic problems of alternative equilibrium and tension" in her found-art sculptures (Lisle, 1990, p. 108). Body thinking is part and parcel of conveying three-dimensional representations of the world.

Painters, too, think bodily about their work. Visual artist John Marin wrote of the need to recognize "the pressure of the air against my body, my body against the air," while "building the picture" (Goldwater and Treves, 1945, p. 467). Painter Susan Rothenberg speaks of a keen awareness while she paints "of my body in space" (cited in Stiles and Selz, 1996, p. 264). Jacques Mandelbrojt (1994) depends upon "an interior muscular identification with the object" he represents (p.186), echoing Henri Matisse, who admonished students to close their eyes and image, not just visually, but bodily: "...[A]ssume the pose of the model yourself; where the strain comes is the key of the movement" (cited in Flam, 1978, p. 43). Similarly, Leon Polk Smith attempts to convey the "weight" of color; he wants nature to be "felt", not seen, in his paintings (cited in Auping, 1989, p. 50). Body thinking is intimately connected to the way things are seen and to the way what is seen is conveyed by hand to canvas.

In the altogether different field of music, body thinking affects aural experience and expression. Pianists such as Vladimir Ashkenazy and Alexis Weissenberg describe the necessity of committing music performance to the muscle memory of fingers (Dubal, 1984, pp. 40, 334). For Ruth Laredo, the entire body is involved in playing the piano. "Your hands are just an extension of your body when you play the piano, and you have to use your body in a special way for each different kind of music" (cited in Dubal, 1984, p. 242). Indeed, says Laredo, she learns most about using the body musically by watching dancers dance. For much the same reason, music scholar Simon Morrison takes ballet in order to understand ballet music (Altmann, 2003). Also thinking with body, the eccentric Glenn Gould spent hours a day imaging rather than actually practicing in order to produce a clear "mental image, which governs what one does...What it all comes down to is that one does not play the piano with one's fingers, one plays the piano with one's mind" (cited in Root-Bernstein and Root-Bernstein, 1999, p. 171). One composes that way, too, with an attendant use of body movements and images—Mozart not only hummed musical ideas, but also enacted them on his fingers (Root-Bernstein, R. and Root-Bernstein, M., 1999, p. 162). Body thinking and body imaging are critical to music.

Body thinking is equally important outside disciplines reliant upon the skilled performance of body or hand. Writers are likely to think in bodily images and intuitions. Poets Derek Walcott and Gary Snyder find verbal stimulus in the felt rhythms of dance and music. Other writers attend to the mute inspirations of body feelings. Robert Frost once observed, "a poem... begins as a lump in the throat, a sense of wrong, a homesickness, a love sickness" (Writers at Work, 1989, p. 68). Isabel Allende builds her novels upon gut responses and inarticulate inclinations that have "not yet made the trip from the belly to the mind" (Epel, 1993, p. 8). "The artist is not a man who describes but a man who FEELS," wrote e.e. cummings, a statement enriched by his own intense study of painting and the parallels he drew between that avocation and his verbal vocation (cited in Root-Bernstein and Root-Bernstein, 1999, p. 8).

Many scientists also rely upon the intuitive and imagistic aspects of body thinking. Norbert Weiner, the inventor of cybernetics (the study of feedback systems in electronics and other fields), wrote that every problem he worked on produced a distinct physical discomfort that became, for him, a "temporary symbol," a personal shorthand, guiding him toward a solution (cited in Root-Bernstein and Root-Bernstein, 1999, p. 173). Mathematician Kalvis Jansons ties string in order to study the mathematical properties of knots. What's more, he remembers in his fingers the feel of tying those knots and works with those kinesthetic images in mind. Similarly, mathematician Stanislaw Ulam sometimes calculated not with numbers but with tactile feelings; Albert Einstein famously worked out his theory of relativity with muscular feeling and bodily sensation; Richard Feynman enacted his understanding of physical forces in the subatomic world by rolling on the floor (Root-Bernstein and Root-Bernstein, 1999). All of these men found it necessary to work out the feel of the system they studied before drawing up equations—a point suggesting that the role of manipulatives in learning mathematics extends far beyond grade school.

There are a good many scientists for whom body thinking

cannot be distinguished from a physical identification with and manipulation of their materials. Cyril Stanley Smith, one of the greatest metallurgists of the 20th century, had a "curiously internal and quite literally sensual" feel for the tactile qualities of metals that was essential to his science (cited in Root-Bernstein and Root-Bernstein, 1999, p. 171). Just as athletic performers benefit from imagining how their bodies will perform in competition, scientists benefit in similar ways by imagining how a physical apparatus will behave when manipulated. "Outstanding execution in scientific experimentation and painting," wrote embryologist C. H. Waddington (1969), "have in common a dependence on ability—probably ultimately muscular—to handle the physical stuff of the world" (p. 158). Knowledge does not come to any profession only, or even mainly, through words or numbers, but from the connection of these to what the body senses and feels.

Body Thinking in the Non-Dance Classroom

Thus far we have argued that body thinking is germane to disciplines such as music or the visual arts in which bodily skill or enactment precedes final expressive products such as sonata scores or sculptures. We have also argued that body thinking plays a fundamental role in disciplines that apparently involve little or no trained body skill—for example, mathematics, physics, and writing. Not surprisingly, then, training in body thinking skills has been found valuable in classrooms across the entire curriculum. At present, most dance-integrated classrooms are at the elementary and secondary level of schooling, which speaks to a baseline of attention to body thinking for children and adolescents (e.g., Zakkai, 1997; Joyce, 1980; Artsource® Curriculum, 2003). But body thinking has also been found necessary to the learning process for college and graduate students, as well as for adult apprentices, in fields ranging from music to science to writing.

For jazz professor Andrew Speight of San Francisco State University, body thinking is essential to the understanding and performance of music. While some musicians argue that the tempo, textures, and dynamics of all music reflect the body's kinetic activity (Arias, 1989), jazz is particularly and historically based on the body rhythms of marching and dancing. In order to master the musical style, jazz students need to understand and feel these rhythms while they play—in essence, they must engage in an historical re-creation of dance style. Speight helps students incorporate these dance rhythms in a number of ways. Initially, he encourages students to march with the music and to tap their feet to the musical pulse. As the syncopations become more complex, they must learn to tap one foot in, say, 4/4 time and the other foot in 2/4 time, off beat, in much the same way dancers learn to layer polyrhythms in different parts of the body (Root-Bernstein and Root-Bernstein, 2003, p. 21). Ultimately, students must learn to incorporate these base rhythms while at the same time flowing with the thematic riffs that also make up the music (A. Speight, personal communication, November 30, 2003).

In this endeavor, the great jazz trumpeter Dizzie Gillespie provides an apt dance model for Speight, because Gillespie often tap danced in front of his band, his feet sounding complex rhythms, his upper body flowing. While Speight does not ask his students to dance the dance, he does ask them to dance the music. He assigns awkward drummers to watch videos of well-known jazz drummers with the sound turned off. He wants them to attend to the "ballet" that aligns the body simultaneously to the music and to the instrument played. Whether that instrument is a set of drums, a bass fiddle balanced on its pin, or an eight pound saxophone slung around the neck, the jazz musician must incorporate necessary changes in posture and technical mastery of sticks, strings, or keys into a bodily feeling for the music.

Over the years Speight has observed that those students who have difficulty cultivating this bodily feeling for jazz trumpeter those who remained stiff, unattached, and at odds with the musical pulse, are often physically inactive outside the classroom. He encourages them to exercise at the gym, to swim, to build body fitness and body awareness. Jazz is most easily mastered when bodily movement, the emotional involvement it triggers, and analytic study all come together to synergize musical training.

Writers can also benefit from exercising the body and body thinking. Though at first blush it may not seem that writing is "an art of the body," as the essayist Wendell Berry puts it, the writer has much to gain from attending to the body in movement (cited in Davenport and Forbes, 1997, p. 299). Certainly this was the experience of rhetoric professor Cheryl Forbes, who, with her dance colleague Donna Davenport, has taught for many years a "bi-disciplinary" course that places dancing and writing side by side in the syllabus. Forbes had little expectation at first that writing—hers or her students'—would really benefit from exposure to dance composition. What she found is that "learning to dance is like learning to write: The two processes share the same mental, even physical, space" (Davenport and Forbes, 1997, p. 294). Structure, style, and other elements of writing possess physical, tangible analogs in dance that enhance the student writer's understanding of and facility with words. In this light, the text, written by hand or typed by computer, becomes a "physical artifact with physical dimensions, qualities, characteristics" (p. 296). Forbes and Davenport conclude that writing has much to gain when approached through the body thinking in dance, goals best achieved by placing writing and dancing on a collaborative par.

An important point for Davenport and Forbes is that neither discipline can be taken for granted, least of all dance and the body thinking it trains for expression. As Forbes discovered, thinking through the body does not come easily to the novice, who finds it difficult at first to imagine movements or execute them as intended or remember and perform complex movement sequences. Even those who would use body thinking for verbal expression "need to be instructed to connect with our bodies as we write, it is not instinctively present" (Davenport and Forbes, pp. 302, 292). Say, rather, that innately present in the species, body thinking must be trained rather than ignored, or it atrophies like an unused muscle. This is the conclusion one of us has drawn from body thinking workshops co-taught with dance professor Lynnette Overby at Michigan State University in an arts/humanities course on the creative process.

After presenting body thinking in general, we introduced the students to body thinking in creative movement, taught them the rudiments of simple dance composition, and challenged them to use movement as an approach to written expression. Only a handful of the students had any experience with artistic writing; even fewer had ever taken ballet or modern dance. Nearly all agreed, however, that their awareness of body thinking had heightened in the course of the bodies-on activities. Moreover, body thinking gave them more and different ideas about prompt objects (bones, shells, bees, nests) than were first apparent to visual and tactile observation. "If you were focusing on a movement," wrote one student, "it gave you a certain feeling." "Different movements brought out different words," concluded another (workshop evaluation, 2002).

Despite this successful outcome, a few students were stymied by a rusty capacity to think with the body. "I learned a lot about body thinking and myself," wrote one of these. "I found myself to be very inferior and conscious with [of?] the rigidness of my body movements. Perhaps I even became embarrassed." A professional writer surveyed after a similar body thinking workshop was presented at a local writers conference said much the same thing. Nevertheless, he realized the value of the exercise. Though he claimed he was not typically aware of body thinking and found it challenging to move in response to a photographic prompt, the moving he did "got me to see what I was paying attention to in the photograph" and helped focus his writing (workshop evaluation, 2003).

Body thinking has also made inroads in the college science classroom. Some years ago Michigan State University biologist Cathy Bristow wondered how to increase student understanding of complex biological processes. She remembered seeing a movie called *Protein Synthesis: An Epic on the Cellular Level* shot at Stanford University in 1971. Following an introduction by Paul Berg (later to win the Nobel Prize), the movie showed, according to the blurb on its cover, "a choreographic interpretation of the current biochemical model.... [in which] the beauty and rhythm in biochemical reactions is revealed in a manner not possible with static drawings." In fact, the movie shows hundreds of students reenacting the genetic synthesis of proteins to the beat of rock music in the Stanford football stadium, filmed from a helicopter! Inspired by this dance-like demonstration, Bristow decided to scale the idea down to classroom size (personal communication, December 8, 2003).

Bristow's goal was to have students translate a DNA sequence into its corresponding protein. Each student was asked to take a role as a DNA base, an mRNA codon, a tRNA anticodon, or an amino acid. The mRNA students had to find the corresponding person on the DNA chain with whom to interact. As the students formed appropriate pair bonds, they clasped each other's shoulders. When all of the mRNA people had found their corresponding DNA base, the mRNA people all linked arms to form the mRNA molecule and moved out of the part of the room designated the nucleus into another part of the room, designated the cytoplasm. There, while the mRNA was being formed, other groups of students representing tRNA anticodons had been searching for their corresponding amino acid people, again forming bonds by linking arms. When the mRNA appeared in the cytoplasm, each tRNA-amino acid pair had to find its appropriate place on the mRNA. Each tRNA anticodon person formed a shoulder bond to its mRNA codon. As these bonds formed, the amino acid people were released from their tRNAs, forming "arm" bonds to their neighboring amino acid. Genetic sequences properly decoded spelled messages that sent the students to candy rewards, all part of the emotional involvement Bristow hoped to create. Bristow subsequently organized bodily re-creations of protein folding and of food web ecologies for college students—mature echoes of the bee dance created by children in Bristow's university-based mentor program for elementary schools (Donovan and Bristow, 2002).

The results in each case were effective. Something happens during the physical reenactment, says Bristow. Students gain a different perspective on the patterns in complex dynamic processes when they walk themselves through them step by step, when they make it happen in their own bodies. They learn to understand biology from the inside out instead of from the outside in. The difference is crucial, according to Nobel laureate Joshua Lederberg, to being a good scientist:

One needs the ability to strip to the essential attributes of some actor or process, the ability to imagine oneself inside a biological situation. I literally had to be able to think, for example, 'What would it be like if I were one of the chemical pieces in a bacterial chromosome?' and try to understand what my environment was, try to know where I was, try to know when I was supposed to function in a certain way, and so forth." (cited in Judson, 1980, p. 6)

An empathic, actor's view of nature can only be learned by thinking with the body.

Bristow's MSU colleague Jim Miller learned this lesson the hard way. For many years he had his graduate students read classic papers about how insects and other animals forage, mate, and perform other activities. He was puzzled and frustrated by their inability to understand and apply what they were reading to the design and interpretation of other experiments. Then he realized that the students were not using what they had learned to become actors in the process. They did not know how to embody their knowledge. So Miller now takes his graduate students to the gym and gives them various tasks meant to raise awareness of their own body thinking behaviors, especially those navigational ones; to allow them to experience simpler sensory and navigational abilities; and to provide sets of self-generated data students can use as a foundation for analyzing insect movements (personal communication, November 14, 2003).

For example, moving from point A to point B is for most people an automatic and unconscious exercise. Miller asks his students to pay attention to the sensory cues they use to walk purposefully across the gym floor or, conversely, to move in random fashion. Then he systematically strips them of these cues with blindfolds and/or Walkman radios that blot out environmental sight and sound. As they set off from the center of the gym toward the gym wall, walking heel-toe or hopping on one foot, students lose all normal sense of their body in space—and gain some idea of "what movement, orientation, and navigation might be like for simpler organisms." Acoustical cues are reintroduced, so that students may have limited feedback on the approach to a target. And at each step of the way, others record the nature of their navigational and movement choices. Eventually, they analyze average elapsed times, optimal navigational strategies, and typical paths for completing each movement task. Miller hopes that such experiences will open students' " 'intellectual eyes and ears' to the possible sensory worlds of other creatures." Miller's ultimate goal is to make better biologists. He does so by placing body thinking at the center of his teaching.

Chemical principles have also been taught through dance.

Award-winning educator Zafra M. Lerman of the Institute for Science Education and Science Communication at Columbia College Chicago has developed many innovative ways to help students from elementary school to university levels—particularly those at risk—learn to take joy in the principles of chemistry. One of the chief ways she does this is to collaborate with dance and theater students at the college to help secondary students choreograph accurate dances about chemical bonding, chemical reactions, the periodic table of the elements, and broader, related concepts such as the environmental effects of ozone. For example, one dance explored the nature of ionic bonds: "A group of dancers representing halogens and another group representing alkali metals meet in a fictional high school dance, where they interact and form ionic bonds. The school deans (Oxygen and two Hydrogens) do not approve of these unions and combine their efforts to break the newly formed bonds." (Lerman, 2001a, p. 4). The clever ploy used in the plot of the dance is that water (H_2O) does, indeed, dissolve compounds (such as NaCl, or salt) made of alkali metals (such as sodium) and halogens (such as chlorine) by breaking their ionic bonds, just as the school deans break up the dancing couples. Lerman says that the fun the students have choreographing and performing their chemical dances only adds to the educational value of their productions (Lerman, 2001b). Many of Lerman's students, who typically do not plan to attend college before taking her classes, go on to win full scholarships, sometimes even taking advanced degrees (Lerman, 2000).

Of course, physicists aren't to be outdone by biologists and chemists. They, too, have explored dance as a medium for learning physical principles. The best-known examples are certainly Kenneth Laws's books, the latest of which is *Physics and the Art of Dance: Understanding Movement* (2002). Laws is a professor of physics emeritus at Dickinson College and his books use the dancer's body and motions as the stuff with which to teach physics itself. For if not self-evident, it surely becomes clear in Laws's hands that the dancer can do nothing that is contrary to physics, and performs best only when her movements make best use of physical principles. The greatest problem for students of physics is not, as is commonly thought, mastering the relevant mathematics of the subject, but translating the meaning of those equations into physical understanding of how real objects, such as their bodies, obey the laws described by the equations (Root-Bernstein and Root-Bernstein, 1999, pp. 14–16).

This translation process is something that George Gollin, a professor of physics at the University of Illinois Urbana-Champaign has undertaken not only for his students but also for the general public. In a collaboration with architecture professor Rebecca Williams and dance professor Linda Lehovec, he has helped to create a series of charettes and interactive exhibits in which visitors become the stuff of physical models. For example, they may simulate subatomic particles forced to move in unexpected ways by the architectural geometries of the exhibits, just as subatomic particles are forced by the geometries of particle accelerators and detectors to move in certain ways and reveal their individual behaviors. Getting people to experience for themselves, through their own bodies, the forces of physics is one of the best ways to teach physical concepts (Gollin).

Body thinking, in sum, is not something that only dancers, athletes and actors "rely on". Body thinking is at the heart of learning everything from making music and poetry to understanding biology and physics.

Dancing for Extra Disciplinary Insight and Expression

Because practitioners of so many different disciplines use body thinking in their creative work, some of them have also discovered that one of best ways to convey their insights is through movement-related skills or even dance itself. We have already noted that Paul Berg of Stanford helped to choreograph and film the classic movie *Protein Synthesis.* Marvin Cohen, professor of physics at the University of California, Berkeley, collaborated with choreographer David Wood in the 1980s on a similar evocation of the principles of superconductivity. In a superconducting substance, electrons move without resistance, so the electrical current never dissipates as random motion or heat as it does in a normal conductor (such as a copper wire). Physicists believe that the motions of the electrons in superconductors are always paired and symmetrical, whereas the motions of electrons in a normal conductor are asymmetrical or random. Cohen and Wood choreographed a dance that explored the various types of symmetrical-paired motions and asymmetrical-unpaired motions that dancers (representing electrons) could attain. Cohen considered the resulting dance, called *Currents,* not only a useful kinesthetic model and illustration of the physics and mathematics of superconductivity, but he also viewed the choreographic experience itself as a form of scientific research. "I told David Wood that if he or the dancers came up with some new ordered state or some new motions I'd appreciate hearing about them," Cohen said. "We're hoping that perhaps he can give us some new ideas" (cited in Root-Bernstein and Root-Bernstein, 1999, p. 286).

Neurologists and biologists, meanwhile, have turned to dance-derived movement notations to record, analyze, and express otherwise intangible insights. It may be odd to consider dance an analytical art, but the dancer and choreographer must break movements and movement sequences into distinct, learnable parts and then reassemble them to create continuous motion. Dance notations have taken this particulate approach to motion to its logical end, isolating the separate movements of each body part in recordable and analyzable forms. It is this combination of analysis and recording intrinsic to dance notations that has drawn the attention of people in medicine and biology.

The earliest use of dance notation in medicine seems to have been suggested by Benesh and McGuinness in 1974 as an aid to understanding movement deficits and their treatment in a wide variety of patients and clinical settings (Benesh and McGuinnes, 1974; McGuinness, 1980; Harrison et al., 1992). Clinical applications of Laban notation followed soon after (Abbie, 1978). Ilan Golani and his colleagues then pioneered the use of Eshkol-Wachmann notation to analyze and record movement deficits caused by severe neurological diseases and trauma (Golani et al., 1979). Subsequent studies have suggested that such movement analysis can be a useful aid in the very early diagnosis of autism in infants (Teitelbaum et al., 1998) and Parkinson's disease in adults (Whishaw et al., 2002).

A less obvious application of movement notation has been to apply it analytically to animal movements. For example, S. M. Pellis, working with Ilan Golani and other collaborators, has examined the stereotypical movements that cats perform when "playing" with mice without killing them, using Eshkol-Wachmann notation. They found that there was no discernable difference between "play" movements and the movements that a cat performed when actually killing a mouse, suggesting that play is practice for predation in cats (Pellis et al., 1988). More recent studies have analyzed play and fight behaviors among rats (Foroud and Pellis, 2003) and explored how rats and raccoons use their forelimbs for grasping and holding things in comparison to human beings (Whishaw et al., 1992; Iwaniuk and Whishaw, 1999). Without some reproducible means to observe, record, dissect, and analyze these very different movements, no useful comparisons could be made. Dancers, by exploring how we move, by learning how to break movements into teachable parts, and by inventing ways to record their insights, have thereby pioneered tools useful to anyone who studies any kind of motion.

We predict that it is only a matter of time before someone begins applying dance logic and analysis to robotics, too. After all, if we want to transfer the best practices of the most skilled workers into the movements of robotic machines, how else can we succeed?

The Paradox in Body Thinking Beyond Dance

Here we come to a fundamental paradox of body thinking beyond dance. As critical as this thinking tool is to physics or music or writing, it is also true that schooling in these disciplines appears designed to repress body thinking after grade school years—the college classrooms discussed above notwithstanding. This is certainly true for the sciences. In an unpublished study presented in seminar in February 2003, Ken Poff and Norm Lownds of Michigan State University examined science textbooks used at elementary, secondary, and college levels for evidence of thinking tool use in classroom instruction. They found that the youngest students are often, if not always, encouraged to observe, image, empathize, body think, etc., their way to scientific understanding. By the time these students reach high school, however, many imaginative thinking tools, except for observing, patterning, and modeling, receive less and less attention, as instruction veers from the hands-on, somatic approach to the rote and analytical. The trend continues through college. Indeed, when students reach this level, according to Poff and Lownds, three tools—playing, empathizing and body thinking—are actively proscribed as anathema to objective, scientific method (personal communication, February 4, 2003).

Nothing could be more wrong-headed. As one of us has written elsewhere, the scientific method taught in school does not adequately or accurately reflect the creative practice of scientists, the best of whom unite a rigorous analysis after the fact to preliminary, imaginative thinking (Root-Bernstein, R. 1989, 1990, 2002). Eugene Ferguson (1993) has made the same point about the necessity of somatic thinking as a prerequisite to engineering skill. In many cases (see above), this preliminary generation of ideas depends on body thinking and related tools such as empathizing—in other words, on somatic knowledge. But where is the budding scientist to acquire and practice these skills? Not in science class! Rather, she must learn and exercise body thinking elsewhere. To the extent that other professions, such as music, sculpture, visual arts, and writing, also depend on body thinking, they, too, rely on incidental, extra disciplinary nurturing and development of that vital skill. There is a void in the schooling of somatic knowledge, and dance can position itself to fill that need in interdisciplinary outreach.

Thinking Tools and the Utility of Dance

Arts advocates and educators understandably hesitate to embrace notions of utility imposed upon the arts from outside their practice. Janice Ross, writing in *Arts Education Policy Review* (2000), asserts that "we need to be vigilant that the arts are not used and valued primarily for their non-art attributes" (p. 7). Nevertheless, in the effort to reverse ongoing decline in public support for dance, she concedes that a case ought to be made for a utility "rooted in the fundamental experience of somatic knowledge" (Ross, 2000, p. 7). In other words, learning body thinking and body expressing with integrity, in a disciplined form such as dance, must be balanced by demonstrating how the acquisition of such skills is, like learning to read, write and do arithmetic, useful to learning in general.

The task of demonstrating learning transfer has hitherto proved more difficult for dance than might be expected. A great deal of research has endeavored to prove that dance, as one of the arts, provides skills and knowledge vital to academic learning (Critical Links, 2002). But these conclusions have been disputed, primarily for lack of rigorous quantitative analysis or a generalizing context for disparate qualitative reports (Winner and Cooper, 2000). What dance needs, argues Karen Bradley (2002), in a recent review of dance research for Critical Links, is a vocabulary for discussing cogently the cognitive skills and processes "that take place during the course of learning dance." "Dance," she reiterates, "...is in need of research that explains the interrelation of its specific dimensions as an arts experience and cognitive processes" (p. 17)—and connects that experience, we add, to the "specific dimensions" of other classroom disciplines. What dance needs, we believe, is a tools-for-thinking approach to integrated classroom pedagogy and research.

We strongly urge the dance education community to consider that thinking tools provide the conceptual focus necessary in demonstrating the vital importance of body thinking and dance to learning across the board. Tools for thinking provide a means of identifying and schooling cognitive skills and imaginative processes that transcend disciplinary boundaries; they provide a predictive basis for research demonstrating what dance develops and trains and transfers to other learning situations; and they provide a theoretical basis for developing a transdisciplinary pedagogy that places dance within the core curriculum.

To learn the thinking tools in dance is to learn how to learn somatically, of and through the body, with built-in bridges to non-body disciplines. If we study not just the techniques of dance, but how we generate and create dance, then we learn how to learn. Individuals who learn to observe carefully through dance, to abstract what they have observed, to find patterns in their abstractions, to form functional analogies between the patterns, and to model and play with these analogies have learned how to learn in any field of endeavor. The observant dancer will also be an observant naturalist. The dancer who can create an abstract dance can also think abstractly about language. The dancer who understands how important it is to play with dance movements also knows how important play is to being a creative thinker of any kind.

This is not a matter of conjecture. As we have argued elsewhere, many of the world's most creative people have mastered thinking tools in one discipline and applied them to another (Root-Bernstein and Root-Bernstein, 1999; 2004). Indeed, creative individuals are often polymaths. This is certainly true of many dance innovators: Loie Fuller was a patented inventor; Vaslav Nijinsky, Oskar Schlemmer, Merce Cunningham, and Trisha Brown were and are visual artists of considerable talent; Graham, de Mille, and Humphrey, to name a few, wrote prolifically (Root-Bernstein and Root-Bernstein, 2003); Alwin Nikolais famously had a hand in every aspect of his "total," multimedia theater, including set design, lighting, and musical composition (Louis, 2003). As many polymaths have expressly noted, well-chosen avocations complement and inform vocations: art stimulates visual imaging for the dancer; dance stimulates body thinking for the sculptor; music stimulates pattern recognizing and forming for the scientist. Tools for thinking thus provide a predictive basis for ascertaining and developing "correlative talents" (Root-Bernstein, R., 1989, 312-340; Root-Bernstein, R. and Root-Bernstein, M., 2004)—complementary sets of disciplinary skills that bridge one subject and another in the classroom.

Indeed, tools for thinking are inherently transdisciplinary, that is, they forge links of common creative process between disparate endeavors that content-focused studies cannot easily connect. By their very nature, the tools provide a method for integrating dance with the arts and with academic disciplines. One such example of a tools-for-thinking method is the dance/writing workshop one of us undertook to help dance students at the high school level think differently about choreography by exploring visual as well as verbal images and patterns (Root-Bernstein, M., 2001). The connections between visual and verbal and dance arts were made explicit for the students by articulating, not special disciplinary vocabularies, but the more general vocabulary of the thinking tool. For example, by focusing on abstracting—the act or process of eliminating all but the essential characteristics of a thing—classroom instruction linked the spare prints of Picasso's Bull series and the equally spare poetry of William Carlos Williams to simple dances composed by the students themselves.

Because these were advanced dance composition students, an explicit and thorough exploration of abstracting meant refocusing at first on the mimetic capacities of the body, for all abstractions begin with what is real. It meant, too, reconsidering step by step the choices a dancer has for refining, altering, and ultimately transforming essential movements. The results were twofold. Students marveled that conscious attention to abstracting and other thinking tools expanded their choreographic powers. As one student put it, her workshop dances "were a little different than other dances because knowing the actual process gave me a new way to explore and change my 'normal' movement" (as cited in Root-Bernstein, M., 2001, p. 140). Conscious attention to thinking tools also allowed the students to transform ideas they mined in art or poetry into analogous ideas in dance. They transposed visual or verbal expression into physical expression, not by illustrating word with gesture, but by referring both word and gesture to one or another of the imaginative thinking tools that support both forms of expression.

At the level of any thinking tool, but body thinking especially, dance can forge similar process links with social studies, language arts, mathematics, and science that enhance learning in these areas by embodying knowledge. It is especially critical that this be done in science, math, writing, and other academic subjects within the core curriculum. It is equally critical that it be done not just on the elementary level, but in secondary and college classrooms. Whether five or 15 and 20 years old, the novice scientist who must learn to observe and understand sub-atomic interactions, the behavior of animals, or the birth and death of stars can also learn to observe and understand interactions, behaviors, and cycles with body movement and body feelings. Not only does this transdisciplinary study cater to multiple learning (and remembering) styles, it also opens a door otherwise shut in science class to the sensory exploration and felt knowledge of organic and inorganic process in space and time. Under the guidance of dance instructors, novice scientists of all ages can learn to express what they know and discover not only in words or numbers, but through movement and dance—and to expand their understanding in the process.

Last but not least, we reiterate that the thinking tools elaborated in these pages can establish transdisciplinary process links that go far beyond the illustrative or "instrumental" use of dance to demonstrate extradisciplinary concepts such as the rain cycle or metaphor. The very best connections between dance and science, between dance and other core subjects, explore ways of thinking about the world vital to both disciplines. Dimensional thinking, as critical to creative movement as body thinking, ties the student dancer's exploration of space to the student geometrician's exploration of x,y coordinates. Body thinking and its attendant kinesthetic empathizing link the dancer's study of group dynamics to the scientist's study of chemical phase change or electrical current. Observing, abstracting and patterning tie the distillation of movement that is modern dance to the spare articulation of verbal image that is poetry. In all instances dance can and should be cultivated not as a handmaiden to math, science, or writing, but as an independent consort capable of transforming commonly shared process and content in its own image. In any event, dance can transfer thinking skills essential to imaginative learning and creative problem-solving—and do so in through the somatic lens that is so particularly its own and yet so necessary to academic disciplines within the core curriculum.

A Transdisciplinary Education

The pioneering education called for here does not propose change in *what* we teach, but in *how* we teach. The thinking tools, by their very nature, can already be found buried within curricular materials used in every discipline, at every educational level. All that needs to be done is to recognize them, use them, and teach them. Given the right take on dance and its component tools, bridges can be built between the dancer's way of knowing and visual, aural, verbal, and mathematical forms of knowledge. And none too soon. When one looks closely at the way humans imagine, create, and problem-solve, disciplinary categories break down. Innovation and invention most often occur at the interstices of disciplinary activity. Education today needs to recognize this fundamental phenomenon. A true liberal arts curriculum for tomorrow must place the arts, and dance especially, on an equal footing with science, technology, and the humanities at every stage of schooling, from kindergarten to college (Eisner, 1986; Gray, 1989; Root-Bernstein, R. and Root-Bernstein, M., 1999). Put more simply, the aRts should be the 4th "R" along with Reading, wRiting, and aRithmetic—and dance should be at the center of the aRts.

Many others before us have called for arts-infused, transdisciplinary schooling. As biologist C. H. Waddington so aptly put it in the early 1970s, "The acute problems of the world can be solved only by whole men [and women], not by people who refuse to be, publicly anything more than a technologist, or a pure scientist, or an artist. In the world of today, you have got to be everything, or you are going to be nothing" (cited in Root-Bernstein and Root-Bernstein, 1999, p. 315). If we are to promote a creative culture in the present world of exponentially increasing, and often suffocating, information, it is time to specialize in breadth of process, rather than in the minutiae of product that constitute current curricula. In this kind of specialization, what counts is not the amount of data an individual has stored in her memory banks; modern technology has made culturally stored knowledge almost instantly available to almost everyone. What matters is whether the individual has the imaginative and creative skills to understand and make use of that vast storehouse of data. What matters is whether the individual can use her creative training to combine and connect dance with sculpture, dance with writing, dance with physics. Dance is an art, a rich repository of subjective, intuitive understanding of the world. It also comprises a science, a somatic way of generating and expressing ideas that is generally useful to all knowledge learning and knowledge making. In the utility of body thinking in and beyond dance lies one of the strongest, most compelling arguments for the inclusion of dance in the core curriculum.

REFERENCES

Abbie, M., (1978). Laban notation and its application to treating clumsy children. *Developmental Medicine and Childhood Neurology 20*, 11–14.

Altmann, J. (2003, October 6). Music scholar pursues research from Russia to the barre. *Princeton Weekly Bulletin*, p. 3.

Arias, E. A. (1989). Music as projection of the kinetic sense. *Music Review, 50*, 1–33.

Artsource® Curriculum—Dance. (2003).The Music Center Study Guide to the Performing Arts. Music Center Education Division. The Music Center / Performing Arts Center of Los Angeles. Retrieved 3 February, 2004, from http://www.musiccenter.org/artsource/dance.html

Ashton, D. (Ed.). (1972). *Picasso on art: A selection of views.* New York: DaCapo.

Auping, M. (Ed.). (1989) *Abstraction geometry painting: Selected geometric abstract painting in America since 1945.* New York: Harry N. Abrams.

Bamberger, J. (1991). The laboratory for making things. In D. Schon (Ed.), *The reflective turn: Case studies in and on educational practice* (pp. 37–62). New York: Teachers College Press.

Benesh, R., & McGuinness, J. (1974). Benesh movement notation and medicine. *Physiotherapy 60*, 176–178.

Bradley, K. (2002). Informing and reforming dance education research. *Critical links: Learning in the arts and student academic and social development.* Arts Education Partnership. Retrieved October 24, 2003, from http://aep-arts.org/Publications&Resources.html

Brown, J. (Ed.). (1979). *The vision of modern dance.* Princeton, NJ: Princeton Book Co.

Cornfield, R. (Ed.). (1998). *Dance writings and poetry, Edwin Denby.* New Haven: Yale University Press.

Crisp, C. & M. Clarke. (1975). *Making a Ballet.* New York: Macmillan.

Critical Links: Learning in the arts and student academic and social development. (2002, May). Arts Education Partnership. Retrieved October 24, 2003, from http://aep-arts.org/Publications&Resources.html

Cunningham, M. (1968). *Changes: Notes on choreography.* New York: Something Else Press.

Damasio, A. (1994). *Descartes' error: Emotion, reason, and the human brain.* New York: G.P. Putnam's Sons.

Davenport, D. and Forbes, C. (1997, Winter) Writing movement / Dancing words: A collaborative pedagogy. *Education, 118* (2), 292–302.

de Mille, A. (1952). *Dance to the piper.* Boston: Little, Brown and Co.

de Mille, A. (1962). *To a young dancer.* Boston: Little, Brown.

de Mille, A. (1991). *Martha: The life and work of Martha Graham.* New York: Random House.

Dewey, J. (1934). *Art as experience.* New York: Minton, Balch.

Donovan, J. and Bristow, C. (2002, Fall). "Get bugged": A university-based mentor program for elementary schools. *American Entomologist, 48* (3), 138–141.

Dubal, D. (1984). *Reflections from the keyboard: The world of the concert pianist.* New York: Summit Books.

Dunning, J. (1999, April 25). For newcomers, an archive in human form. *The New York Times,* pp. AR 8, 25.

Eisner, E. (1986). The role of the arts in cognition and curriculum. *Journal of Art & Design Education, 5* (11,2), 57–67.

Epel, N. (Ed.). (1993). *Writers dreaming.* New York: Vintage Press.

Ferguson, E. S. (1992). *Engineering and the mind's eye.* Cambridge: MIT Press.

Flam, J. (1973). *Matisse on Art.* Reprint, 1978. New York: Dutton.

Foroud, A. and Pellis, S. M. (2003). The development of "roughness" in the play fighting of rats: a Laban Movement Analysis perspective. *Developmental Psychobiology 42,* 35–43.

Gardner, H. (1983). *Frames of mind: The theory of multiple intelligences.* New York: Basic Books.

Gladstone, V. (1998, May 24). A taskmaster tells his troupe, surprise me. *The New York Times,* pp. AR26, 34.

Golani, I., Wolgin, D. L., & Teitelbaum, P. (1979). A proposed natural geometry of recovery from akinesia in the lateral hypothalamic rat. *Brain Research 164,* 237–267.

Goldwater, R. & Treves, M. (Eds.). (1945). *Artists on art, from the XIV to the XX century.* New York: Pantheon Books.

Gollin, G. (n.d.A) Joint *explorations: Architecture, dance, and physics.* Retrieved January 5, 2004, from http://web.hep.uiuc.edu/home/g-gollin/architecture_dance_physics/

Gollin, G. (n.d.B) *Physics and dance.* Retrieved January 5, 2004, from http://web/hep.uiuc.edu/home/g-gollin/dance/dance_physics.html

Graham, M. (1991). *Blood memory.* New York: Doubleday.

Gray, J. A. (1989). *Dance instruction, science applied to the art of movement.* Champaign, IL: Human Kinetics Books.

Greenburg, J. and Jordan, S. (1993). *The sculptor's eye: Looking at contemporary American art.* New York: Delacorte Press.

Hanna, J. (1979). *To dance is human, A theory of nonverbal communication.* Austin: University of Texas Press.

Hanna, J. (2001). The language of dance. *JOPERD 72* (4), 40–53.

Harrison, M. A., Atkinson, H., De Weerdt, W. (1992). Benesh Movement Notation. A tool to record observational assessment. *International Journal of Technological Assessment of Health Care 8*, 44–54.

Horosko, M. (Ed.). (1991). *Martha Graham: The evolution of her dance theory and training, 1926-1991.* Chicago: a cappella books/Chicago Review Press.

Humphrey, D. (1959). *The art of making dances.* Ed. Barbara Pollock. New York: Grove Press.

Hutchinson, E. D. (1959). *How to think creatively.* New York: Abington-Cokesbury Press.

Iwaniuk, A. N. & Whishaw, I. Q. (1999). How skilled are the skilled limb movements of the racoon (Procyon lotor)? *Behavior and Brain Research 99*, 35–44.

Johnson, M. (1987). *The body in the mind: The bodily basis of meaning, imagination, and reason.* Chicago: University of Chicago Press.

John-Stein, V. (1985). *Notebooks of the mind: Explorations of thinking.* Albuquerque: University of New Mexico Press.

Joyce, M. (1980). *First steps in teaching creative dance to children (2nd ed.).* Mountain View, CA: Mayfield Publishing.

Judson, H. (1980). *The search for solutions.* New York: Holt, Rinehart and Winston.

Kisselgoff, A. (1984, February 19). Martha Graham. *New York Times Magazine*, p. 51.

Laws, K.L. (2002). *Physics and the art of dance: Understanding movement.* New York: Oxford University Press.

Lehman, A. & Richardson. B. (Eds.). (1986). *Oskar Schlemmer.* Baltimore: Baltimore Museum of Art.

Lerman, Z. (2000, April 5). Making an impact. *Graduating Engineer and Computer Careers Online.* Retrieved December 15, 2003 from http://www.graduatingengineer.com/articles/feature/04-05-00sb6.html

Lerman, Z. (2001a, December). Alternative methods to teach and assess science. *Chemistry in Israel, Bulletin of the Israel Chemical Society, 8.* Retrieved December 15, 2003, from http://www.weizmann.ac.il/ICS/booklet/8/con8.html

Lerman, Z. (2001b, August 3). Visualizing the Chemical Bond. *Chemical Education International, 2* (1). Retrieved December 15, 2003, from http://cssj.chem.sci.hiroshima-u.ac.jp/ctc/

Lisle, L. (1990). *Louise Nevelson: A passionate life.* New York: Summit Books.

Louis, M. (2003, October 26). Multimedia's multitasking pioneer. *New York Times*, AR 8.

Maloof, Sam. (1983). *Sam Maloof, woodworker.* New York: Kodansha International.

Mandelbrojt, J. (1994). In search of the specificity of art. *Leonardo, 27*, 185–88.

200   *Michele Root-Bernstein and Robert Root-Bernstein*

Marks, P. (2001, May 10). Creating the moment, one step at a time. *New York Times*, pp. B1, 4.

McGuinness, S. J. (1982). Benesh movement notation. An introduction to recording clinical data. Part 12: An historical perspective and clinical uses. *Physiotherapy 68*, 182–184.

Minton S & J. Steffen. (1992). The development of a spatial kinesthetic awareness measuring instrument for use with beginning dance students. In L. Overby & J. Humphrey (eds.), *Dance: Current Selected Research, 3* (pp. 73–80). New York: AMS Press.

Montessori, M. (1984). *The absorbent mind.* (C. Claremont, trans.). New York: Bantam Doubleday Dell Publishing Group. (Original work published 1949)

Nijinska, B. (1981). *Early memoirs.* (I. Nijinska & J. Rawlinson, trans.). New York: Holt, Rinehart and Winston.

Noguchi, I. (1994). *Isamu Noguchi: Essays and conversations*, Diane Apostolos-Cappadona & Bruce Altschuler (eds.). New York: Harry N. Abrams and Isamu Noguchi Foundation.

Overby, L. (1992). A comparison of novice and experienced dancers' body awareness. In L. Overby & J. Humphrey (eds.), *Dance, Current Selected Research, 3* (pp. 57–72). New York: AMS Press.

Pellis, S. M., O'Brien, D. P., Pellis, V. C., Teitelbaum, P., Wolgin, D. L., Kennedy, S. (1988). Escalation of feline predation along a gradient from avoidance through "play" to killing. *Behavioral Neuroscience 102*, 760–777.

Read, H. (1956). *Education through art (3rd ed.).* New York: Pantheon Books.

Root-Bernstein, M. (2001). Abstracting bulls: A dancing words / writing dance workshop. *Journal of Dance Education, 1*(4), 134–141.

Root-Bernstein, M. & Root-Bernstein, R. (2003). Martha Graham, dance, and the polymathic imagination, a case for multiple intelligences or universal thinking tools? *Journal of Dance Education, 3*(1), 16–27.

Root-Bernstein, R. (1989). *Discovering. Inventing and solving problems at the frontiers of knowledge.* Cambridge: Harvard University Press.

Root-Bernstein, R. (1990, Sept./Oct.). Sensual education. *The Sciences*, 12–14.

Root-Bernstein, R. (2002). Aesthetic cognition. *International Journal of the Philosophy of Science, 16*, 61–77.

Root-Bernstein, R. & Root-Bernstein, M. (1999). *Sparks of genius: The thirteen thinking tools of the world's most creative people.* Boston: Houghton Mifflin Co.

Root-Bernstein, R. & Root-Bernstein, M. (2004). Polymathy and the creative imagination. In R. Sternberg, E. Grigorenko & J. Singer (eds.). *Creativity: From potential to realization*, American Psychological Association.

Ross, J. (2000, July/August). Arts education in the information age: a new place for somatic wisdom. *Arts Education Policy Review, 101*(6), 27–32. Retrieved October 22, 2003, from First Search database.

Seitz, J. (1992). The development of bodily-kinesthetic intelligence in children: Implications for education and artistry. *Holistic Education Review, 5* (2), 35–39.

Seitz, J. (1993, March/April). I move...therefore I am. *Psychology Today, 26* (2), 50–55.

Seitz, J. (2000). The bodily basis of thought. *New Ideas in Psychology: An International Journal of Innovative Theory in Psychology, 18* (1), 23–40.

Sorell, W. (ed.). (1992) *The dance has many faces (3rd rev ed.)*. Chicago: a cappella books/Chicago Review Press.

Steinberg, C. (ed.). (1980). *The dance anthology.* New York: New American Library.

Stiles, K. & Selz, P. (1996). *Theories and documents of contemporary art: A Sourcebook of artists' writings.* Berkeley: University of California Press.

Taylor, P. (1987). *Private domain.* New York: Alfred A. Knopf.

Teitelbaum, P., Teitelbaum, O., Nye, J., Fryman, J. & Maurer, R. G. (1998). Movement analysis in infancy may be useful for early diagnosis of autism. *Proceedings of the National Academy of Sciences, U. S. A. 95*, 13982–7.

Tharp, T. (2003). *The creative habit: Learn it and use it for life.* (Mark Reiter, collaborator). New York: Simon & Schuster.

Todd. J. (2001). Body knowledge, empathy, and the body politic. *The Humanist 61*(2), 23–28.

Turner, M. (1996). *The literary mind.* New York: Oxford University Press.

Waddington, C.H. (1969). *Behind appearance: A study of the relations between painting and the natural sciences in this century.* Cambridge, Mass.: MIT Press.

Whishaw, I. Q., Pellis, S. M. & Gorny, B. P. (1992). Skilled reaching in rats and humans: Evidence for parallel development or homology. *Behavior and Brain Research 47*, 59-70.

Whishaw, I. Q., Suchowersky, O., Davis, L, Sama, J., Metz, G. A. & Pellis, S. M. (2002). Impairment of pronation, supination and body co-ordination in reach-to-grasp tasks in human Parkinson's disease (PD) reveals homology to deficits in animal models. *Behavior and Brain Research, 133*, 165-176.

Winner, E. & Cooper, M. (2000). Mute those claims: No evidence (yet) for a causal link between arts study and academic achievement. *Journal of Aesthetic Education, 34* (3/4), 10-75.

Writers at work: The Paris Review interviews, 1963-1984. Series 1-6. New York: Viking Press.

Zakkai, J. D. (1997). *Dance as a way of knowing.* York, ME: Stenhouse Publishers/The Galef Institute.

6

Body Language and Learning:
Insights for K-12 Education

Judith Lynne Hanna, Ph.D.

A key reason to offer dance education to children in grades K-12 is that dance is communication and its body language can contribute to the "mental" mission of K-12 education to develop students' skills in sending and receiving messages. This article summarizes some research that suggests the cognitive potential of dance in K-12, findings critical to grounding dance in the academic realm. Verbal language is the recognized medium for learning. In many ways similar to verbal language in communication, dance intertwines the cognitive, affective, and physical. Multisensorily fusing inner feelings and ideas with outer body kinetic design, dance can engage students in the teaching and learning process. If the brain, vocal organ, and ears for speech, eyes for reading, and body language for emphasis and elaboration allow us to communicate, consider how the brain, total body, and various senses allow us to send and receive messages.

"Good dancers have mostly better heels than heads" is, unfortunately, one of many proverbs that convey common misperceptions. Many people relegate dance to the realms of play, physical exercise, recreation, and theater performance. Some think Martha Graham is a snack (Americans for the Arts 2004).

So why might schools even consider offering dance education as part of an already full K-12 curricula, in addition to the emphasis on standardized testing in reading and math, and scarce economic resources? One reason that advocates put forth is that the National Education Goals[1] include dance as one of the arts (along with music, theater, and the visual arts), and thus as a core subject of the same significance as English, math, and science for all children. In

---

[1] Conference Report on H.R. 1804, Goals 2000: Educate America Act. 1994, *Congressional Record*, 140(32), H1625-H1684; Goals 2000 Legislation PL 103-227.

a first for a U.S. Secretary of Education, Rod Paige sent a letter in July 2004 on the value of the arts in education to each of 16,000 superintendents of education in the United States. He wrote "the arts are a core academic subject under the No Child Left Behind Act (NCLB). I believe the arts have a significant role in education both for their intrinsic value and for the ways in which they can enhance general academic achievement and improve students' social and emotional development." On January 26, 2005, in *Education Week*, Secretary Paige with Governor of Arkansas and chairman of the Education Commission of the States (2004-06), Mike Huckabee, argued for putting the arts front and center.

A more important reason for schools to offer dance education in K-12 is that research shows the biological bases and potency of nonverbal communication, of which dance is one form. This research supports the argument that dance is communication and its body language can contribute to the "mental" mission of K-12 education to develop students' skills in sending and receiving messages.

When I first began my research on dance in the 1960s, I looked for theoretical grounding. I turned to dance therapy: what helped to explain how dance communication could be used in the healing process? At the time I found both psychological and dance theories insufficient. When I entered the graduate program in anthropology at Columbia University, I asked in each of the required, interrelated, four-field courses (cultural, linguistic, archaeological, and physical), how does this subject help me to understand dance? Linguistic study led me to explore how dance is language-like. If the brain, vocal organ, and ears for speech, eyes for reading, and body language for emphasis and elaboration allow us to communicate, how would the brain, total body, and various senses allow us to send and receive messages? More recently the research on hand gestures led to the question, if one body part can communicate, what about the use of other body parts? The purpose of this article is to summarize some research that suggests the cognitive potential of dance in K-12, findings critical to grounding dance in the academic realm.

The Body "Talks" and "Stretches" the Mind— An Evolutionary Tool

Attending to motion is an evolutionary tool for survival. Evolutionary biologists note that humans need to distinguish quickly prey, predator, and sexual selection. Humans have to anticipate another's actions and respond accordingly. Infants track movement and anticipate what will come, as in the peek-a-boo game. People participate in and respond to dance, a particular kind of motion.

Merging body, emotion, and cognition (Damasio 1994, Goleman et al. 2002, Moore & Oaksford 2002), dance can be powerful, engaging communication not only because its motion attracts attention, but because dance is language-like (Barko 1977, Goellner & Murphy 1995, Hanna 1987, 2001) and nonverbal communication is salient. Nonverbal communication constitutes a central feature of human development, knowing, and learning (dePaulo 1992, Roth 2001). Moreover, nonverbal communication is important in children's development because it gives them an important way of interacting with other people (Doherty-Sneddon 2003). Language is power and, according to Vygotsky (1962), knowledge of language is a determinant of thought. We learn and think through English, and we can do likewise through dance. The body gives clues. It "talks" and people "listen."

Over thirty years ago, anthropologist Gordon Hewes (1973) argued that the body was not mute and in fact language was based on the innate cognitive structure of gesture. Corballis (2002) argues that gesture was a way humans communicated, and it served as a platform upon which to build a language. Other researchers have documented how the body communicates through proximity (Hall 1966, Burgoon et al. 1996), touch (Thayer 1982, Lynn & McCall 2000), eye gaze (Leathers 1986, p. 42), facial expression (Ekman 2003; note, a babbling baby's mouth positions change when it is trying to communicate, Duenwald 2002), smell (Stoddart 1991), posture, physical appearance, and emotion in gesture and locomotion (Hanna 1983). The advent of the printing press and the Industrial Revolution diminished the importance of the body and its use. However, during the mid-twentieth century, psychologists began to reevaluate the body's expressiveness and study nonverbal communication. With television, computers, and video games, the need to read images in motion has become increasingly important.

Recent research by psychologists Susan Goldin-Meadow and her colleagues supports Hewes's theory and documents the strength of nonverbal communication, sometimes even more compelling than verbal communication. This research focuses on hand gesture, merely one of the dancer's repertoires of body parts used to communicate. The investigators found that when produced beside speech, gesture becomes image and analog. However, when called upon to carry the full burden of communication, gesture takes a language-like form using word and sentence level structure.

Among congenitally deaf children who had hearing parents and were not exposed to a conventional sign language, segmented and hierarchically combined gestures carried the primary burden of communication (Singleton et al. 1993, Goldin-Meadow et al. 1996, Alibali et al. 1997, Goldin-Meadow 1997, Goldin-Meadow and Mylander 1998, Goldin-Meadow 1999, Goldin-Meadow and

Sandhofer 1999). Youngsters referred to information that was spatially and temporally displaced from the location of the speaker and the listener.

Researchers also found that congenitally blind speakers gestured despite their lack of a visual model, even when speaking to a blind listener. Gesture, in this case, required neither a model nor an observant partner to appear in conversation. Blind children gesturally conveyed to seeing adults substantive information that was not found anywhere in the children's speech. Moreover, when speech and gesture conveyed different information, gesture diminished a listener's ability to recognize a spoken message if gestures conveyed a different message (Iverson 1998, Goldin-Meadow and Sandhofer 1999).

A study of children not visually or aurally challenged found that a child's gestures convey information to ordinary listeners when it conveys different information from speech. Gestures offer insight into a child's thoughts, mental processes, and representations by reflecting knowledge that the child possesses but does not verbalize. Researchers suggest that "knowledge expressed in gesture is not fully explicit, simply because in many instances it is not found anywhere in a child's speech and thus appears to be inaccessible to verbal report" (Garber et al. 1998:82, Goldin-Meadow 2000). Goldin-Meadow (2000:231) says,

> that gesture may be involved in the process of cognitive change itself...through two mechanisms which are not mutually exclusive: (1) indirectly, by communicating unspoken aspects of the learner's cognitive state to potential agents of change (parents, teachers, siblings, friends); and (2) directly by offering the learner a simpler way to express and explore ideas that may be difficult to think through in a verbal format, thus easing the learner's cognitive burden.

Linguists who have studied Nicaraguan sign language, a system developed spontaneously by children at a school for the deaf founded in 1997, and Al Sayyid Bedouin sign language, spontaneously developed in a village of about 3,500 people in the Negev desert of Israel, confirm that gesture is an integral part of language. Moreover, linguists believe that signing features may reflect the innate neural circuitry that governs the brain's faculty for language (Wade 2005).

Researchers found elementary school teachers' gestures contributed to cognitive and affective components of teaching mathematical equivalence as it applies to addition. Gesture that matched speech was more effective than speech alone (Goldin-Meadow, Kim & Singer 1999).

Beyond Hand Gestures

The communicative potential of hand gesture is magnified many times in dance, a fuller embodied expression. Dance uses hand gesture *and* gesture and locomotion of other bodily parts to communicate. The entire body is the instrument of dance as it sends and receives messages.

Like American Sign Language, dance draws upon the same components in the brain for conceptualization, creativity, and memory, as does verbal language in speaking and writing. Both dance and verbal language have vocabulary (locomotion and gestures in dance) and grammar (rules for putting the vocabulary together and, in dance, how one movement can follow another). And both dance and verbal language have semantics (meaning). Verbal language strings together sequences of words, and dance strings together sequences of movement, to make phrases and sentences (see Table 1). Although spoken language can simply be meaningless sounds, and movements can be mere motion, listeners and viewers tend to read meaning into what they hear and see.

Table 1

Comparison of VERBAL LANGUAGE & DANCE (body language)

Commonalities
Verbal Language & Dance Both Have:
Vocabulary
Meaning
Ambiguity
Emotion
Symbolism
Grammar
Context

Differences	
Verbal Language	*Dance*
Uses mostly prose, some poetry	Uses mostly poetry, some pros
Exists in time and volume	Exists in time, space, and effort
Communicates through words (sound and sight)	Communicates through movements (sight, smell, proximity and touch), costume and music

Both verbal language and dance contain ambiguity and engender cultural transmission. Both also have arbitrariness (many of their characteristics have no predictability), discreteness (separateness), displacement (reference can be made to something not immediately present), productivity (messages never created before can be sent and understood within a set of structural principles), duality of patterning (a system of physical action and a system of meaning), affectivity (expression of an internal state with the potential for changing moods and situations), and a wide range in the number of potential participants in the communication processes.

Certainly, there are differences between dance and verbal language. In dance, the motor, visual, and kinesthetic channels predominate. Dance is an autonomous system of communication. In verbal language, vocal and auditory channels predominate. Verbal language exists solely in a temporal dimension. Dance involves the temporal plus three dimensions in space. It is more difficult to communicate complex logical structures with dance than it is with verbal language. With its symbolic potential, dance more often resembles modern poetry than prose. Poetry has multiple, suggestive, and elusive meanings. Renowned modern dancer Martha Graham held this sentiment in the 1980s, although she first described dance as emotional expression in the 1930s prior to the development of the field of nonverbal communication in psychology. *New York Times* writers, from the arts to politics, refer to "dance as a form of speaking, words as a dance of thoughts" (Anderson 1997) and "a lexicon of wordlessness...silent speech" (Safire 1991).

Because gesture and locomotion in dance rest on different representational devices from speech and are not dictated by the standards of the speech form which is linear and non-spatial, dance has the potential to offer a different view into the mind of the dancer. Dance can also communicate content not easily communicated in verbal language. Modern dance pioneer Isadora Duncan is widely reported to have said, "If I could *tell* you what I mean, there would be no point in dancing." Of course, dance can communicate forms and abstraction (Dalva 1988, Dunning 1997, 1998). But even so, the observer can read stories into the performance.

There is new research that suggests the power of dance to cause positive plastic changes in the brain. Neurologist Joe Verghese's team (2003) studied what activities stretched minds and lowered the risk of seniors developing Alzheimer's disease. The results were surprising. Those who did crossword puzzles cut the risk by 38 percent, those who played instruments, 69 percent, those who played board games, 74 percent, and dancing lowered the risk by 76 percent. Physical activities like group exercise of team games had no significant impact in warding off the onset of Alzheimer's. However ballroom dancing has the mental demands of remembering dance steps and executing them in response to music and coordination with a partner or group in space without bumping into other dancers (see Coyle 2003). Requiring dance–making in addition to remembering movement patterns, responding to music, and working with others, as common in dance education, is surely transforming.

Meaning in Movement

Although literature moves human experience a step away from the body in its attempt to express bodily sensations, dance remains at the basic level of human expression. Movement is our mother tongue and primordial thought.

> Dance communicates through the sight of performers moving in time and space (the spectator sees muscle contraction and release, and tension and relaxation, as the dancer moves, as well as the costume; the sounds of physical movement, breathing, accompanying music and talk; the smell of the dancers' breath, physical exertion; the tactile sense of body parts touching the ground, other body parts or props, and air about the dancers, and dancers touching another person; the sense of spatial distance between people; and the sense of empathy with a performer's bodily movement and energy. The eyes indicate degrees of attentiveness and arousal, influence attitude change, and regulate interaction. In addition, the eyes define power and status relationships (Leathers 1986:42).

The meanings of dance come from the meanings of social behavior, movements, and sensory elements in everyday life. These meanings have a history and culture. People "read" and "write" verbal language and dance from the perspectives of their cultures, personal experiences, knowledge of the dance form, sex, political group, social class, and so on. Perception of dance is subject to the dancer's and observer's individual interpretations.

Over the years I have been examining dance as nonverbal communication in an approach much like that of a sociolinguist or semiotician examining verbal language (for example, 1987, 1988a, 1989a, 1998, 2001). Both "dance" and verbal "language" are generic terms. One does not speak "language," but rather one speaks English, Igbo, or some other specific tongue. Similarly, one dances, for example, ballet or Bharata Natyam. Contrary to conventional wisdom, dance is not a universal "language" but many languages and dialects. There are close to 6,000 verbal languages, and probably that many dance languages. Peter Martins,

Judith Lynne Hanna

director of the New York City Ballet, has said that classical ballet and modern dance are different dialects of the same language (Solway 1988). By contrast, classical Indian dance, with its ancient, elaborate system of codified gestures, is a different language altogether.

Translating a verbal language from one language family to another can be problematic. So it is not surprising that translating one mode of communication, such as dance, into another, such as verbal language, is daunting. However, the transformation of emotions, ideas, and data from one medium to another can offer creative insight. Such transformations may make knowledge more accessible and also show an understanding of subject matter by demonstrating its use in a different context. This creative expression contrasts with rote learning.

To help describe physical movement and to help determine what dance moves mean, Laban analysis and a semantic grid (see Table 2) are available. Just as verbal language has symbolic ways of communication, so, too, does dance. There were various notation systems to describe physical movement. Yet, there was no tool to probe for meaning in dance. To fill this gap, I discovered ways of

Table 2

Ways of Conveying Meaning in Dance

SPHERES ⟋ DEVICE	Event	Body in Action	Whole Perfor- mance	Discursive Perfor- mance	Specific Move- ment	Inter- mesh with Other	Presence
Concreti- zation							
Icon							
Styliza- tion							
Metonym							
Metaphor							
Actuali- zation							

conveying meaning to embody the imagination in dance and developed a semantic grid with devices and spheres as a tool to probe for meaning in dance (1979). These are briefly noted to suggest the sophisticated semantic potential of dance. Note that students can learn to mime and represent something realistically in dance, and they can also learn to use abstraction. As they mature intellectually, they can acquire skills to use more complex symbolism. Symbolization, a fundamental cognitive activity that people use on an ongoing basis is integral to dance.

Dancers may use one or more of at least six symbolic DEVICES to convey meaning. *Concretization* is movement that produces the outward aspect of something. Examples include a warrior dance displaying advance and retreat battle tactics, a dancer depicting an historical figure such as Nijinsky, and a wide-open mouth denoting a scream. An *icon* represents most characteristics of something and is responded to as if it actually were what it represents. For example, a Haitian dancer manifesting through a specific dance the presence of Ghede, the god of love and death, is treated by fellow Haitians with genuine awe and gender-appropriate behavior—as if the dancer were actually the god himself. A *stylization* encompasses arbitrary and conventional gestures or movements. Examples are a Western ballet *danseur* points to his heart as a sign of love for his lady, and a swing dancer shakes a finger in the lindy hop as a sign of joy in moving well. A *metonym* is a motional conceptualization of one thing representing another, of which it is a part. An example is a romantic duet representing a more encompassing relationship, such as an affair or marriage. The most common way of encoding meaning in dance is through *metaphor*, the expression of one thought, experience, or phenomenon in place of another that it resembles. Illustrative of joining different domains are contrastive movement patterns for men and women referring to their distinct biological and social roles, dancers performing as animal characters to comment on human behavior, mechanical movement symbolizing the rigidity of bureaucracy, and dance virtuosity representing human aspiration to transcend the limits of the body. Students are most likely to use metaphors and metonyms in their dance making. *Actualization* is a portrayal of one or several of a dancer's usual roles. Examples include a woman who performs in a dance for mothers to convey her maternal role, and a dancer who has a romantic interest in a spectator brings that person onto the stage to participate in the dance. As in verbal speech, dance may reflect a person's actual personality through movement energy. A performer who is known to have AIDS can evoke awe during a dance due to this fact.

The devices for encapsulating meaning in dance seem to operate within one or more of eight SPHERES of communication. An example of the meaning of dance being in the *dance event* itself is when people attend a social dance to be seen, perhaps as participants in a fund-raising charity ball. The meaning of dance may be in the sphere of the *total human body in action*. For example, meaning is found in a woman or a man's self-presentation. The *whole pattern of performance*, emphasizing structure, style, feeling, or drama, may be the locus of meaning. Focus is on the interrelation of parts of a dance that give it a distinctiveness, as in a sacred dance, or a style of dance such as ballet. Meaning may be centered in the *sequence of unfolding movement*, including who does what to whom and how in dramatic episodes. Narrative ballets like "Sleeping Beauty," "The Nutcracker," and "The Last Supper at Uncle Tom's Cabin" are illustrative. *Specific movements* and how they are performed may be significant, as when a male dancer parodies a woman by dancing *en pointe*. The intermesh of movements with other communication modes, such as song (speech) or costume, may be where meaning lies, for example, in the Broadway hit, "The Lion King." Another example is dance movement for a masquerade that becomes significant when the performer dons the mask and becomes what the mask represents. Meaning may be in the sphere of *dance as a vehicle for another medium*. An example is dance as a backdrop for a performer's song or rap recitation. The sphere of meaning may be centered in *presence*, the emotional impact of projected sensuality, raw animalism, charisma, or "the magic of dance." Presence is the electrical energy that passes between dancers and to the audience. Meaning in dance also relies upon who does what, when, where, why and how, alone and with whom. Such variables may bespeak of gender roles, as well as ethnic, national, and other group identities, which may promote self-esteem and separatism (Hanna 1992, 1997).

Of course, just as some children learn to read and do other complex tasks on their own, some children learn from watching peers and television how to express their concerns through dance. African-American children's spontaneous dance in a desegregated magnet elementary school was a creative commentary through devices and spheres of encoding meaning about race relations, patterns of authority, and personal identity (Hanna 1986, 1988b). Dance was an arena in which African Americans could dominate and gain recognition and establish a prideful group identity in face of external threats to their identity. Through dance themes, participation criteria, and places of performance in a white-controlled school system, youngsters metaphorically identified themselves as distinct from the "shuffling black" stereotypes of earlier historical periods and from the whites of today. They declared a wished-for privileged status and, in a sense, they attained it through dance.

We speak of time, space, and effort as key elements of dance.

The meaning of these comes from meanings in proxemics, spatial distances between people, touch, and gaze in everyday life.

Hall's research on the meaning of the use of space in daily life (1966) found this: In American culture, *intimate* distance has a close phase (0-6 inches, such as in love-making, wrestling, comforting, and protecting) and a far phase (6-18 inches for less intense but still intimate interaction). A romantic relationship in American culture commonly includes a dinner or nightclub date with the pair seated proximate and touching as a metaphoric sign of attraction. Hall also found that *personal* distance, the usual space we maintain between ourselves and others also has a close phase (½ to 2½ feet for people bonded in some ways, such as family members) as well as a far phase (2½ to 4 feet used for discussing subjects of personal interest and involvement). *Social* distance has a close phase of 4 to 7 feet, used for impersonal business, and a far phase of 7 to 12 feet for formal business as in an office or home. Finally, *public* distance has a close phase of 12 to 25 feet, such as in a presentation to a small audience, and a far phase of 25 feet or more.

Physical proximity in a social interaction conveys a message and an expectation about the level of intimacy appropriate or desired for that interaction (Burgoon et al. 1996). Grammer et al. (1998) found that "…communication in courtship shows a process in which the sender slowly reveals his/her intentions and the receiver seems to sum up different combinations of courtship signals over time. Basically women control male approaches and elicit male self-presentation. In contrast to females, males seem to make their decisions on the basis of interpersonal attraction" (p. 7).

Proximity permits the dancer and observer to receive feedback (for example, signs of interest include pupil dilation and eye widening) from each other, and thus to communicate effectively, both participating in the performance. This is the attraction of live performance. Ekman in *Emotions Revealed* (2003) describes micro expressions—ultra-rapid facial actions, some lasting as little as one-twentieth of a second—that lay bare our feelings and cross our faces spontaneously and involuntarily.

The use of space between spectator and performer is a key communicative tool all kinds of dancers. Dancers may invite audience members onto the stage or perform in the audience area. Proximity involves the audience member in the performance and creates a feeling of immediacy: a sense of "here and now." Dancers perform in close proximity to the audience in flamenco in the caves of Granada, at weddings among Arabs and Jews, for various occasions in numerous African cultures, and in adult entertainment exotic dance clubs. Some religious services create a sense of closeness and immediacy by dancing the gospel into the pews where the congregation sits.

Astarte by the Joffrey Ballet began with a dancer actually seated in the audience, inches away from paying patrons. Award-winning modern dancer B.T. Jones has physically interacted with audience members during choreographed pieces. On April 10, 1998, I saw *Ritual* at the John F. Kennedy Center for the Performing Arts, Washington, D.C., in which about 60 performers were dancing in audience areas, perched on arms of empty seats to the front, side, and back of spectators, leaning over them. Performers also danced in spaces leading to the theater, on couches, benches and the floor and even in rest rooms. They took audience members by hand to invite them to participate in the dance (see Table 3).

Touch, with biological roots in the mother and child connection, is humankind's earliest form of communication, "clearly one of the most basic and commanding forms of human communicative behavior"—an imperative to the establishment of social attachment (Grammer et al. 1998, p. 59; Vedantam 2002). The variety and amount of interpersonal touch can disclose the state and style of relationships between people (Floyd 1997).

Touch communicates many different feelings and ideas—from comfort, rapport, empathy, humor, playfulness, sentience, immediacy and cordiality to sensuality, and intimacy. The context and duration of touch and whether it is active or passive influence meaning. Hall (1966) noted that touch can be sensual, utilitarian, and/or friendly (see Table 4).

Our sense of self is connected to the physical experience of touch with its power to establish boundaries of contact and separation, to stimulate and arouse, or to pacify and calm. The body is the location for physical sensations that trigger social memories. Intentional and incidental touch is certainly expressive in life from birth to death. Meanings depend on who are the toucher and touched, the place and strength of touch, and the setting.

Thayer states, "Even a fleeting, impersonal touch between strangers can have a powerful emotional impact" (1982: 281). Touch is part of attentiveness that includes gaze, smile, direct face-to-face body orientation, and forward lean.

Conclusion

When scarce resources tend to preclude sequential programs in dance as a core subject, the question is what can be learned from dance offered in other ways? Verbal language is the recognized medium for learning. In many ways similar to verbal language, dance intertwines the cognitive, affective, and physical. Multisensorily fusing inner feelings and ideas with outer body kinetic designs, dance can engage students in the teaching and learning process. In fact, dance is a time-honored way of learning,

Table 3

Proximity in Dance Symbolizes Proximity in Everyday Life:

Messages of Proximity	Messages of Absence of Proximity
Comfort/Support	Distance
Friendliness	Coldness
Trust	Disinterest
Inclusion	Distrust
Immediacy	Dislike
Humanity	Exclusion
Play	Rejection
Affection	Alienation
Sensuality	Violated Expectations
Desirability	Rudeness
Love	Inhumanity

Table 4

Touch in Dance and Everyday Life

Touch in Dance Expresses theMeaning of Touch in Everyday Life:	Examples of Public Displays of Touch in Everyday Life:	Absence of Touch Expresses:
		Distance
	Handshake	Coldness
Comfort/Support	Kiss (on one or both	Disinterest
Friendliness	cheeks or lips)	Distrust
Trust	Hug	Dislike
Inclusion	Hand-holding	Exclusion
Immediacy	Arms Entwined	Rejection
Humanity	Arm Around Shoulder	Alienation
Play	Pat on the Head	Violated Expectations
Affection		Rudeness
Sensuality		Inhumanity
Desirability		
Love		

knowing, and expressing. Community, religious and governmental institutions attest to dance as a means of communication. For example, the government of China used ballet to convey its values (Christopher 1979). Many countries use dance as a symbol of unity among diverse sectors of their population (Sircar 1972, Daniel 1995, Shay 1999). Societies teach what it is to be male or female and how to "speak" about stress through danced images (Hanna 1988a, 1989a, 1992, 1997, 2005). Sometimes dance communicates anti-establishment values (Hanna 1998, 1999, 2003). Throughout history there have been attempts to control dance (Wagner 1997). Around longer than science and the humanities, dance can also be a serious mode of inquiry and discovery.

Expression through language is a form of thinking. So, too, is expression through the nonverbal medium of dance. Dance can express emotions and ideas, including themes in English history and geography as well as problems in math and physics. Dance can communicate new knowledge, reinforce, and assess learning. Translating concepts from the verbal to nonverbal and the nonverbal to verbal requires building vocabulary and understanding. A well-developed dance education program propels students to become aware of a need to know the "3Rs." In the twenty-first century technological era, dancers must be able to read, write, and calculate. The language of dance fosters multilingualism in its role as a language of learning other subjects. Given a student's familiarity with dance elements, dance can be a means of testing a student's understanding of non-dance subject material. Being able to transfer knowledge and use it in new situations is closely related to truly understanding a concept. Translating ideas from one domain of knowledge into another, such as thinking metaphorically through a physical embodiment of information, can reveal what further instruction is necessary. Student evaluation of each other's work can sharpen the assessment. Recall the Goldin-Meadows study mentioned earlier: gesture offers insight into a knowledge a child possesses but does not verbalize.

Not only does dance draw upon verbal language, embodying poems or stories, for example, but vernacular and literary writers use dance metaphors" (Hanna 1983, ch. 12, "The Punch of Performance: Re-Creation") because of their communicative value. Illustrations include statements such as "he waltzed around the subject," "they choreographed the battle," and "the abortion minuet." Shakespeare allowed lovers to speak indirectly to one another by using dance as a metaphor for love in *Much Ado About Nothing* (for example, Beatrice speaks of the "hot and hasty" quality of the jig).

Dance is an untapped resource to help students realize their communicative potential. Learning in, about, and through dance offers unlimited possibilities for cognitive growth. Knowledge about the evolutionary importance of attending to movement and nonverbal communication contributes to the constellation of understanding that undergirds a case made for a two-fold role for dance in the schools: (1) as a distinct discipline with sequential curricula in making dances, being a performing art meritorious in itself, and (2) as an applied art with potential to acquire, reinforce, and assess non-dance knowledge (Hanna 1999a).

REFERENCES

Alibali, M.W., Flevares, L. & Goldin-Meadow, S. (1997). Assessing knowledge conveyed in gesture: Do teachers have the upper hand? *Journal of Educational Psychology, 89*(1):183-193.

Americans for the Arts (2003, January 22). No wonder people think Martha Graham is a snack cracker: There is not enough art in our schools. *New York Times*, p. B10.

Anderson, J. (1997, March 14). Musings on mortality and courage," *New York Times*, p. B10.

Barko, C. (1977). The dancer and the becoming of language. *Yale French Studies, 54:* 173–187.

Burgoon, J.K., Buller, D.B. & Woodall, W.G. (1996). *Nonverbal communication: The unspoken dialogue.* New York: Harper Collins.

Christopher, L.S. (1979). Pirouettes with bayonets: Classical ballet metamorphosed as dance-drama and its use in the People's Republic of China as a tool of political socialization. Unpublished doctoral dissertation, American University.

Corballis, M.C. (2002). *From hand to mouth: The origins of language.* Princeton: Princeton University Press.

Coyle, J.T. (2003). Use it or lose it. Do effortful mental activities protect against dementia? *The New England Journal of Medicine, 348*(25):2489–2490, June 19.

Crowder, E.M. (1996). Gestures at work in sense-making science talk. *The Journal of the Learning Sciences, 5:* 173–208.

Dalva, N.V. (1988). The I Ching and me: A conversation with Merce Cunningham. *Dance Magazine, 62*(3): 58–61.

Damasio, A. (1994). *Descartes' error: Emotion, reason, and the human brain.* New York: Bard/Avon.

Daniel, Y. (1995). *Rumba: Dance and social change in contemporary Cuba.* Bloomington, IN: Indiana University Press.

DePaulo, B.M. (1992). Nonverbal behavior and self-presentation. *Psychological Review*, 111: 203–243.

Doherty-Sneddon, G. (2003). *Children's unspoken language.* London: Jessica Kingsley Publishers.

Duenwald, M. (2002). Deciphering "da da da." *New York Times*, October

1, p. D5.

Dunning, J. (1997, October 4). A dancer returns, abstract and storied. *New York Times*, p. B1.

Dunning, J. (1998, April 6). To see, even to enjoy, but perhaps not to understand. *New York Times,* p. B2.

Ekman, P. (2003). *Emotions revealed.* New York: Times Books.

Floyd, K. (1997). Communicating affection in dyadic relationships: An assessment of behavior expectancies. *Communication Quarterly, 45*(1):68–80.

Garber, P., Alibali, M.W. & Goldin-Meadow, S. (1998). Knowledge conveyed in gesture is not tied to the hands. *Child Development, 69*(1): 5–84.

Goellner, E.W. & Murphy, J.S. (Eds.). (1995). *Bodies of the text: Dance as theory, literature as dance.* New Brunswick, NJ: Rutgers University Press.

Goldin-Meadow, S. (1997). When gestures and words speak differently. *Current Directions in Psychological Science, 6*(5):138–143.

Goldin-Meadow, S. (1999). The role of gesture in communication and thinking. *Trends in Cognitive Sciences, 3*(11):419–429.

Goldin-Meadow, S. (2000, January/February). Beyond words: The importance of gesture to researchers and learners. *Child Development, 71*(1):231–239.

Goldin-Meadow, S., Kim, S., & Singer, M. (1999). What the teacher's hands tell the student's mind about math. *Journal of Educational Psychology, 91*(4):720–730.

Goldin-Meadow, S., McNeill, D. & Singleton, J. (1996). Silence is liberating: Removing the handcuffs on grammatical expression in the manual modality. *Psychological Review, 103*(1):34–55.

Goldin-Meadow, S. & Mylander, C. (1998, January 15). Spontaneous sign systems created by deaf children in two cultures. *Nature, 391*:279–281.

Goldin-Meadow, S. & Sandhofer, C.M. (1999). Gestures convey substantive information about a child's thoughts to ordinary listeners. *Developmental Science, 2*(1):67–74.

Goleman, D., Boyatzis, R. & McKee, A. (2002). *Primal leadership: Realizing the power of emotional intelligence.* Watertown, MA: Harvard Business School Press.

Grammer, K., Kirsten B., Kruck, K.B. & Manusson, M.S. (1998). The courtship dance: Patterns of nonverbal synchronization in opposite-sex encounters. *Journal of Nonverbal Behavior, 22*(1): 3–29.

Hall, E.T. (1966). *The hidden dimension.* New York: Doubleday.

Hanna, J.L. (1979). Toward semantic analysis of movement behavior. *Semiotica, 25*(1–2):77–110.

Hanna, J.L. (1983). *The performer-audience connection: Emotion to metaphor in dance and society.* Austin, TX: University of Texas Press.

Hanna, J.L. (1986). Interethnic communication in children's own dance, play, and protest. In Y. Y. Kim (Ed.), *Interethnic communication, vol. 10: International and Intercultural Communication Annual* (pp. 176–198). Newbury Park, CA: Sage.

Hanna, J L. (1987). *To dance is human: A theory of nonverbal communication* (rev. ed.). Chicago: University of Chicago Press.

Hanna, J.L. (1988a). *Dance, sex, and gender: Signs of identity, dominance, defiance, and desire.* Chicago: University of Chicago Press.

Hanna, J.L. (1988b). *Disruptive school behavior: Class, race, and culture.* New York: Holmes & Meier.

Hanna, J.L. (1989a). African dance frame by frame: Revelation of sex roles through distinctive feature analysis and comments on field research, film, and notation. *Journal of Black Studies, 19*(4):422–441.

Hanna, J.L. (1989b). The anthropology of dance. In L.Y. Overby & J. H. Humphrey (Eds.), *Dance: Current selected research, I:* (pp, 219–237). New York: AMS.

Hanna, J.L. (1992). Moving messages: Identity and desire in dance. In J. Lull (Ed.), *Popular music and communication* (2nd ed.), (pp. 176–195). Newbury Park, CA: Sage.

Hanna, J.L. (1997). "Ubakala, we are coming": Searching for meaning in dance. In E. Dagan (Ed.), *The spirit's dance in Africa* (pp. 90–93). Montreal, Canada: Galerie Amrad.

Hanna, J.L. (1998). Undressing the first amendment and corseting the striptease dancer. *The Drama Review,* (T158) 42(2), 38–69.

Hanna, J.L. (1999a). *Partnering dance and education: Intelligent moves for changing times.* Champaign, IL: Human Kinetics Press. Forthcoming Korean translation: Jungdam

Hanna, J L. (1999b). Toying with the striptease dancer and the first amendment. In S. Reifel (ed.), *Play and culture studies, 2*:37–56. Greenwich, CT: Ablex.

Hanna, J.L. (2001). The language of dance," *Journal of Physical Education, Recreation and Dance, 72*(4):40–45, 53.

Hanna, J.L. (2003). Exotic dance adult entertainment: Ethnography challenges false mythology. *City and Society 15*(2):165–193.

Hanna, J.L. (forthcoming, 2005). *Dance-Stress connections: Healing and harm.* Walnut Creek, CA: AltaMira Press.

Hewes, G. W. (1973). Primitive communication and the gestural origin of language. *Current Anthropology, 14*(1–2), 5–24.

Iverson, J.M. (1998). Gesture when there is no visual model. *New Directions for Child Development, 79*:80–100.

Leathers, D. (1986). *Successful nonverbal communication Principles and applications.* New York: Macmillan.

Lynn, M. & McCall, M. (2000). Gratitude and gratuity: A meta-analysis of research on the service-tipping relationship. *Journal of Socio-Economics, 29*:203–214.

Morford, J.P. & Goldin-Meadow, S. (1997). From here and now to there and then: The development of displaced reference in homesign and English. *Child Development, 68*(3):420–435.

Moore, S.C. & Oaksford, M., eds. (2002). *Emotional cognition: From brain to behaviour* (Advances in Consciousness Research, 44, Series B) (Philadelphia: John Benjamins.

Roth, W-M. (2001) Gestures: Their role in teaching and learning, *Review of Educational Research, 71*(3):365–392.

Safire, W. (1991, April 29). On language. *New York Times Magazine*, p. 16.

Shay, A. (1999). Parallel traditions: State folk dance ensembles and folk dance in "The Field." *Dance Research Journal, 31*(1):29–56.

Singleton, J.L., Morford, J.P. & Goldin-Meadow, S. (1993). Once is not enough: Standards of well-formedness in manual communication created over three different timespans. *Language, 69*(4):683–715.

Sircar, M.C. (1972), Community of dancers in Calcutta. In S. Sinha (Ed.), *Cultural profile of Calcutta.* (pp.190-198). Calcutta: Indian Anthropological Society.

Solway, D. (1988, April 24). City ballet moves in an American beat. *New York Times*, pp. H1, 40.

Stoddart, M.D. (1991). *The scented ape: The biology and culture of human odour.* New York: Cambridge University Press.

Thayer, S. (1982). Social touching. In W. Schiff & E. Foulke (eds.). *Tactual Perception* (pp. 263–304). Cambridge, UK: Cambridge University Press.

Vedantam, S. (2002, July 29). Understanding that loving feeling: In a study of the brain, special nerves registered the emotional context of a pleasurable touch. *Washington Post*, p. A2.

Verghese, J., Lipton, R.B., Katz, M.J., Hall, C.B., Derby, C.A., G., Ambrose, A.F., Sliwinski, M. & Buschke, H. (2003, June 19). Leisure activities and the risk of dementia in the elderly, *The New England Journal of Medicine, 348*(25): 2508–2516.

Vygotsky, L.S. (1962). *Thought and language.* Cambridge, MA: Cambridge University Press.

Wade, N.B. (2005). A new language arises, and scientists watch it evolve. *New York Times*, Feb 1, p. D3.

Wagner, A. (1997). *Adversaries of dance: From the puritans to the present.* Urbana: University of Illinois Press.

7

THE VOICES OF TEACHERS: THE IMPACT OF PROFESSIONAL DEVELOPMENT ON THE INTERDISCIPLINARY TEACHING OF DANCE

Lynnette Young Overby

Since 1999, under the umbrella of the Program for Interdisciplinary Learning through the Arts (PILA), classroom teachers have participated in summer institutes with follow-up professional development opportunities and have learned to integrate creative dance into the curriculum. Three of the teachers are the focus of this paper. They include a first grade teacher from a suburban school system, a music teacher from an urban school system, and a preschool teacher from a university based child development center. A multiple case study design was used to determine change in attitudes and behavior regarding the integration of dance into the curriculum.

"But I can't dance!" Many teachers who attend the creative dance professional development workshops share these sentiments. Immediately they imagine being required to learn a complex combination of steps, while at once moving to music that is too fast, and feeling embarrassed about the whole ordeal. However, by the end of creative dance professional development sessions, they are excited about the possibilities and ready to embrace another tool for teaching and learning. What brings about this transformation? This paper will include a theoretical background of interdisciplinary teaching, the voices of three teachers involved in professional development, and suggestions for the development of successful professional development programs.

Although most states have developed educational standards for dance education, creative dance is rarely included in schools. Creative dance is an art form that involves expression through the body. When children are involved in creative dance activities, they are engaged in problem solving and expressions of feelings. Moreover, they learn to collaborate, think creatively, and gain an aesthetic appreciation for movement. While children are learning about movement they are also learning about themselves, their classmates, and their environment. The holistic nature of creative dance makes this art form a viable tool for integrative learning. However, most classroom teachers are unprepared with little to no background in teaching dance (Macdonald, C., 1991; Overby, 2000). Preservice programs in elementary and early childhood education rarely prepare classroom teachers to feel competent in creative dance. Although many anecdotal reports exist that attest to the power of creative dance in integrating the curriculum, few research studies have been conducted to provide unequivocal support for this claim. For example, after using a variety of search methods to locate articles both published and unpublished since 1950, researchers identified only four true experimental studies with control groups and quantified outcomes, that were designed to assess the impact of creative dance on reading (Keinanen, M., Hetland, L., & Winner, E. 2000).

Professional development is a method designed to alleviate the inadequacies of pre-professional training in various aspects of the curriculum, including creative dance. Professional development can take several forms—from one two-hour workshop to a year-long intervention program. The most effective professional development includes theory, demonstration, practice, feedback and coaching (Joyce & Showers, 1995). Recent research in staff development reveals that virtually all teachers can learn the most powerful and complex teaching strategies provided staff development is designed properly. Interdisciplinarity in teaching dance is the focus of the professional development presented in this paper.

Interdisciplinary Understanding

Students demonstrate interdisciplinary understanding when they are able to use what they have learned to solve problems, create products, or explain phenomena. (Boix-Mansilla, Miller & Gardner, 2000). Interdisciplinary understanding includes an emphasis on knowledge use. A careful treatment of each discipline involved and appropriate interaction between disciplines. (Boix-Mansilla, Miller & Gardner, 2000). In applying this definition to arts integration, the disciplines must be treated with equal importance. Equal importance does not necessarily mean equal in training and experience. For example, the teacher who teaches the water cycle, should clearly understand this particular concept—not all content involved in earth science; similarly, the same teacher should have a clear understanding of the dance/movement vocabulary, so that essential connections can be made. Only then can the knowledge of the art and the curricular discipline lead to a transformation of knowledge, a knowledge that transcends both disciplines.

Interdisciplinary Teaching Models

Many different models exist that allow a variety of interdisciplinary methods. They include models that occur within a single discipline, across several disciplines, within learners, and across a network of learners (Fogerty, 1991). I have utilized the shared model that occurs across disciplines. The shared model views the curriculum through binoculars, bringing two distinct disciplines together into a single focused image.

Theoretical Perspective

It is very important that work be guided by a theoretical perspective that provides the lenses, by which we develop initiatives, implement programs and evaluate the results. Constructivism provides such a lens. The constructivist believes that each person must construct meaning for him- or her self. Learning must be connected to preexisting knowledge, experiences, and conceptualizations. (Brooks, J.C. & Brooks, M.G., 1993; Glasersfeld, 1989). In applying this notion to the interdisciplinary teaching approach, the specific method of instruction involves building knowledge of the art form and the curricular connection, then devising activities that require active hands-on-minds-on learning. Next, reflection involves an articulation of meanings constructed during the learning process. Finally, assessment provides evidence of both content and conceptual knowledge and applications.

For example, in a lesson on the water cycle, teachers, like the students they will teach, are introduced to the stages of the water cycle. These stages are connected to movement elements; for example, water in a stream is connected to free-flowing movement, while a rainstorm is connected to high to low level, strong movement. They next are guided in a movement story about the journey of a drop of water. The dance requires the students to move in self space and general space, alone and in partners. Understanding of the water cycle builds on previous knowledge and demands an internalization of the water cycle content during a movement re-interpretation. Figure 1 describes the connections between the science and movement concepts.

Figure 1:
Connecting dance and curricular content of the water cycle

Connecting Science with Movement - Movement Chart

Movement Concepts	Science Concepts:			
Stream	Evaporation	Condensation	Precipitation	
Space (Place, levels, Directions, Pathways)	General Space, middle and low level,	General Space and self space, low level to high level	Self space, high levels	General space, high to low level
Time (Slow, medium. Fast)	Slow	Fast	Slow	Medium to fast
Force (Energy, weight, flow)	Smooth, light, free	Smooth, light, free	Smooth	Sharp
Body Movement (Locomotor & nonlocomotor)	Stretching, bending, gliding	Floating, rising	Shapes	Bending, Jumping to low level, pounding the floor

Story Dance—The Water Cycle

1. The water in the stream moves gently as it flows up the river (free flowing slow locomotor movements).
2. Molecules of water become hot and move into the air then spread out moving faster (fast movement, light movement, high level movement).
3. As the water vapor rises higher, it reaches cooler air. The cool air makes the water vapor slow down and move closer together. A cloud is formed (group shapes with scarves).
4. Soon the water drops become too heavy to remain in the air as clouds, and gravity brings them down to earth as rain.
5. Rain drops strike the ground like tiny bombs, flinging up the earth. (high to low level movement hitting the ground).
6. Some rain drops seep slowly into the ground while others form tiny streams, and others cling to plant leaves. (Take on shape of a plant) (Overby, Post, & Newman, In Press)

The performance of the water cycle is a demonstration of knowledge that can be easily assessed by self, peers, or teachers. This type of learning also addresses the need to devise lessons that meet the needs of a variety of learners. Many students learn best through kinesthetic means. Arts based learning provides additional strategies and methods of instruction.

Methodology

The present study was guided by the following question—will professional development in interdisciplinary teaching of dance affect the attitudes and practices of classroom teachers? The methodology for this study was a multiple case study design. The data flowed from questionnaires, interviews, observations, and inspection of journals. The subjects of this research are three teachers—an early childhood educator, a first grade teacher, and a music teacher.

The teachers attended 15 hours of professional development summer institute, where they became familiar with the following information: (a) the elements of dance, space, time, force and body movement; (b) state standards and benchmarks; (3) dance explorations (4) pedagogical information, and (5) designing, teaching, and assessing interdisciplinary lessons.

Before and immediately following the summer institute, the teachers completed a questionnaire that included questions related to their understanding of creative dance. During the summer institute, the teachers developed plans for incorporating creative dance in the curriculum. They included these plans in the post-summer institute questionnaire (see Table A).

The teachers received follow up assistance of two additional visits to the home school. The teachers were observed teaching interdisciplinary lessons, and were given feedback. Seven months after the summer institute, the teachers rated their attitude, behavior, and competence regarding interdisciplinary teaching of creative dance on a 1 (low) to 10 (high) scale at the beginning of the seventh month interview.

Post-Summer Institute Interviews

The teachers were interviewed seven months following the summer institute. The purpose of the post-summer institute interview was to collecting information about specific examples of experiences where dance was integrated in the curriculum.

Teacher 1

Joyce is a preschool teacher at a university child development laboratory. She has been a teacher educator for 15 years where she teaches a class of three and four year olds. She also supervises and trains university students who are child development majors. She has incorporated drama and dance into her curriculum for many years. She made the following comments about her use of creative dance. "The dance concepts enriched and informed the way I plan for creative dance whenever I teach." She continued with "I am

Table A

Attitudes, Behavior, and Competence—Creative Dance

Attitude

Teacher	Attitude (Pre-)	Attitude (Post-)
Teacher 1 (preschool)	10	10
Teacher 2 (1st grade)	6	9
Teacher 3 (music)	2	8

Behavior

Teacher 1 (preschool)	daily	daily
Teacher 2 (1st grade)	4 x per year	1 x per week
Teacher 3 (music)	1 x per month	2–3 x per week

Comment on use of movement - in the past two years my work has a true dance basis instead of just movement. I am using truer dance elements, word movements, and concepts in a true dance way, which makes the movement activities stronger.

Competence

Teacher	Pre-	Post-
Teacher 1 (preschool)	5	8
Teacher 2 (1st grade)	6	9
Teacher 3 (Music)	1	8

more informed and committed." She also commented on the time and resources, as needing more time and a need to make better use of her resources. Comments were also made about the children's learning. "The children are more aware of themselves as movers and dancers—not just responders to the teacher. She also indicated the need for continued work. "Some children still follow as I lead, so when I get into free movement they are more at a loss. Finally, she commented on her university students—and the impact of her deeper understanding of dance movement. "One of my university students did a whole science unit using movement. They told the story of Swimmie. She talked to the children about how fish move—she focused on the movement first. A bigger focus was on literacy, acting out, sequencing, and working as a group. I observed wonderful social growth in the children" She continued with her discussion about the university student by saying, "I am trying to do enough to help the student teachers use movement as a tool."

Joyce has successfully integrated creative dance into her curriculum for her three- and four-year-old students. She is also providing guidance in the integration of dance and science for pre-service child development majors.

Teacher 2

Tina, a first grade teacher for 20 years, had no previous experience with creative dance. In the post-summer institute questionnaire, Tina was questioned about her feeling of confidence regarding the effectiveness of her creative dance plan. She stated, "I don't really have a plan as of yet other than having involvement with the presenter. Hopefully, using movement will give my students another way to learn information."

At the seventh month interview, Tina perceived her attitude, behavior, and competence in creative dance as much improved:

Categories	Pre-	Post-
Attitude	6-7	9
Behavior	4 x per year	1 x per week
Competence	6	9

After the summer institute she was assigned a student assistant to work with her in her classroom. She commented on this assistance during her interview:

Question: How have you used movement/dance in the classroom?

"I use dance a lot more—especially when the students were here on a regular basis." With the help of the students she was able to build on her knowledge and application of dance. She continues with a specific example: "I find dance/movement to be very useful—a non-threatening way to introduce concepts.

Examples—The concept of space in the classroom was applied to proximity of the planets to the earth and moon."

Although Tina began the professional development with the least experience and competence of the three teachers, she has been able to successfully incorporate dance into her curriculum. She has also proven to be a great mentor for university preservice education students, who teach creative dance in her school as a service learning requirement in creative dance and creative dramatics. She values creative dance.

Teacher 3

Karen is a music teacher in an urban school district. She teaches K-5 grade students for approximately five classes each day. Each class is 30 to 40 minutes long. In the post-summer institute questionnaire, she made this comment. "The summer institute has opened my eyes to the possibilities of integration in new subject areas. She responded to the question, "How do you feel about implementing your plan?" with: "Good. I know that the results may not be as aesthetically pleasing as one's idea of "dance" but the process is what is important."

Post-Summer Institute Interview

After the summer institute, Karen became an enthusiastic implementer of creative dance in her music classroom. "I have seen how important it is for kids to use their bodies to move. Dance is another language for them." She described an activity that tied into her music curriculum. "Dance supports my work in the music room. For example, in a lesson on pitches, I placed students in small groups and, they made up high, medium, and low movements with their bodies. Before [the summer institute] I was afraid it might look silly. Now, I no longer see movement as something silly and fun- in fact- some children use movement as their primary mode of communication."

Karen commented on her use of movement with upper grade students:

I had students find the strongest beat in a group of meters. 1-2-3-4. They created a statue every time the strong beat sounded, and they had to change to a new shape. Change, hold, hold, hold. Repeat. They absolutely loved it! I for sure would not have tried this with a 4th grade class.

She had concerns about her children's ability to make dances: "I feel weak on how to help them create their own dances." She described an activity where the students created a rainstorm with their bodies, and she wondered how to structure the rainstorm into a dance:

I had them create a storm. Started with rubbing hands, snapping fingers, clapping, panting legs, and stomping feet. Reverse and the storm goes away. Also with instruments—rubbing sand blocks, tapping wood blocks, Clapping hand drums, Patting thighs. Timpani drum.

This was a wonderful teachable moment, as I explained that by simply utilizing a shape movement shape pattern, the rainstorm activities become a dance with a beginning, middle and ending. During the interview, we also discussed problems and concerns. She recognized that exploration was an important component of dance making. She described the following experience as a failure for the students but a learning experience for her. "It didn't work because I didn't explore different ways of movement. We have to do a lot of exploring first in force, levels, etc. I need to give them a dance vocabulary for their bodies."

During the month of May, Karen taught a week-long topic on the human body systems and creative dance. She had the students maintain a journal of movement elements. The procedure was to spend 45 minutes per day on movement. "The students explored the movement vocabulary—levels, pathways, time, force, weight, and body movement, shapes and then writing about them. They were introduced to the science vocabulary."

The final project was a dance created for each of the systems by groups of students. Each of the groups demonstrated their understanding of the body systems through their dances. Karen provided the following descriptions of the student choreography:

Group 2—Circulatory system
"Four girls started with a strong shape. They chose music by kataro. The dance started with 2 girls lying on their sides. Continuously bending and straightening for the whole dance. A Learning disabled girl was the lungs. She stood above the heart. A 4th girl continued to run around the heart and lungs, circulating blood. The girls collapsed on the floor at the end, like a heart stopped beating. They really seemed to understand the concept of the circulatory system."

Group 3—Digestive system
"Seven boys were in this group. They started in a straight line with their backs to the audience. I didn't know what was going to happen. When the curtain opened all turned around. One boy started rapping and chanted—"It starts in your mouth chew real good.—Esophagus—he continued to name all of the parts of the digestive system in the song. The chorus acted out the words, which were more or less choreographed." She continues, "I was delighted they were able to make up dances and do them by themselves. I gave them 15 to 20 minutes to create the dances, then on to the stage for the performance. It was very successful. The classroom teacher was delighted. She could tell what they were trying to portray."

At the next summer institute, Karen presented a video of the final dances created by her students. They created dances depicting the skeletal system, the circulatory system and the digestive system.

Summary and Conclusion

Since 1999, as a component of the Program for Interdisciplinary Learning through the Arts, teachers have attended summer institutes and returned to their schools with an openness and a confidence that dance can and should be utilized across the curriculum. The three teachers included in this paper were successfully able to apply their knowledge to their specific teaching environment. All three teachers needed and benefited from additional follow-up workshops, observations, and support.

In sum, non-dance teachers are capable of gaining a working knowledge of creative dance and gain the ability to apply the concepts in a classroom setting. With support and guidance, they begin to connect dance to many areas of the curriculum. They are witness to the power of creative dance, as their students respond in a positive manner.

The Learning Continues

I have learned a great deal since beginning these institutes in 1999. One important lesson has been the need for additional professional development. The summer institutes have evolved into supplementary experiences including, workshops throughout the school year, on-line discussion forum, and follow-up assistance with students trained in creative dance. Another lesson has been in providing teachers with specific strategies for making a dance. Basic compositional forms, that is ABA, theme, variation, and narrative form have enabled teachers to make many concepts dance. Finally, I have learned that most teachers are very willing to utilize dance in their curriculum—they simply need more experience. The three teachers in this study provided necessary information so that future professional development opportunities will be planned to make a positive impact on teacher's attitude, behavior, and competence as they integrate dance into the curriculum.

REFERENCES

Boix Mansilla, V., Miller, W., & Gardner, H. (2000). On disciplinary lenses and interdisciplinary work. In *Interdisciplinary Curriculum*, Wineburg, S. & Grossman, P.(eds). New York: Teachers College Press, 17–38.

Fogerty, R. (1991). Ten ways to integrate curriculum. *Educational Leadership,* 61–65.

Glasersfeld, E. V. (1989). Cognition, construction of knowledge and teaching. *Synthese 80,* 121–140.

Joyce, B. & Showers, B. (1995). *Student Achievement through Staff Development.* New York: Longman, Inc.

Keinanen, M., Heltand, L. & Winner, E. Teaching cognitive skills through dance: Evidence for near but not far transfer. (2000). *Journal of Aesthetic Education, 34.* 296–306.

MacDonald, C.J. (1992). Effects of an in-service program on eight teachers' attitudes and practices regarding creative dance. *The Elementary School Journal, 80,* 99–115.

Overby, L. (2000). The voices of teachers: The effect of professional development on the knowledge and behavior of classroom teachers. Presented at the Annual Conference of the National Dance Education Organization. Salt Lake City, Utah.

8

DANCING OUT LOUD: CHILDREN'S USE OF LANGUAGE WHILE CREATING DANCES

Theresa Purcell Cone

The excitement that young children experience as they express their thoughts, understandings, and feelings through dance is not only evident in their spontaneous urge to move but also in their use of language and vocal sounds. In this study, 24 first-grade children, organized into eight groups of three, each attended three 20-minute sessions in which they created dances in response to the same story. The teacher's role was to read the story with the children, ask them to create a dance with minimal teacher direction, and then videotape the sessions. As I reviewed the videotapes I observed and heard the children readily improvise dance movements as they simultaneously laughed, talked, shouted, and made a variety of vocal sounds.

Analysis of the videotapes included writing descriptions and then examining the descriptions to locate conceptual themes that emerged. One aspect of the findings was the interconnectivity between the actions and language of the children during their process of creating the dances. As a result of the analysis, I identified nine categories which identify how children integrated language with their actions. The categories include: initiating the creative process, claiming a leadership role and directing others, identifying as a character, speaking as a story character, describing an action, making vocal sounds as an emotional response, describing a scene from the story, using collaborative language, and describing spatial locations and creating imaginary environments.

For young children, the integration of language and movement appears to be a natural connection. Children not only think and create through language, but also through movement. In this way their ideas, understandings and feelings are uncovered and explored. In some dance classes, children are asked to only be expressive through movement and keep their voices quiet, letting the dancing

233

speak for them. This method of teaching may be appropriate for selected situations, although a child's process for creating can be limited when language is prohibited. Noisy classes can be viewed as places of high creativity and personal expression where the innate connection of language and the process of creating dance is encouraged and celebrated.

On a beautiful summer morning I was standing on my deck absorbing the warmth of the summer sun and taking a moment to listen to the wonderful sounds of nature. From my neighbor's yard was the melodic voice of Olivia, the three-year-old child who lives next door. I leaned out from the deck to see what she was doing and observed her running and spinning and swinging her arms while she was singing, laughing and talking. She was absorbed in what appeared to be an imaginative story expressed out loud through movement and voice. For me, that moment illuminated the similarity between the research findings in this study and how movement and language can be inextricably linked to the creative process of children at any time.

This study investigated how first-grade children created dances in response to hearing and reading a story and viewing the illustrations. One aspect of the creative process that emerged was their frequent use of language while creating dances. Shouts, whispers, vocal sounds, shrieks, laughter, singing and lively dialogue; were the sounds that characterized the children's creative dance experience. The dancing space was filled with the voices of discovery, exploration and improvisation. For these young children, vocal articulations were integrated with their process of creation from the moment they were introduced to the story. Dance educator Ruth Murray (1963) supports the appropriateness of a noisy atmosphere in children's dance sessions. She notes, "One by-product of creative work in dance with children which is always present is noise…when groups work together there will be much talk, even some argument" (p.404). Children learn early in life to express their needs, feelings and ideas through both language and movement. These basic means of communication are naturally carried over into their creative dance experiences. In this study, children created dances within a collaborative context leading to a lively exchange of ideas where children verbalized much of their thinking. The social dimension to the experience initiated comments about where to move, how to move, who would do the movements and when to move. Children used language to negotiate for leadership, define character identity and tell about their understanding of the story. In this environment, children generated a dynamic and creative energy as they expressed their meaning through a fusion of dance and language. The opportunity pedagogy as a framework that values what children bring to the experience. Stinson asserts, "It is essential, however, that students have opportunities to speak, to find their own voice in words as well as movement, and to share that with others" (p. 40). The spontaneous emergence of language partners with movement to provide a child with multiple means of expression and communication.

The framework of the study consisted of 24 first-grade children, organized into eight groups of three, with each group attending three twenty-minute sessions. In the first session, the children listened to a reading of the story picture book, *Big Al* (Clements, 1998), and then were asked to create a dance about the story. The story depicts a big ugly fish that tries a variety of ways to make friends with a school of little fish. He is unsuccessful because of his size and appearance until the little fish are caught in a fisherman's net and Big Al bites the net to release the little fish. As a result, the little fish see how Big Al can be helpful and caring and as a result they are not afraid and all become friends.

In the second session, children could choose to repeat or change their previous dance or create a new one. Interviews with the children about their experiences were conducted in the third session and time was provided for the children to draw pictures about their dances. The first two sessions were videotaped. The design and interpretative analysis of this qualitative research drew from philosophical perspectives that included aspects of phenomenology and feminist and constructivist approaches to teaching. I approached the research without prior assumptions about what the children would create and I chose not to form a hypothesis to guide the data collection and analysis. I wanted to gain fresh insights into what children would do with the freedom to create dances from their point of view based on their understanding and experiences. My role as the participant/observer was to read the story with the children, ask them to create a dance and then step behind the video camera and watch them create their dances. I was interested in gaining insights about the children's process of creating dances with minimal teacher influence and I was also interested in how their dances reflected their meaning of the literature.

The data analysis was based on three primary sources of evidence: written descriptions of the videotaped sessions, the interview transcripts, and the drawings. During the implementation of the research, writing of the video description, transcription of the interviews and completion of the drawing identification matrix, I bracketed my interpretation of the data to remain neutral and open to all the activity of the children. After repeated readings and reflection on the data, I identified several themes that characterized the different approaches children used to create their dances. This

Theresa Purcell Cone

article chapter focuses on one prominent theme that appeared in all of the groups; how children naturally integrated language and vocal sounds with their movements as they created the dances.

As I watched and listened to the videotapes, I could hear children frequently talking, yelling and making sounds. Although I could not clearly hear every word, I included in the written description the words and vocal sounds that were audible. While reading the descriptions of each group's videotape I noticed that I had repeatedly written phrases that mentioned how the children were constantly talking about what they are doing, or that some children narrated a story while the others danced, or that children yelled and ran around the space. As a result of the analysis, I identified nine conceptual categories of language use. For this study, the term "language" is used to mean all the vocal sounds and words that appeared while the children were engaged in creating dances.

Initially, language appeared during the reading. Some students asked questions, made comments about the illustrations, laughed, made predictions, related their own experiences and read the story out loud along with me. The children's feelings and thoughts about the content of the text and illustrations were spontaneously transformed into vocal expressions. During the reading, I did not discourage any comments or sounds that emerged. I was seeking to understand the natural lived experience of a first grade student interacting with a story and to illuminate how and when the creative process for dancing begins.

The nine conceptual categories of language use that appeared during the process of creating the dances represent the findings of all the groups although each category was not equally evident in all groups. Some groups talked and made vocal sounds constantly as they danced while others made only a few comments. The discussion of each category includes examples of the children's comments.

Category One: Initiating the Creative Process

Language was the children's initial means of expressing their response to the story. Here, children shared comments that started the flow of spontaneous movements. While some children flipped the pages of the book and talked about which scene they wanted to use in their dance, others called out the character they wanted to portray or where they wanted to move in the space. Immediately upon the conclusion of reading the story one child cried out, "I got a great idea for a dance." Another child described a specific scene from the book that he wanted to dance about first when he stated, "Let's pretend that we are swimming along and we get caught in the net." Other children used language to negotiate ideas as they

"Let's pretend that we are swimming along and we get caught in the net." Other children used language to negotiate ideas as they stated, "First we are going to talk about it," and, "Do you want to start it?" Children used language to communicate their ideas for transforming the story into dance. It was during these conversations that the creative process began.

Category Two: Claiming Leadership Roles and Directing Others

This category of language use was highly prevalent during the creative process. In some groups, one child dominated the dialogue while in other groups all children offered comments to an equal extent. Students often shared their ideas for how to use movement to express their interpretation of what they heard and saw in the story. In several groups, one child assumed the role of choreographer and told others what movements to perform. As one child said, "You have to pretend you are in the seaweed. You have to do it like this." or, "You have to roll into a ball. I'll show you." Another child stated, "When we jump over you, then you have to chase us. You have to be laying down." In one group, a child narrated the actions of the dance and added new characters and actions to extend the original story. He stated, "The shark is hiding. You swim away then the shark comes." The children in his group readily performed his suggested movements in response to his comment. In this next example a child is lying on the front of her body and pointing to a page in the book and states to the other two children, "You have to get low like this." Then, while she leans on her hands and feet facing the floor and shakes her body she adds, "Now this is the part where he goes like this, you have to go like this." Another child in the group takes over as the leader when she returns to the book, flips through the pages and states, "I'll show you the pages and you guys can do it, okay you guys just go around and dance." These comments demonstrate how the children communicated their ideas about what they wanted to happen in the dance through movement and language. Some suggestions were rejected, "No I don't want to do that," or altered "Let's do it over here instead," while other suggestions stimulated immediate action.

Category Three: Identifying Themselves as Characters

Children in this study eagerly claimed their imaginary identity through announcing what character they wanted to be in the dance. One child boldly stated at the end of the reading, "I want to be Big Al." Their words become the agents of transformation as they imaginatively changed themselves into dancers portraying fish characters. Their character announcement also informed the others about who they have become in the dance. Character roles were clearly stated in these examples from the video descriptions, "I'll be the little fish," "I'll be the Big Al," "I am a penguin," "Okay you're the penguin." One child mentioned to another, "You have to be Big Al," and the other child replied, "We can alternate," as they negotiated different roles in the dance. The character roles that children chose to dance were verbally articulated as a way to claim their part and express their preference for creating movements.

Category Four: Speaking as a Story Character

Children not only created dance movements to represent their interpretation of how the characters appeared in the story, but they also invented dialogue to accompany their movements. As they gave voice to the characters, they verbalized the actions and feelings portrayed in the story. When one child was dancing to represent a little fish caught in the net, she yelled out, "Help I am stuck, help I can't get out," as she lay on the floor frantically waving her arms and legs. While another child dancing the same role called out, "I am tangled in the net." This next example of a brief exchange between children demonstrates how they engaged in conversation as story characters. The first child, dancing in the role of Big Al, waved his arms and said, "I saved you," as the second child, a little fish, who is also waving her arms replied, "I know, I know." Next, the first child happily stated, "You are my friends, you are my friends." In another group, a child dancing the scene in the story where Big Al is covered with seaweed exclaims loudly, "I am seaweed." A few moments later depicting a scene where Big Al is covered in the sand the child moves her body in an exaggerated sneezing movement and called out, "Achoo!" a word used in the story. The invented dialogue naturally flowed as children created their interpretation of the story. These imaginary characters became real to the children as they embodied the character's actions and gave the character a voice.

Category Five: Making Vocal Sounds as an Emotional Response

Children used their voices to express and emphasize their feelings while the story was read as well as while they were dancing. These vocalizations were not clearly articulated words but expressive sounds. Children yelled, screamed, roared and shrieked to express excitement or portray the sound of a character in action. Some children, dancing as little fish, ran and shrieked to express fear as the child portraying Big Al chased them in the space. Another child made the sound, "Boom" to accompany his sharp reaching movement to indicate that he has freed the little fish captured in the net. In one group, as the students turned the pages of the book, one child stood up, wiggled, and said, "And all the little fishes like whoooooo whooooooo," to express her emotional interpretation of dancing as a fish. Also, while viewing the illustration of Big Al on the first page one child expressed the sound, "Oooooo," pointed her finger and leaned forward as a spontaneous reaction. The volume of the children's voices reflected to the energy of their action. Big, fast, strong movements were usually accompanied by loud, low pitch sounds while smaller and lighter movements were paired with whispers, high pitched sounds, or short squeaks. The joy and intensity of the dancing clearly emanated through a range of vocal articulations.

Category Six: Describing a Scene From the Story

This category demonstrates what information the children recalled and comprehended after listening to the story. I observed the direct connection between the content of the story and the movements children expressed in their dance. The children used language to verbally share what they remembered and understood which inspired their dance movements. One child recalled, "Remember when he [Big Al] was covered with seaweed?" This comment was followed with creating movements that expressed the children's interpretation of their meaning of this story scene. Other comments the children made while dancing that describe scenes in the story include, "Then the little fishes go away," "Next I do the puffed up part," "Pretend you are stuck," "Now the seaweed," and "Now you are being different colors." Each comment a student offered revealed his or her understanding of what they remembered, felt and comprehended about the text and illustrations. The dancing expanded, confirmed and communicated these understandings.

Category Seven: Using Collaborative Language

In each group the children worked collaboratively to create ideas for the dancing. The social nature of creating and the intrinsic need of peer collaboration were evident in the interactions between the children. They shared character roles, made suggestions for what part of the story to dance about, turned pages of the book together and moved at the same time. Language became the way they expressed their thoughts and negotiated their actions. The awareness that they were sharing a collective experience was evident in what they said while dancing. Frequently, the plural pronouns *we* and *us* were used in directive statements and expressions of the experience. Examples of these are: "We all have to do it together," "First we are going to talk about it," "We can make up our own dance," "Let's start over," "We're stuck we're stuck," and "Let's read the story again." The children did not view themselves as isolated creators but as a cooperative group sharing ideas, experiences and meanings. Each child who presented an idea through movement or words influenced the thinking and movements of the other children. Some comments related to a movement idea were rejected, "No that is not the dance we want to do," while others were readily accepted, "Let's try it from the beginning." The synthesis of movements and language reveals this collaborative nature of children to interact with each other as creators and dancers.

Category Eight: Describing an Action

This category represents how children used language to describe their actions while dancing. They used words to describe the actual movement such as, "I am jumping," "Look a walking fish," or "I am rolling around." They also used words that expressed an action such as, "Chop Chop Chop Chop" while moving an arm up and down and, "I am getting bigger and bigger," as arms were stretched out to the side to depict a large shape or "I am flapping like a fishy," while running and swinging arms up and down.

For these children, language was used to explain to others the intent of their action or as a self-confirmation about what action that they were performing. During the interviews, I gained insights into what words or phrases the children used to describe their movements. I found that action words dominated the descriptions and only a few children used terms that described movement qualities such as, tempo, force, range, level, or direction. Some children mentioned specific body parts and used terms that also appeared in the story such as bumped, sneezing, swimming, puffed, wiggled, and caught. The following poetically arranged list of words (Cone, 2002) was drawn from the video description and interview transcripts and depicts words the children used to describe their actions in the dances:

Feet, Hands, Head, Tummy
Bumped
Puffed
Pulled
Fell Down
Running
Curling
Jumping
Standing
Stuck
Laid down

Trapping
Eating
Wiggling
Rolling
Sneezing
Hitting
Chopping
Swimming
Turning
Kicking
Spinning
Catch
Slamming down (p.231)

Category Nine: Describing Spatial Locations and Creating Imaginary Environments

The research took place in a 40'x40'foot gymnasium with three 4' piles of folding gymnastics mats placed against the wall, and in several sessions the mats were laid out along the wall. In the center of the room was a 10'-diameter black circle painted on the floor. During the process of creating their dances, I observed the children naturally appropriating the structure of the room and objects in the room to create places for the dancing. They used the circle as the fisherman's net, corners of the room as places for a character to enter the space or a location for a particular scene, a 12' wooden bench as the fisherman's boat, and paper streamers as seaweed and costumes. Language became the means to designate and communicate the imaginary use of these objects and locations. In one session, a child pointed to the circle and commented to the two others in her group, "This is the net, the circle is the net." In another group, a child ran over to the tan and blue striped mats near the wall and stated, "It [the mat] can be the water and the sand because it is blue and tan." And one child viewed the dancing space as stage when she stated, "I am off the stage. Now you are looking for me." In one session a small pile of 3'-long paper streamers was laying on the floor. One child called out, "Do we have any seaweed around here?" and then answered his question by pointing to the streamers and saying, "On that, that." Immediately after he designated the streamers as seaweed another child picked up the streamers and placed them on his shoulders and stated, "Remember when he [Big Al] was covered in seaweed?" Incorporating objects into the dancing appeared to help the children create a setting for their dance. As they shaped the existing environment to support their dance ideas they used language to communicate with each other the newly assigned role of objects illustrated by this child's statement from the interview, "It is like the floor is the water and the fish are swimming in it."

Pedagogical Implications

For children, the opportunity to create dance movements becomes an exciting adventure that stirs the imagination releasing a surge of ideas. In the process of creating dance movements children frequently use vocal sounds and words to communicate and express their thoughts and feelings about an idea for a dance movement. Language becomes an important link between thought and action. When creating dances children use all of their resources, both language and movement, to express their ideas, feelings and understandings. Their natural inclusion of language becomes a way to express what they cannot say through movement. These media of expression compliment each other.

Expressive vocal sounds, laughter or rhythmic shouts frequently accompany the joy a child experiences by running across an open space or spinning on the floor. As educators, we can promote a culture of vocal silence in a dance class when we say, "Express your ideas through your movements and not your voice, Shhh!" Although we want children to learn to use movement to express their thoughts and feelings, words and vocal sounds intuitively appear. However, all vocal sounds may not be appropriate all the time and the teacher may need to set volume limits or define the types of sounds that can support expression. Yet, children should feel free to use their voices as they create and perform dances, share ideas for movement, direct the action of others or create dances where vocal sounds or words are a planned element of the dance. The collaborative nature of creating dances encourages discussion, negotiation and a vocal discourse that recognizes the value that multiple perspectives bring to the creative process. Movement and language dialogue with each other in the children's world of creating dances; both means of expression appear to be necessary for creative ideas to emerge and take shape.

This article began with an illustration of how one child spontaneously fused language and movement while creating an imaginary experience. I close by sharing another experience, this one related to how the words a teacher uses in a dance class influences what children learn. As I was looking over information I had collected related to dance assessment, I found several samples of a tool I had used to assess what first grade children learned in a dance lesson. The children had written sentences describing what they had learned on 2' strips of colored paper. One paper stated, "I learned that when you dance you should not talk," another stated, "I learned that you should not talk because you can't think," and "What I learned about the dance, don't talk right in the middle of the dance." In reading these, I was at first embarrassed by what I had found, but also relieved to know that over the years I changed my way of teaching to allow for more student dialogue. As a researcher and teacher I have learned to let go of the "mythical silence" that can hang over a dance class. I encourage language and I listen, really listen, to what children say as they create. Here, I gain valuable insights into their way of creating, knowing, and making meaning.

REFERENCES

Cone, T. (2002). Off the page: Children's creative dance as a response to children's literature. Unpublished doctoral dissertation. Temple University, Philadelphia, PA.

Clements, A. (1988). *Big Al.* New York: Simon & Schuster Books for Young Readers.

Murray, R. (1963). *Dance in elementary education.* New York: Harper & Row Publishers.

Stinson, S. (1998). Seeking a feminist pedagogy for children's dance. In S. Shapiro (ed.), *Dance, power and difference: Critical and feminist perspectives on dance education* (pp. 23-47). Champaign, IL: Human Kinetics.

9

KINETIC AWARENESS™ PEDAGOGY: ELAINE SUMMERS AND SECOND-GENERATION PRACTITIONERS

Jill Green

This study explores the pedagogy of Kinetic Awareness,™ a somatic practice developed by Elaine Summers. I trace the legacy of Summers and the work of future practitioners through a qualitative research project. As a Kinetic Awareness teacher, I, as researcher, discuss my own insider status and subjective positionality during the project. The major data collection tool was one four-hour interview. Additionally, I spent two weekends with Summers, interviewing her, spending time with her, working on Kinetic Awareness board activities, and conducting an extensive member check by asking her to review my manuscript and make changes accordingly. Thus, field notes and observation, as well as a systematized self-reflexivity, were also included. Summers and I spent much time sharing sometimes conflicting perspectives and discussing directions of the work. The study may be characterized as postpositivist since I juxtapose the diverse ways Kinetic Awareness may be perceived, applied, and conceptualized. I do not attempt to find one "truth" but layers of complexity in describing and characterizing the work.

Readers may be aware that I usually address and write about critical theory and postmodern issues in dance education and somatic practice. I believe it is important to look at issues such as gender, race, culture, etc., to bring to awareness those who may be marginalized in dance classes. I explore how power enters dance technique classes (see Green 1999, 2001–a, 2001–b, 2001–c, 2002–3). Thus, I find it significant to deconstruct traditional notions of what it means to teach and do research about dance pedagogy and somatics.

However, this study may be a bit different from my previous research. Although I utilize a postpositivist framework for my research in the sense that I seek diverse perspectives and different "truths" about the pedagogy of Kinetic Awareness (KA), I also wish to pay homage to Elaine Summers. As I grow older, I see the need to recognize those who came before, and as the field of somatics in dance education continues to develop, I feel a need to distinguish those who contributed so greatly to the practice and pedagogy of the work. However, while I strive to bring recognition to my mentor and friend, I do so while searching for diverse directions the work is taking and may continue to take in the future.

For this reason, I, as researcher, must be aware of my insider status within this research project. At the same time, I do not believe that researchers cannot be objective and separate themselves completely from the research context.

Postpositivist Inquiry

Since I am not a historian but rather an educational researcher, I trace Summers's pedagogy through a qualitative/postpositivist research approach. In other words, I present my own experiences and interactions with her as part of my methodology. Besides accessing the materials written about Summers's and KA, I conducted an interview with her to collect data about her work and legacy as well as the work of later generations of KA teachers and practitioners. I was interested in exploring the power of her pedagogy through her own words as well as those who came after her, including myself. For this reason, I am a participant in this investigation, too. Because qualitative/postpositivist research methods recognize the subjective stance of the researcher, I note how this work has had an effect on me as well as others.

I use the term "postpositivism" as either a worldview or approach to scientific inquiry and as a qualitative methodological strategy. As a worldview, postpositivism re-evaluates what has come to be known as "natural science" and recognizes the limitations of the positivist tradition in research (Green and Stinson, 1999). For example, while most positivist researchers attempt to find objective methods that uncover a given reality, many postpositivist researchers reject the claim that research can be value-free or that one sole truth can be found through objective research methods (Denzin, 1989; Eisner, 1989; Lather, 1986b; Lincoln and Guba, 1985; McLaren, 1989; Nielsen, 1990). Some postpositivists claim that some level of subjectivity may even help researchers and participants gain a more meaningful and nuanced understanding of people and research themes (Fetterman, 1989; Kvale, 1983; Maguire, 1987).

Furthermore, while positivist methods strive to determine measurable truths that can be generalized, postpositivists claim that we construct reality according to our experience (see Guba and Lincoln, 1989), the researcher cannot know what constructions will be introduced during the investigation, and cannot predict beforehand what claims, concerns, and issues will arise (1989). For this reason research designs and questions must be flexible.

Because postpositivism tends to acknowledge the role of the investigator during the research process, much postpositivist research utilizes a methodology that is based on a reflexive perspective and approach (Bogdan & Biklen, 1992; Erickson, 1986; Kvale, 1983; Lather, 1986-a, 1991, in press; Lather & Smithers, 1997; Peshkin, 1988; Soltis, 1989).

Moreover, some postpositivists argue that the act of writing up data, or constructing the written report, necessarily involves the process of interpretation based on social constructions and the writer's preconceived assumptions about what it means to do research. Laurel Richardson (1990) claims that all writing is inscribed by our values and reflects metaphors that we use to communicate how we see the world. Since writing is inscribed by our experiences, no data can be neutral. Therefore, according to this perspective, it is effective to make one's subjectivity visible and display how one's voice enters the text. Thus, the first-person voice is often used in postpositivist research in an attempt to recognize the researcher's presence and bring a sense of self-responsibility to the process of assembling data.

Postpositivist research necessitates that I look at disconfirming evidence and places where my own feelings "bump up" against the data (see Green, 1996-a, 1996-b, 1999; Green & Stinson, 1999). Therefore, I discuss how my own ideas about KA differ with those of Summers and how my conclusions do not resonate with the data. Because this is a qualitative study, I do not attempt to generalize findings. Rather, my intention here is to pay homage and explore the ways the work has grown and changed through new generations.

My conversations with Elaine Summers convey more than an attempt to discuss her work. Beyond depicting the legacy of a somatic educator, I attempt to look at Kinetic Awareness from the perspective of its developer as well as from a multitude of possible lenses and applications. In one sense, this study is presented as a narrative about my communication with Summers. In another sense, it traces the directions and diverse developments of the work.

Methodology

The major data collection tool for this study was one four-hour interview with Summers. Although this may seem to be a quite limited data collection project, the methodology is much more complex. In addition to this long interview, I researched literature about second-generation KA practitioners and the various directions of the work. Thus, a triangulation of data (Guba & Lincoln, 1989; Lincoln & Guba, 1985) was established through working with a number of sources (Summers, other practitioners, and myself) and through working with a number of theories (Summers's humanist and experiential perspective and my own more postmodern view). Further, I, as an additional participant and researcher, took field notes and conducted a number of more informal interviews with Summers. I spent two weekends with Summers, interviewing her, spending time with her, working on Kinetic Awareness board activities and conducting an extensive member check by asking her to review my manuscript and make changes accordingly. Thus, field notes and observation, as well as a systematized self-reflexivity, were also included (Lather, 1986-a, 1986-b, 1991, 1995).

Ms. Summers and I spent much time sharing sometimes conflicting perspectives and discussing directions of the work. The study may be characterized as postpositivist because I juxtapose the diverse ways Kinetic Awareness may be perceived, applied, and conceptualized. I do not attempt to find one "truth" but layers of complexity in describing and characterizing the work. In order to demonstrate the multiple perspectives in the text of this chapter, I have chosen to represent the narrator voice in regular typeface, Summers's voice during our series of meetings in **bold**, my KA teacher and student selves in *italic,* and other KA educators in *script.*

Elaine Summers

When thinking about someone like Elaine Summers, I realize the significance of tracing the power of her life and work because she has affected the field of dance on so many levels and in so many ways. In fact, Elaine Summers has left us with a number of legacies. You may know Elaine through her choreography and as one of the members of the Judson Dance Theater in the 60s and 70s.[1] You may know Elaine through her work with the visual arts, as a known filmmaker and prominent member of the downtown New York visual arts community. I know her mainly through her work with the development of Kinetic Awareness™ (KA). It is through the teaching of this body-mind work that I have seen her touch so many dance lives.

Background

> *KA is an approach to somatic education that provides an opportunity to explore movement potential and develop movement possibilities. This system of body-mind reeducation...focuses on increased movement efficacy and ease through heightened awareness*

of automatic and conscious movement. It enhances the understanding of the language that the body uses to communicate with ourselves. (Green, 1992, p. 61)

Because this system uses rubber balls to enhance body awareness and release excess muscular tension, KA is often referred to as "the ball work": "Balls placed under various parts of the body provide contact with inner sensations, bringing awareness to inefficient patterns and psycho-physical processes" (p. 61).

However, the ball work is actually only one part of the practice. KA is really a way of looking at the body in dance. This attitude and pedagogy of the body was developed from the experiences and vision of Elaine Summers. Thus, Summers provided us with an approach, not just to help us move our bodies more easily, but also a way to explore bodily meaning, understanding, and influence within a number of contexts.

The first time Summers injured herself was when she was young and did not really consider herself a professional dancer. She was rehearsing and kicked a piece of furniture, dislocating her patella. It was then that she began to learn that you simply cannot fix an injury; for example, ligaments will not simply spring back into action. She became fascinated with books on anatomy and kinesiology, and as she said in her interview, as she learned about her injury she was "**falling in love with bodies**" and came to see them in a way she had never imagined before.

Another experience compelled Summers to further study the body. According to an account by Robin Powell, informed by an earlier interview with Summers,

In the 1950s… [after being accepted to Julliard she] was told by doctors that her osteoarthritis would cripple her and confine her to a wheelchair. At the recommendation of a friend [and therapist], Summers, not quite 30, [sic 29], began classes with Charlotte Selver. Selver, who had studied with Elsa Gindler in Germany, used aspects of Gindler's work and Zen meditation in developing her own technique, Sensory Awareness, during the 1940s. Two years later Summer began work with Carola Speads, Gindler's associate and master teacher. After healing her body enough to resume her dance career, Summer continued exploring body awareness principles. From 1958 to 1968 she…developed Kinetic Awareness. (Powell, 1987, p. 39)

Elaine's difficulties with her body and dance career inspired her to learn more about the body in order to be able to dance. Additionally, she attributes the wealth of knowledge and sharing about body awareness, which was present at the time and is generally known as the "human potential movement," for her somatic explorations and discoveries. For example, although she did not directly know Moshe Feldenkrais, she was aware of his work and was introduced to it through colleagues and acquaintances. With this explosion of bodywork, Elaine was able to work on her own body and develop her approach.

Development of KA and Pedagogy

I want to reiterate that this work is not merely an approach to deal with body issues and problems. Summers was working on a way of understanding the body. Epistemologically speaking, she was articulating a framework for how we learn to know our bodies and communicate the bodily knowledge that is in us. Rather than relying solely on external information, Summers was interested in helping dancers take ownership of their bodies and *"reclaim their bodies"* (Powell, 1987, p. 39).

Subsequently, Summers relied on a very particular type of pedagogy to help her with this goal. Although, she probably would not consider herself mainly a dance educator, she does have a degree in art education and she has often acknowledged the importance of facilitating the creative self. For example, Summers said,

> **I would love to do a whole thing about my teachers and inspirations and why they have been so important ... and how serendipitously they seem to open up a world for you through their understanding.**

So, believing in the power of teaching, and attempting to help people take ownership of their bodies and explore their kinesthetic intelligences, Summers developed KA, which combined elements of Selver's sensory awareness and Gindler's breathing strategies but began to explore a specific approach based on bodily knowledge, balls and other tools and props, alignment, dance, and a student-centered system for relying on one's own body knowledge and exploration.

This body reeducation system as described by Summers is based on an attitude towards the body that **"the body is yours and you need to understand it; you need to listen to it**.*"* Summers explained the origins of the use of balls as a development of her work with Selver and Gindler. She remembered,

> **You would lie with your spine on a bamboo stick and your spine would start making adjustments so the next thing you knew you were perfectly comfortable on the bamboo stick. So that's the same as the balls, the concept of how elastic**

your body is and how it will adjust...and you have no idea how it's going to do this, but it's important to give your body the chance to do it, to practice it.

Thus, at first Summers was only thinking about how she could dance and what she needed to do to help her body move with more ease and help rehabilitate her osteoarthritic hip joints. But through practicing the work and through her teaching (when her students began to request a system for teaching the work), she began to recognize that we know more about our bodies than anyone else, including so-called "experts" in the field. This is what Don Johnson refers to as *experiential authority* (1992). It is a way of looking inwardly to help us understand and own our bodily experiences.

I remember Elaine referring to an internalized outside authority figure as "Aunt Matilda", who represents any authority that imposes his or her own view about the body on us. She would tell us to stop listening to Aunt Matilda or whomever she represented in us and start hearing the wisdom of our own bodies. Summers referred to what Isaac Asimov describes as "protoplasmic streaming" and Wilhelm Reich's description of "organic energy"—or our ability to feel, to explain the cellular knowledge and somatic communication possible in the body. And this process, for her, is part of an ownership of the body.

In explaining this process, and another significant concept for her, the idea of "**tension as an ally,**" Summers said,

I started teaching very early. I started teaching by including Kinetic Awareness ideas with thinking about [ideas such as] this is your body. What do your bones feel like? How can you feel where the pain is? And then [I was] leading right into modern dance, which I had always taught creatively [for] children and [for] everyone. I became involved with the ball work after six months of thinking that I had to give up dance because of the three doctors that I consulted about osteoarthritis. I began to work many hours alone in the studio and study with Charlotte and Carola. At that time I began to teach KA, which included an hour of KA and an hour of straight modern dance. Part of this work was based on giving each other a massage so that people could feel the difference in tension levels and what that meant in how tense a body felt as opposed to a collapsed body, that relaxation was not collapsation [sic], and I had also realized that one of the big problems for people was that the idea was being sold as the "relaxation technique," that stress was very bad, that tension was terrible. It was the idea that "you must relax."

In other words, Summers feels that we have to be careful about how ideas are presented and marketed, and that such a selling of ideas changes everybody's attitudes and bodily being. She detests the idea of "no pain no gain" and relaxation as always being good and tension as being bad. She prefers to explore levels of tension through its continuum, with habitual or frozen tension as unhealthy, because there is no choice or exploration involved, but considers the conscious use of tension as an ally. As Summers explained,

> The only way we move, or anything moves, is with tension. Even when you are holding tension, for example, frozen tension in a shoulder, it is necessary to keep sending the same amount of tension to the same place, creating lactic acid.

Further, she does not believe in selling the work because she wants each person to explore it or use it in her or his own ways. She prefers to get the practice out through word-of-mouth. This may be why KA is not as popular as some of the other more marketed somatic practices. *I believe that this is one way that this work may be considered liberatory. It involves personalized exploration that is not standardized or marketed as a commodity.*

Thus, Summers has left a legacy with KA, not just of exploring and communicating a specific way to articulate and rehabilitate the body in dance. She has also left a pedagogical legacy and a way of viewing and articulating the body and of freeing the body from specific political or socio-cultural norms about what the body should be or how it should look. As she said about to her dance company, **"I always wanted a dance company that wasn't cookie-cutter, and I learned through teaching that people with all kinds of bodies look wonderful dancing."**

Second Generation Practitioners and Teachers

Summers helped develop and nurture the careers of many of her present and former students. It makes sense that these careers were immensely diverse because Summers worked hard to ensure that her students took ownership of their own bodies and futures. Although the group of current somatic practitioners and thinkers is small compared to other movement reeducation systems, Elaine's students have done much to extend her legacy. For example, Ellen Saltonstall teaches yoga as well as KA and incorporates KA principles into her work with yoga. She also teaches KA to yoga teachers and has written a book about Kinetic Awareness (Saltonstall, 1988). Robin Powell, who has a doctorate in dance and advanced degrees in social work and psychological therapy, works with psychological trauma as well as pain management. Her system allows you to feel which tensions are emotional. Although Summers chooses not to work this way, she respects it. As she said,

> **Although I feel that is true, that the body development and injuries may be psychologically caused or be a component of your total body experience or development, I prefer to limit my teaching to the actual kinetic, physiological, neurological, or any of the body system's actual structures. Since all of our experiences are connected to our psychological selves, it is important to investigate and explore the psychological in our being. In my teaching, I feel it is helpful not to be teaching the kinetic psychological part because in both psychology and kinetics there is resistance to change. I find it more effective when the student comes upon psychological emotional responses that I listen and recommend psychological therapy by another therapist, as I might recommend an acupuncturist or chiropractor.**

So although Robin took a different approach and expanded the work in a different direction, and Elaine would rather work with the movement itself, KA allows for this type of diversity via its communication and practice.

Frances Becker, another former KA student, takes the work into her dance and choreographic life. She explores Kinetic Awareness as a dance technique and creative tool. Like Elaine, Frances incorporates KA into dance and creative work in her classes. She picked up on this element of the work and has explored KA with contact improvisation and the teaching of choreography. She worked with a system of integrating KA with contact improvisation with her colleague Nina Martin in New York in studio workshops and at the Laban Institute, Movement Research, and at the Experimental Theatre Wing at New York University (Becker, 1993; Martin, 1993).

These are just some examples of the directions the work has taken. Many other practitioners are working in a number of contexts and venues. My intention here is to trace some of the diversity of approaches and pathways that emanated from the KA practice and approach.

My Own Direction

For myself, I see my work as extending KA in other directions. As an educator, scholar, and researcher, my own work has led to using KA within a number of theoretical as well as practical contexts. When I first started, I too was interested in healing an injury, to my plantaris muscle in my calf. Michelle Berne, one of the first KA master teachers, was teaching a class I was taking at NYU at the time. Because I was going to be on crutches for three months, she told me that I had to go to Summers to do the ball work. I had no idea what she was talking about but decided to go. I found that this work changed my life in many ways. Besides healing my injury, the work became something that facilitated change on a number of levels, including psychological, emotional, and physical, and really how I felt in my body. While prior to my accident I felt hard like steel, I soon found a more responsive and articulate body capable of feeling deeply and adapting to change so much more easily. This really made life more meaningful and deeper.

Later, when I was working on my doctorate, I began to explore a number of theories, including social theory and postmodern theory. I began addressing bodily issues in dance such as how our bodies are socially constructed and I began to question essentialist claims that our bodies are the same and that bodily experience is value-free or not influenced by culture and society. So through my teaching, research, and scholarship I am beginning to explore theoretical as well as practical concerns about how societal bodies are taught to behave and how we can understand our own somatic responses.

I have come to the conclusion that engagement in practices such as Kinetic Awareness is subversive² because it upsets a dominant paradigm based on giving our bodies to others, i.e., to the experts, to manipulate and control. I believe that, particularly in this country and many others, we are purposely habitually taught to separate body and mind in an effort to weaken us so that we can be controlled and manipulated more easily. These ideas are also found in the theories of scholars such as Don Johnson, a somatic thinker, and Michel Foucault, a well-known French postmodern thinker (see Green, 1999). I use KA and other somatic practices as pedagogical and research tools to investigate how our bodies are habitually trained and socially constructed, and I believe that this is a liberatory and subversive act.

However, I must say that Summers does not necessarily share these opinions and theories. Interestingly, when I asked her whether she thought the work was subversive, Summers said that she did not like the term subversive. But I think it is helpful to use the term so that we can consciously explore social issues. Further, I do not believe that somatic practice in and of itself is necessarily good or problem-free. I am suspect about blindly using somatic practices without the recognition that they are tools used to get to a particular place. I do not believe that they are necessarily a panacea for all the world's ills. In fact, as Johnson suggests, they can be used to numb the body and help perpetuate social inaction (1992) or even be destructive. For example, I knew someone who was not trained as a therapist but used somatic work with victims of trauma and sexual abuse. His idea of using somatics to help these people (who were all women) was literally to get on top of them in order to help them relive the past trauma and he gladly said that he was working somatically.

My point here is that bodily experiences are not neutral or value-free and we cannot simply know bodily truth just by going inwardly to ourselves. Bodily truth is based on our backgrounds, early experiences, culture, and how we have learned to live within our bodies.

I believe that our bodies are more fluid than we tend to think, that we have trained our bodies to behave in ways that we may not be aware of in order to meet a social standard or cultural requirement. For example, as Johnson points out, when Westerners attempt to practice yoga and move themselves into positions that they may see as contorted and unnatural, they invariably get hurt when forcing themselves into these positions. However, what we may not understand is that people who do get themselves into these positions and difficult movements have been trained to do so from an early age by sitting on the floor at low tables while they ate meals. This physical patterning is really a part of a cultural education. When Westerners, who use chairs to sit at a dinner table, try to do this they have many difficulties because they have not trained their bodies to do this from a young age. These are different bodies with different orthopedic abilities and requirements.

Of course, I am not saying that these are essentially different bodies, that the genetics are different. I mean to say that the social acculturation has been different and that the bodies have adapted differently. This is why science cannot explain all bodily issues and problems because some behaviors are taught and socially acquired.

Final Thoughts

Summers recognizes this social factor as relevant and significant. She addresses how our bodies are informed and taught; this was evidenced with her reference to "Aunt Mathilda" and the effect of body images on the health and life of our bodies. Additionally, Summers addressed issues of power and oppression in our interview and she so often talked about respecting the voices of those who may be silenced. This to me signifies what I mean by *subversive*. However, I think she interpreted the term *subversive* to mean destructive and negative, which is not really how I meant it. We had an intense discussion that clarified the presentation of our ideas linguistically, and we found that our understandings and concepts were based on the specific qualities or differences between the functional and genetic aspects of the work.

Summers does prefer to see the work in relationship to concepts such as harmony, support, and community. She said that *subversive* is a word she tries to avoid. She does not focus on the political because she believes that **"everything includes the spiritual and hugeness of the world."** She prefers to **"build towards light."** She wants everyone to experience the joy and ease of movement. As she said at the end of out interview,

> It's not being subversive but supporting the reality of the tremendous myriad, marvelous multiple ways that our body is ... so that the work that we're doing here joins in the work the Buddha did, don't kill anything...not even a fly...I want to learn a way to evolve myself and in the doing that...and our job is to explore the creative force, the creative self in us...to build on it ... but destruction is bad...We can help each other to see and act...and fight exploitation through choice...We have choice...KA gives us control through understanding how [the body] works.

No matter how Summers views the work and in what directions she is willing to take it, it is clear to me that she opened a valuable door to look at the work in so many significant contexts and possible applications, practically and theoretically. While doing this she encouraged others to find new ways to look at the work, even though she may not personally agree with these ways all the time. For me, this work has been a treasure personally, emotionally, physically, theoretically, professionally, politically, culturally and in ways I probably have not yet imagined or visualized. I thank Elaine for these extraordinary gifts.

REFERENCES

Becker, F. (1993, Summer/Fall). Kinetic Awareness. *Contact Quarterly,* 2 (18), 53-55.

Bogdan, R. C., & Biklen, S. K. (1992). *Qualitative research for education: An introduction to theory and methods* (2nd ed.). Boston, MA: Allyn and Bacon.

Denzin, N. K. (1989). *The research act: A theoretical introduction to sociological methods* (3rd ed.). Englewood Cliffs, NJ: Prentice Hall.

Eisner, E. (1989). Objectivity and subjectivity in qualitative research and evaluation. In E. W. Eisner & A. M. Peshkin (eds.), *Qualitative studies in education*. New York: Teachers College Press.

Erickson, F. (1986). Qualitative methods in research on teaching. In M. C. Wottrock (ed.), *Handbook of research on teaching* (3rd ed., pp. 119–161). New York: Macmillan.

Fetterman, D. M. (1989). *Ethnography step by step.* Newburry Park, CA: Sage.

Green, J. (1992). The use of balls in Kinetic Awareness. *Journal of Physical Education, Recreation and Dance, 63*(8), 61–64.

Green, J. (1996-a). Moving through and against multiple paradigms: Postpositivist research in somatics and creativity—Part I. *Journal of Interdisciplinary Research in Physical Education, 1*(1), 43–54.

Green, J. (1996-a). Moving through and against multiple paradigms: Postpositivist research in somatics and creativity—Part II. *Journal of Interdisciplinary Research in Physical Education, 1*(1), 73–86.

Green, J. (1999). Somatic authority and the myth of the ideal body in dance education. *Dance Research Journal, 31*(2), 80–100.

Green, J. (2001-a). Social somatic theory, practice and research: An inclusive approach in higher education. *Conference proceedings, dancing in the millennium: An international conference* (pp. 213–217). Washington, D.C.

Green, J. (2001-b). Socially constructed bodies in American dance classrooms. *Research in Dance Education, 2*(2), 155–173.

Green, J. (2001-c). Emancipatory pedagogy?: Women's bodies and the creative process in dance. *Frontiers, 21*(3), 124–140.

Green, J. (2002-03), Foucault and the training of ideal bodies in dance education. *Arts and Learning Research Journal, 19.*

Green, J., & Stinson, S. W. (1999). Postpositivist research in dance. In S. H. Fraleigh & P. Hanstein (Eds.), *Researching dance: Evolving modes of inquiry* (pp. 91–123), Pittsburgh, PA: University of Pittsburgh Press.

Guba, E. & Lincoln, Y. (1989). *Fourth-generation evaluation.* Newburry Park, CA: Sage.

Kvale, S. (1983). The qualitative research interview: A phenomenological and hermeneutical mode of understanding. *Journal of Phenomenological Psychology, 14*, 171–196.

Johnson, D. (1992). *Body: Recovering our sensual wisdom.* Berkeley, CA: North Atlantic Books and Somatic Resources.

Lather, P. (1986-a). Research as praxis. *Harvard Educational Review, 56*(3), 257–277.

Lather, P. (1986-b). Issues of validity in openly ideological research: Between a rock and a soft place. *Interchange, 17*(4), 63–84.

Lather, P. (1991). *Getting smart: Feminist research and pedagogy with/in the postmodern.* New York: Routledge.

Lather, P. (in press). Applied Derrida: (Mis) Reading the work of mourning in educational research. *Journal of Philosophy and Education.*

Lather, P. & Smithies, (1997). *Troubling the angels: Women living with HIV/AIDS.* Boulder: Westview/HarperCollins.

Lincoln, Y. S. & Guba, E. G. (1985). *Naturalistic inquiry.* Beverly Hills: Sage.

Maguire, P. (1987). *Doing participatory research: A feminist approach.* Amherst, MA: Center for International Education.

Martin, N. (1993, Summer/Fall). Kinetic Awareness. *Contact Quarterly, 18*, (2), 58.

McLaren, P. (1989). *Life in schools: An introduction to critical pedagogy in the foundations of education.* New York: Longman.

Nielsen, J. M. (1990). Introduction. In J. M. Nielsen (ed.), *Feminist research methods: Exemplary readings in the social sciences* (pp. 1–37). Boulder: Westview Press.

Peshkin, A. (1988). In search of subjectivity–one's own. *Educational Researcher, 17*(18), 17–21.

Powell, R. (1987). Body therapies: Body awareness techniques. *Journal of Holistic Nursing 5*(1), 36–42.

Richardson, L. (1990). *Writing strategies: Reaching diverse audiences* (Qualitative Research Methods Series 21). Newburry Park, CA: Sage.

Saltonstall, E. (1988). *Kinetic Awareness: Discovering your bodymind.* New York, New York: Kinetic Awareness Center.

Soltis, J. F. (1989). The ethics of qualitative research. *Qualitative Studies in Education, 2*(2), 123–130.

NOTES

1. Much of this work continues today through the sponsorship of Movement Research with performance at Judson by choreographers and dancers all over the country.

2. Summers and I went back and forth about the term *subversive.* She hated the term and preferred to think more positively. This may be one example of how ideas can "bump up" against each other in postmodern research.

10

KINETIC LITERACY: MOTIF WRITING IN K-5 DANCE EDUCATION

Mila Parrish

This article offers an approach to teaching kinetic literacy through Laban Motif Writing. The research was conducted over a two-year period in both New York and New Jersey Public Schools. It advocates a form of symbolic learning called Motif Writing, a literacy tool for children in dance making, dance analysis, and dance inquiry. Symbol systems such as mathematics and music are comparable to Motif Writing, as they entail movements, pictures, signs, and sounds and provide a "language" with which to describe and elicit ideas. Symbol systems guide the development of intelligence, present children with numerous choices for communicating, and can greatly expand children's capabilities to think. This research examines the acquisition and development of symbolic modes of representation using Motif Writing, which provides a foundation for intellectual perception.

This article includes a review of literature on dance notation as applied to K-12 dance education and presents a brief look at the development of Motif Writing. An explanation of the rationale and methodology applied in the research, as well as personal conclusions, practical application, and frameworks for a curricular-based, dance-literacy program called Literacy in Motion are included. The Literacy in Motion curriculum is designed for professionals in the fields of K-5 curricular education, physical education, and dance education.

At a small K-3 public school, minutes north of New York City, something unusual is happening. Voices and bodies stir with excitement in a classroom. Children are moving from resource table to wall chart, from teacher to small work groups. Unrestricted by linear arrangements of desks and chairs, they find new meaning in their bodies. Creating nouns, verbs, and adjectives in moving sentences, the children are building connections through the creative process. The personal investment, commitment, interest, and enthusiasm are contagious and clearly visible. Children are moving in conjunction with their curriculum, discovering a long-

abandoned resource: their kinetic literacy. As class continues, the
children create, organize, and share original movement scores.
Themes that they have physicalized include prey and predators,
glaciers, icebergs, and properties of water. They feel the
importance of their work because they have tapped their kinetic
intelligence and are using it to bring their curriculum alive.

Why is this unusual? These third-graders have had five 45-
minute dance classes, and in a short time, they have found new
ways to express, expand, and organize their knowledge. They are
spirited, with an understanding of the basics of moving safely in
space; creating and remembering movement; cooperating with a
partner in developing movement ideas; observing and analyzing
other students' creative work; and writing their work in a special
"secret" dance language called Motif Writing. They can create a
movement score (similar to a music score) to organize, record,
document, and analyze their dances. In short, they feel the power
of their own creations embodying their curriculum and have found
a new language, a kinetic language.

A baby's developmental milestones are measured by acts such
as bending, twisting, rolling, standing, and walking, which are
based on muscular sensations of tension and relaxation. Movement
is the basis of early intellectual development; without physical
stimulation, infants fail to thrive and eventually die. Cognitive
psychologist Jean Piaget's research in child development cites the
intellectual importance of kinetic experience in the Sensory Motor
Stage, in which a child learns to deal with physical existence
exclusively from the five senses and motor activity. Kinetic
interactions assist our perception and structuring of our world.
Therefore, we can presume that kinetic expression is a child's first
language.

Kinetic literacy has received little recognition in current
educational circles. Most of our nation's classroom curriculum is
set up for verbal and analytic structures. Children with aptitudes in
reading, reasoning, and conceptual skills thrive, whereas children
with strengths in creative imagination, mechanical reasoning, and
intuitive perception may fail. Through this research, I investigate
movement as a kinetic language and develop a curricular
framework, which leads to the development of K-5 kinetic literacy.
In this article I will discuss a form of symbolic learning called
Motif Writing, a literacy tool for children's knowledge
construction in dance, and share a K-5 interdisciplinary dance
curriculum called Literacy in Motion.

Over a two-year period I taught this material in both New York
and New Jersey Public Schools. The student population was
varied: The participants cited were kindergarten–5th grade with
about a 50/50 mix of girls and boys. Class sizes ranged from 19 to
27 students. Each lesson was between 50 and 60 minutes long.

Individually and in small groups, students created short Motif dances based on curricular themes by manipulating Motif symbol cut-outs. At the end of each class, the children shared their creations, cited their observations, and discussed future possibilities. The following was a typical class format:

- Movement exploration and discussion on the curricular theme of the day;
- Improvisation and directed activity to introduce the Motif vocabulary;
- Introduction of the symbols which may have included a short writing or reading activity;
- Development of movement phase and documentation through Motif;
- Writing or ordering cut-out symbols and, on occasion, reading their scores to another student;
- Presenting dances; and
- Discussion and reflection.

Activities in each thematic unit were created, including dance sharing with friends and family, homework assignments, worksheets, art projects, and movement practice (to be done before or after movement sessions). A homework sheet could contain a review of material covered in a previous class, a glossary of Motif, a variety of activity games, or visual arts assignments. These were used to stimulate reflection and promote synthesis of the material.

In this research I am interested in defining viable applications of Motif Writing and to observe its use with various curricula. Using children's classwork, symbolic recall, and dance documentation through their artwork, dance making, movement scores, and discussions, I noted their comprehension of material through observation, cooperative learning groups, and reflective comments. I interviewed many children and their teachers regarding their experiences and insights with Motif Writing to ascertain its effectiveness. The research culminates with a curriculum framework covering three unit themes to support the incorporation of Motif Writing into the public school curriculum.

My approach in developing curricular applications for Motif Writing across the K-5 curriculum began with a thorough review of all related written materials. This provided a valuable understanding of the applications and research materials in the fields of interdisciplinary education, movement analysis, and dance education. I observed educators utilizing Motif Writing in dance and other subject areas and evaluated their teaching strategies. I interviewed leading dance educators in the field of Motif Writing about current developments to identify trends in the application and acceptance of Motif. I had the privilege of training with three of the prominent leaders in Motif Writing: Ann Hutchinson Guest, Lucy Venable, and Ann Kipling Brown.

Rationale

The field of dance in public education has been suffering. The arts are often thought of as extravagant and, in tough economic times, funding ceases, resulting in the elimination of arts programs. Currently movement and dance education has experienced a resurgence of interest and an increase in scholarship. The three factors driving this resurgence are: The Goals 2000: Educate America Act, and the National Standards for Arts Education (1994); Howard Gardner's theory of multiple intelligence, which specifies the importance of bodily-kinesthetic intelligence (1993); and the ceaseless efforts of dance educators, university professors, school boards, parents' organizations, classroom teachers, and students. These efforts provide encouragement for dance educators in their fight for credibility in a largely unknown field.

I believe that Motif brings intellectual understanding and a heightened awareness of the power of kinesthetic literacy in the schools, whether in the classroom or in the gymnasium. Dance educators probe for techniques to lend credibility and clarity to their profession. Motif is a method of dance notation utilizing symbols to communicate human movement. Motif provides a system of organizing movement, allowing children to communicate in a "language" much the same as the languages of math and music. Through Motif a child can put the elements of movement into meaningful visual patterns. By including Motif in the dance curriculum, students—as well as their teachers, parents, principals, and superintendents—are educated in the understanding of dance within an educational framework.

Although there is little research on the benefits of Motif Writing with K-12 curriculum, literature on Labanotation, dance education, and curricular interdisciplinary education is extensive. Scholarship exists in each of the distinct subject areas, but there is little documentation on the integration of Motif with curricular-based K-5 dance education. The following literature and hands-on training with specialists in the field of dance notation and motif writing have been essential in the development of this curriculum.

An author, researcher, scholar, and international guest speaker on dance notation, Ann Hutchinson-Guest, trained at the Jooss-Leeder School (where Laban frequently lectured) in England. Hutchinson-Guest notated Jooss's *The Green Table* and other seminal works advancing the field of Labanotation around the world. Her books, journals, teacher training seminars, and interviews have been essential to this research. In one of her many books examining the development of notations systems, *Choreo-*

graphics (1989), Hutchinson-Guest examines the multitude of notation systems in particular strengths regarding the premise of each system, the elements of timing, and the level of movement analysis. Each notation system is presented through identical movement material so direct comparison can be made.

In addition to Hutchinson-Guest, Valerie Preston-Dunlop worked to explore the concept of Motif Writing, and both published material on the application of Motif to analysis and education. In 1967 Preston-Dunlop wrote a series of four workbooks called *Readers in Kinetography Laban*, which presents a methodology for learning and dance making using Kinetography Laban (known as Labanotation in the United States). Although not specifically called Motif Writing, Preston-Dunlop's methodology states that the purpose of Kinetography Laban is individual interpretation consistent with contemporary definition of Motif Writing. Preston-Dunlop emphasizes bodily kinesthetic intelligence in recall, stating that a person must physicalize to understand, since the "body" memory is more powerful than the "brain" memory of the series of symbols on a page.

Your Move: A New Approach to the Study of Movement and Dance (1995), by Hutchinson-Guest, is a three-part handbook for movement analysis and description. The text provides clear insight into the Motif Writing notation system and teaching approach utilizing a textbook, a workbook, and an audio tape for reading studies. Hutchinson-Guest states that Motif Writing is not based on, or limited by, any one form or style of movement, but on the basis of all movement, exploring its fundamental truths. *Your Move* builds a framework for kinetic literacy and also provides an introduction into the exploration of movement, information as to what the student is doing and why, tips for technique and performance, and an initial venture into movement composition and choreography. In my opinion, this text is the handbook for Motif Writing. Each chapter includes an in-depth analysis, with useful and humorous illustrations, and several reading studies and homework sheets to solidify concepts. On several occasions, I had the opportunity to observe (and later assist) Hutchinson-Guest while she was working with students.

Also influential was the work of Ann Kipling-Brown, professor and scholar of children's dance, who has written articles on the application of Motif Writing and Labanotation for the dance educator. During the summers of 1994 and 1995, I had the pleasure of participating in two teacher training courses at Ohio State University and Teachers College, Columbia University, during which Kipling-Brown presented her methods. Kipling-Brown's work assisted in an application of the Motif as it applies to children.

Also important was the research and instruction of Lucy Venable. Venable's work in the field has ranged from dancer with the José Limón Company to rehearsal assistant for Doris Humphrey, from past president of the Dance Notation Bureau to Professor Emeritus at Ohio State University. Her lectures, writings, and interviews have been integral to my technical understanding of Motif and its application to dance literacy.

In addition to reading the published material on notation and Motif, I gained much insight into this field from the observation of distinguished dance educators who work with Motif and children. In a Motif workshop, I observed Karen King-Calvin, a primary school dance educator from Ohio, teach a fourth-grade interdisciplinary Motif lesson on the Underground Railroad, and Linda Yoder, also a dance educator from Ohio, present a Motif class on interpersonal skills and relationships for high school students.

Next, I will discuss Rudolf Laban, artist, educator, and inventor of Labanotation; explore how he invented this movement language; and investigate the usefulness of this system for K-5 dance education.

Writing Dance

For more than 500 years, dance enthusiasts, professionals, and scholars have tried to devise a system of recording dance onto paper. Today there are 124 notation systems, 53 of which have been successfully used to a limited degree to contribute to the recording of movement and dance (Hutchinson-Guest, 1984). Each system had been devised with the intent of providing a clear terminology to adequately represent the nonverbal language of movement and dance. In the last century, the symbol system called Labanotation has led to the development of nonverbal dance notation and is considered a comprehensive codified "language of movement."

Rudolf Laban (1879-1958) developed Labanotation, a system of identifying, investigating, and recording all forms of human movement from the simplest to the most complex. Labanotation presents an objective record of movement, and as Causeley (1969) explains, provides "a common denominator for thinking and communicating, independent of any theory, style or technique" (p. 13).

Movement consists of actions: to wave, to nod, to squint; each action expresses meaning which may be cultural or specific. Complex physical actions and human gestures have multiple symbolic and cultural meanings. As complex beings we have constructed elaborate systems based on signs, which may be oral, visual, or written, to communicate. The human body holds a powerful kinesthetic intelligence that is innate. The significance of movement in life and dance has been investigated in depth by Laban, whose system of notation harvests this body intelligence and presents methods for the observation, evaluation, analysis, documentation, and creation of motion.

Laban was not the first to develop a system of notation. Others, such as Raoul Auger Feuillet and Beauchamp, founded their own notation systems over 300 years before Laban (Laban, 1956, p. iv). In fact, the French parliament recognized Beauchamp, the ballet master of Louis XIV, as the inventor of dance notation in 1666, and Feuillet published dances written in this notation around 1700 (Laban, 1956, p. v). Laban, in his book *Dance Script* (1928), states that his notation and movement language uses the principles in Beauchamp and Feuillet's notations. Laban spent years exploring the benefits of other notation systems before founding his own.

Laban was interested in finding the common denominator of all human movement and in bringing dance to the same prominence as all other art forms, arguing "that no temporal art can achieve a full development without the notation which can capture, preserve and examine its ephemeral creations" (1922, p. 675). Moreover, Laban (1920) wrote, "It is necessary to determine the symbols of dance in writing because a tradition which will make possible a deeper evaluation of artistic achievements in dance can only arise from comparison, examination, repetition and recreation" (p. 65).

Laban's research has categorized Labanotation into three forms of movement description: Structural, Effort Shape, and Motif Writing. Structural Description depicts movement in clearly defined and measurable terms and is essential for the preservation of choreographic works. Effort-Shape Description describes movement in terms of its quality and expression. Motif Writing describes movement as a broad and general statement, noting only the most salient features of a movement.

Motif Writing

Motif Writing is a system of notation used to record, analyze, document, generate and create a movement *without* capturing all the details. It is symbolic vocabulary that is easy to learn. It can be thought of as an elementary form of Labanotation, and can be used to varying degrees of complexity (Hutchinson-Guest, 1995; Venable, 1996; Kipling-Brown, 1989). Motif provides a tangible means of representing the "raw materials" of movement, which are body, effort, shape, and space, as well as the elements of composition. It can be compared to a painter's primary colors, a musician's scales or a poet's words. Laban Motif Writing is a language of movement used to assist in the communication, creation, and education of dance, thereby advancing dance literacy.

Hutchinson-Guest (1996) furthers the endowment of Motif as an essential tool of dance literacy when she says,

> composing dance sequences, creating movement through the use of the basic alphabet, opens the door to greater exploration and hence to greater creativity. Like the sculptor who must get to know his materials—how clay reacts to his handling, how wood responds to his chisel or stone to his hammer—so the dancer needs to have an intimate knowledge of the raw materials of dance. (p. 2)

Motif's symbol system states the general idea behind a movement and allows for exploration, improvisation, and composition of that basic idea or theme. In relation to Labanotation, Hutchinson-Guest (1995) states, "In Motif, you are writing very little because you want the interpreters to bring their own ideas and improvisation, their own creativity to it; whereas with a structured score, there will be a personal interpretation on a clearly established choreographic form." Valerie Preston-Dunlop (1967) addresses the plasticity of Motif when she states,

> Motif Writing is a system of notation which gives the outline of a movement, its motivation without describing in detail how the action is to be performed.... The interpretation of motif writing is left up to the reader, so that it is a perfect vehicle for describing movement, as is the case in educational work. (preface)

Motif Writing has numerous applications in the fields of movement studies and dance education. Students and teachers alike benefit from integrating Motif Writing into their lessons (Dunlop, 1966; Topaz, 1972; Chilkovsky, 1976; Venable, 1978; Redfern, 1978; Kipling-Brown, 1986, 1989; King-Calvin, 1994; Yoder, 1994). Motif provides a way to communicate basic movement concepts. In teaching, it can help the educator organize and structure lessons. Preston-Dunlop (1966) states that Motif Writing "clarifies [the teachers'] point of view on movement education and helps them to see how they might aid their students more than they have been doing, and how their range of teaching methods might be enlarged" (p. 19). When integrating the symbolic representation of Motif Writing, students become kinetic explorers, grasping ownership of the tools of dance and, therefore, becoming less dependent on teacher supervision and direction. Venable (1994b) concurs by stating that as educators become more articulate: "Our students get clearer and seem to have more resources independent of the teacher. The ability to symbolize movement ideas seems to help support this independence and to challenge new explorations, new combinations" (p. 2).

In addition to teacher education, preparation, and organization of lessons, Motif Writing displays the components of dance composition, which can be sequenced, revised, analyzed, and documented. Consequently, a student can create a dance score in one lesson and revise and complete it in future lessons. Because Motif Writing provides the vocabulary to study all aspects of human movement, it especially assists in compositional and analytical skills for choreography and the development of an aesthetic appreciation of dance. Lucy Venable, who has employed Motif Writing in dance composition courses at The Ohio State University, states:

> Motif is a great aid for exploring movement, ordering movement, sticking to the theme or motif, sorting out the main ideas, critiquing one's own movement and that of others. It is giving a stronger underpinning to what and how we teach dance, no matter what the form. (Venable 1994b, p. 2)

When Motif Writing is used as a tool for movement examination, analysis, and dance composition, the notation presents a language which we can use to articulate concisely the basis of movement. As Betty Redfern (1978) states, "Not only as a tool for recording any form of dance, but as a means too of learning to think in terms of movement and thus to compose dances other than by improvisation or spontaneous response to stimulus" (p. 10).

Motif Writing has provided university, secondary, and primary school students with an aesthetically enriching experience: they benefit from both the plastic nature of the symbols and the immeasurable possibilities for creative stimulus. It is highly valuable in the field of dance education; as Venable (1994a) states, "[the] interpretation of Motif Writing is left to the reader ... it is a perfect vehicle for describing movement activities where the creative invention of the mover is of prime importance" (p. 1). She (1996) continues, "Motif is more prescriptive, so it gives you an outline of what you might then fill up. It can be used in more of a creative way. You are not going to get into the facts and in a way, you don't want to."

When used as an integral element in designing a dance education curriculum, Motif Writing has several advantages. It:

- provides a visual aid to comprehension, giving a fresh look at movement for those with or without training.
- provides an introduction into the exploration of movement and allows and encourages freedom in interpretation.

- assists in developing a child's creative resources for movement possibilities.
- assists in the increased development of motor vocabulary by providing the student with the knowledge of what he is doing and why, which can help further technique and performance.
- assists in movement observation, thereby increasing a student's awareness and range.
- provides a vehicle for learning about the structure of composition and choreography.

The symbolic representation found in Motif Writing fosters a recognition and keen understanding of the value of kinesthetic literacy, whether united with a curricular base or as a separate dance content area. There is increasing interest in the application of Motif Writing in classroom education, physical education, and dance education. Dori Jenks, a dance educator using Motif, said, "Students at all grade levels became more articulate about their dances, both physically and verbally. The symbols helped to make abstract concepts of time, space and energy more tangible to the elementary students" (1994, p. 2).

In conclusion, the Motif Writing symbols provide an "alphabet of movement" which allows the student to remember and document movement ideas for later performance or study, to enhance compositional analysis, to heighten aesthetic awareness, to build esteem through authorship, and to unite the historic concepts of dance to children's dance scores. By incorporating this unique nonverbal symbolic language with the process of creation, students receive the tools necessary to articulate themselves and their thoughts in movement. Their kinesthetic intelligence has voice, which leads to innovation in other forms of literacy.

Notation and Expression

Kinesthetic experiences intrinsically bring together artistry and cognition. When combined with a conceptual approach to dance education, Motif presents children with a broad knowledge base and capability for significant personal expression. When dance experience combines both written and physical learning modalities, it empowers children with information to convey their ideas. Moira Logan comments on the impact of artistic kinesthetic experience by stating,

Like the other arts, dance gives us access to a nonverbal, metaphoric dimension of experience, one that has to be experienced to be understood...The realm of sensory experience ...forms the basis for aesthetic experience...When movement activities and the sensation of moving are connected to the expressive and imaginative powers of the mover, dance begins to happen. Dance and its appreciation involve a heightened kinesthetic awareness, a bodily intelligence and a sharpened perception of movement as a dimension of aesthetic experience. (Tuttle, 1985, p. 38)

In addition, Motif allows for multiple interpretations, fostering individual voice and style. Motif can encourage the child to be a historian, a critic, a notator, or a creative artist. Dance literacy serves as a catalyst for a variety of cognitive functions, as noted author and educator Gladys Fleming states:

Movement experiences can be initiated and presented in such a way that children are eager to respond to new complex situations. Dance is...concerned with developing, inventing and controlling movement simultaneously with thinking, sensing, responding, feeling and inquiring. (Krause, 1981, p. 269)

Logan and Fleming recognize that the doing and the making of dance fosters kinesthetic intelligence, a result found in no other learning modalities. When blended with symbolic language such as Motif, a transformational learning or literacy in learning occurs.

Notation as Language

Language, whether symbolic, physical, or written, is designed to communicate. When written, language is a vehicle to transmit and receive ideas, information, and knowledge across space and time. Motif Writing is a vocabulary of tangible symbols to document any style or form of dance, thus offering users a versatile mode for communicating their ideas. As Kipling-Brown (1987) states, "The importance of using symbols to attain and to organize ideas and beliefs has altered the conception of intelligence from the acquisition of factual and sense data to the ability to use data in building concepts and communicating expressively" (p. 13). Motif gives children a language they can use to create, communicate, and document their thoughts and ideas through dance. These actions and ideas are conveyed through a selected symbolic vocabulary, and authorship (choreography) is achieved by converting movement ideas to symbols and writing them on paper or by translating actions from a score (notation on paper) and creating a movement representation. Motif provides a mental exchange between concept and creation. This written symbolic vocabulary propels children to artistry and provides intrinsic satisfaction, since their ideas can be shared and understood. By communicating in a common language, children become more enthusiastic as they acquire and master new concepts and symbols and learn to communicate more creatively and effectively.

Motif Writing provides students as young as three with a language to assist their inquiry and communication through movement. Contemporary educational belief is that children be presented with diverse modes of learning. It should not occur simply by spoken word or teacher-directed actions, but through the use of concrete materials and engaging activities; therefore, the integration of physical, kinesthetic action and plastic hand-held manipulatives increases a child's intellectual stimulation and development. The tools found in Motif assist the concepts of ordering, sequencing, designing, and facilitating cooperative learning strategies that produce greater class participation.

It has been my observation that the integration of Motif in the dance curriculum increases student interest and commitment by providing a framework for them to organize their movement ideas. For example, when students shy away from a dance-making activity due to the unfamiliarity of using the body as a tool for creative expression, or hold the common misconception that dance is *ballet* and, therefore, "only for girls," Motif captures their attention and gives them the freedom to explore without stereotype. It is my experience that students find Motif intellectually challenging, artistically empowering, and physically enjoyable. In one class I taught, a fourth-grade boy wrote, "If you think dance is ballet or some other thing, you are wrong." Another fourth-grader wrote, "We have to work very hard....We learn a lot of symbols like twist and turn....I enjoy making dances, sharing, and performing for an audience. " Another student wrote, "Dance makes you feel free and it's not just for girls....The kinds of things you do in dance is express yourself, make dances, learn symbols, and have fun" and "I learned in dance how to use symbols [in] making dances. " Students commented on preferences for creative process or physical action with observations such as, "I like making dances and sharing them with everybody," "I enjoy making dances because you can use your imagination....Sharing dances can be fun too," and "In dance, you do dances you never saw or did [before], you make up a title and learn a special dance language....I enjoy making the dances because you have to make up your dance and memorize it. "

Notation and Interdisciplinary Education

Interdisciplinary units are dynamic learning situations where several educational disciplines are blended together to enhance cognition. Interdisciplinary education is defined as a curriculum approach that consciously applies methodology and language from more than one discipline to examine a central theme, issue, problem, topic, or experience (Hayes-Jacobs 1989, p. 8). When dance is linked with curricular themes, the rewards are immediate through sensations, connections, and insights. Participants physically invest (embody) themselves in the process, communicating their learning through the whole self. Heidi Hayes Jacobs, a noted author on interdisciplinary education, concurs that there is validity beyond the discipline, and the layering of two subjects can create dynamic learning environments. Jacobs (1989) states, "Students can learn not only the usual concepts (and perhaps learn them better), but they can also get a metaconceptual bonus—'a powerful idea,' a cross-cutting idea, a perspective on perspective taking a dimension of experience that may be of great value" (p. 29).

Through dance the "powerful idea" is physicalized and is retained longer than usual by the participants. The linking of learning domains can act to elevate the relevancy of a subject. Jacobs (1989) asserts,

> No matter what the content, we can design active linkages between fields of knowledge....Integrated curriculum attempts should not be seen as interesting diversion but as a more effective means of presenting the curriculum....The curriculum becomes more relevant where there are connections between subjects rather than strict isolation. " (p. 5)

Jacobs (1989) states further that when subjects are taught in isolation, "accumulation of knowledge is the focus," and when subjects are taught in tandem they "demand higher-order connection-making and synthesis that promote real, long-term understanding" (p. 43). Interdisciplinary experiences present an opportunity for pertinent and stimulating moments for students. When these experiences are well designed, students may break from the conventional conception of learning and begin to foster a philosophy which will help them in the working world.

In the Literacy in Motion curriculum, dance is used as a vehicle for illustrating and embodying another subject. This pedagogical perspective is outlined by the *Minnesota Dance Education Curriculum Guide* (1993), which states that through interdisciplinary dance education, "students may problem solve through movement exploration, then create a dance which may be shared and discussed with others. This experience combines many levels of physical, social, and intellectual activity" (p. 104). Throughout this research I have chosen several themes and designed the learning experiences to teach dance and curricular content areas simultaneously, working with the premise that students will integrate knowledge better by experiencing the different disciplines together than by experiencing them alone.

An essential aspect of the Literacy in Motion curriculum is the cultivation of new learning modalities and development of links between dance and the classroom curriculum. Interdisciplinary learning is fostered in the Literacy in Motion framework by:

- Forming connections between content (curricular classroom knowledge) and dance making through inquiry of topic and exploration.
- Fostering levels of abstraction in students' thinking skills that they are not likely to reach in other parts of the curriculum.
- Engaging in thinking strategies for analysis and understanding.
- Developing inventive solutions through physicalizing their knowledge.

The Literacy in Motion curriculum places strong emphasis on the process of learning. Students not only study about the dance they make, but they experience cooperative learning and higher-order thinking skills. Interdisciplinary work can be interesting and stimulating; it encourages children to want more from their study. Interdisciplinary work also has school-wide influences. Interdisciplinary classroom teacher Judith C. Gilbert noticed that attendance rose and that "[there was] greater student, teacher, and parent involvement, increased cooperation among teachers, and student development of life-long learning skills such as responsibility and self-direction, independent study, research, and time management" (Hayes-Jacobs, p. 47). My experiences concur with Gilbert's, as the enthusiasm in interdisciplinary dance was inspiring in the schools, and administrative, community, and parental support rose. Funding increased following the supervisor's visit, 60 parents attended their children's dance sharing, and parents donated time and transportation of costumes and sets for school interdisciplinary dance units.

As noted dance educator Mary Joyce (1980) states, "When [children are] exposed to more than one art form concurrently, it is reasonable to assume that a dynamic interaction of perceptions takes place" (p. 5). This curriculum integrates current interdisciplinary educational practices and presents how dance can be employed to augment curricular literacy.

Curriculum

Dance is kinetic expression, artistry, cognition, and communication. Dance conveys ideas which cannot be rendered in sounds, in words, or in pictures, or communicated in any other form than through a moving body. Dance is a kinetic human language that we can use to reach and empower our children and in which instantaneous pedagogy gives children voice in their expression.

An interdisciplinary model for teaching is employed in Literacy in Motion. It uses Motif Writing to provide the tools for intellectual inquiry and analysis, and it is based on the belief that dance provides an opportunity for linking our kinetic physical development and intellectual development. Experiences in dance are presented for exploration, discovery, analysis, communication, expression, and interpretation, which gives children opportunities to work physically, socially, and intellectually as well as to discover their own artistic originality.

The framework is grounded in the educational philosophies of John Dewey (the importance of the nature of experience and the experimental continuum, 1938), Howard Gardner (the theory of multiple intelligences, 1993), and Jean Piaget (stages of cognition and construction of knowledge, 1973). Literacy in Motion educates through the experience of dance itself, which is immediate and engages children in the learning process.

Goals

Literacy in Motion goals are the following:

- Children will be able to comprehend that dance is a kinesthetic means of communication, with its own language of Motif Writing, and that the body is the vehicle for expression.
- Children will be able to comprehend the connection between dance and classroom curriculum.
- Children will be able to learn to create original dances and celebrate the value of a student's own choreography.
- Children will be able to learn the elements of dance and compositional tools used for dance making.

Framework

The Literacy in Motion framework is designed for teaching children's dance in the elementary school. It focuses principally on grades K–5, providing a medium for teachers to use in their classrooms, but can successfully be implemented in grades 6 to 8. It employs interdisciplinary constructs as a vehicle for student inquiry, exploration, and the introduction of Motif Writing. Students learn, manipulate, and create dance by using the Motif Writing symbol system of notation.

The framework reflects a conceptual approach to dance education in which many content areas: elements of dance, dance inquiry and exploration, dance making, dance sharing, and dance analysis are fostered. The center for the framework is Motif Writing, which feeds all the content areas. This curriculum can be conceptualized as mobile, with dance content areas flowing from the center to the endpoints and back again, expanding participants' knowledge as their experiences grow.

This framework embodies five conceptual content areas, grouping each element presented in all units and classes in varying degrees. These are:

Elements of Dance: The elements of energy, time, space, and relationship that are basic to the appreciation of dance as an art form.

Inquiry & Exploration: Inquiry and exploration provide the ideas that become the dance.

Dance Making: The creation of original dances and movements is a method for students to communicate. Movement experimentation, problem solving, improvisation, and composition assist students in making choices and in discriminating and forming movement phrases.

Dance Sharing: Dancing with and for other students, assists in the development of group unity and cooperation. Individual encouragement is achieved through reciprocal supportive comments during class and informal group sharing, which results in successful creative work.

Dance Analysis: The act of observing and reviewing dance works fosters analytical skills necessary for students to evaluate their own individual and other group efforts.

Instructional Method

The students experience dance through the five content areas, with Motif Writing and curricular theme woven into the framework. The curriculum is designed to provide experiences that enable the students to learn and apply selected symbols and principles of notation within the context of the dance experience. In each class students examine an aspect of a curricular theme, explore modes of embodying that theme, learn new Motif Writing symbols relating to the theme, and create dances. Each class ends with an informal dance sharing or performance followed by students' observations and reflections.

Numerous instructional methods can be employed within this framework. However, in this research two methods were most successful as a way of evaluating participant retention: Compose-then-Move method and Move-then-Compose method. Compose-then-Move experiences call for students to be skilled in the reading of notation materials. In this method, students from one dance class would conceptualize and notate a dance on a curricular theme (e.g., properties of water) and send it to another class for them to read and perform, thereby creating "e-mail dances" and "postcard dances. " This activity not only facilitated interaction between classes, but it presented historical references regarding the development of the notation system. The "e-mail dances" served as a means of re-creating the original purpose of this notation system as its creator Rudolf Laban, had intended.

The Move-then-Compose experiences call for one individual to create and share a very short dance while two other students observe and notate the movement sequence. While it is usually employed in small work groups, Compose-then-Move method can also be implemented in large groups. In this method, the class would form a large circle and individual children would volunteer to create a short dance to perform in the center. Other classmates, using a packet of laminated symbols, would notate and comment on the dance they had seen. Immediate reward was thereby granted, and each child was made to feel valued by receiving personal attention for originality, phrasing, and physical prowess. Participants were equally interested in the observation, analysis, and scoring as well as the physical creating and dancing. This experience was called "Name that Dance."

Other teaching materials employed in this framework included videos of Native American dancers and time-lapse footage of plants growing, penguins swimming, and glaciers and icebergs changing shape. Children's literature and poetry were chosen for themes and movement investigations, and photographs and illustrations were employed to foster visual references and stimulate imagination for active embodiment. A variety of music assisted in setting the atmosphere for inspiration and assisting in the dance-sharing portion of class.

Handwriting the notation symbols was time-consuming and difficult; therefore, at the beginning of the sessions, children used laminated hand-held Motif symbols to expedite the dance analysis and the creative process. In later sessions, students recorded by hand their dance scores complete with illustrations (see Images 1 and 2). On occasion the children's dances were videotaped and viewed in class. The classroom was decorated with large, colored, Motif Writing symbols with English subtitles that provided a dance glossary for quick reference. The students' illustrations brightened the walls, publicizing the activity in class. Flip charts were used for brainstorming.

Children's movement possibilities were more developed compared to their notation vocabulary. Sometimes children requested additional symbols for particular actions in their dances, for example, rolling, which was not covered in the syllabus. I provided these without great explanation. The additional symbols seemed to heighten the appeal of Motif Writing without hindering

Image 1. Students processing and scoring a dance.

Image 2. Students dancing their notation in the classroom; notice Motif information on the blackboard.

the creative work. As the class progressed, the children grew fascinated with the history and development of this language and consequently developed their own symbols. They became invested as owners of their language of dance by actively furthering its usage.

Different children bring different aptitudes to the dance class. One child might explore kinetically before beginning to create, while another might need to write the dance before exploring with movement. Whether or not a child is quick to innovate, explore, and memorize, his/her method is as acceptable as another child's. In this research, I observed that a child's creative processes in dance making are unique and personal.

The class format included exploration of movement concepts, discussion of curricular themes, explanation and manipulation of symbols, dance making, and dance sharing. Covered within this framework are symbols for the basic movement action of the body (Basic Body Action); symbols for level change, directional movement, and pathway (Spatial Indications); the sequencing of symbols on the staff, sequence of action, either simultaneous or successive, and intensity of action (Graphic Design); and duration of actions (Duration of Actions). Below is a list of the symbolic vocabulary covered within Literacy in Motion.

SYMBOLIC VOCABULARY

Basic Body Actions:
- to move and to find stillness
- to contract and to expand
- to contract a lot and to expand a lot
- to jump and to wiggle
- to turn and to twist
- to balance and to fall

Spatial Indications (shown by symbol shape and shading):
- levels: low, middle, and high
- directions: forward, backward, and sideways
- pathways: straight, curving, meandering, and circular

Graphic Design:
- notation is written and read vertically beginning at the bottom of the page and moving to the top. The dance in Figure 1 reads: expand, pause, and two jumps.
- double horizontal lines mark the beginning and ending of the dance.

Figure 1.

Figure 2.

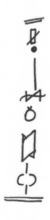

Figure 3.

Figure 4.

Figure 5.

Duration of Actions:
- timing is indicated by the placement of the symbol on the staff.
- duration is shown by the length of the symbol. Figure 2 reads: expand for a much longer than the pause and two jumps combined.
- sequence is shown by the order of symbols on the staff. Figure 3 reads: jump, turn, stillness, expand for twice as long and fall.
- simultaneous actions are shown by side-to-side placement of symbols on the staff. Figure 4 reads: Simultaneous action of expanding and contracting, simultaneous action of turning and balancing, simultaneous action of falling and contraction.
- intensity of actions are show by the selection of the symbol. Figure 5 reads: strong contraction followed by a turn, an expand, and a less intense contraction. (see Fig. #5)

Scope and Sequencing

The Literacy in Motion framework consists of 24 classes comprised of three units of study, with eight classes in each unit. Each class is 50 minutes and is based on exploration of selected themes in the children's classroom curriculum and the related symbols and principles of Motif Writing. The Motif Writing vocabulary taught within this framework is straightforward and relates to the particular curricular concept covered. The classes are cumulative, allowing for continued manipulation and integration of the symbols acquired from previous classes. The framework is designed for ease in acquisition of new concepts. Literacy in Motion curriculum is accessible to all students whether or not they have a dance background.

Assessment

Portfolio assessment was used to evaluate students' comprehension and learning throughout the year. A journal of artifacts (chosen by each child) represented the students' efforts over the span of the classes. The portfolio contains:

- selected notations with reflective comments on their dances, including how they like to move and what they saw in classmates' dances, and constructive comments on their own choreography;
- class participation and students' reflective comments or in-class observations;
- evidence of teamwork, cooperation, and support of others;

- student drawings and artwork which represent the classroom dance experience. (See Figures 6 and 7).
- written discoveries, comments, and thoughts regarding the dance class;
- video documentation of a child's process and creative dance making; record of parent/student/teacher conferences;
- the student's self-assessment worksheets.

Conclusion

Motif Writing, a derivative of Labanotation, can be integrated within all levels and styles of dance. In this research, I have demonstrated that using Motif Writing within a conceptual framework provides a tool for students to acquire a working knowledge of dance as a physical, intellectual, and expressive art form.

The Literacy in Motion curriculum framework, for K-5 students, is grounded in an interdisciplinary partnership between dance education and classroom curriculum using Motif Writing. By uniting Motif Writing with curricular themes, the curriculum is embodied and expands into multi-layered learning. This curriculum framework targets the concepts of sequencing, cooperation, group dynamics, and communication skills.

Motif Writing provides a key for elementary-age children to understand movement concepts by presenting a structured method for exploration, organization, and documentation of their work. During this process, students develop an awareness of their bodies, moving through space, in time, and with dynamic energy. Motif Writing assists their inquiry and design, and prepares them to use their analytical skills when viewing other students' dances or restructuring their own.

In the Literacy in Motion framework, children were given opportunities for problem solving, for building independent and cooperative creative work, and for developing a means of communicating their ideas. These experiences increased students' verbal clarity and kinetic expression on the curricular topic. Following each dance class, students were eager to bring their dance experience back to their classroom. On occasion, classroom teachers would lead a visual art activity following the dance class to integrate the students' experiences. Sue Johnson, a third-grade teacher, said that the movement class carried over into her classroom activities. "Children definitely made the connection between content area…and dance. They often asked to use dance to express what they have learned." Students' knowledge and understanding of dance concepts and their curriculum produced memorable learning experiences as a result.

Figure 6. Student drawing of the motif experience.

Figure 7. Drawing of a student's dance experience.

While conducting this research, I discovered that Motif Writing provided a fresh approach to both the manner and the clarity of my teaching, which brought insights into the appropriate progression of this material. Using Motif Writing at the center of this dance curriculum, I was able to reach a large population of students, dissolve stereotypes of dance, and address participants' diversity of learning styles. Caryl Greenblatt, a fourth-grade teacher, commented on the transformational quality of this type of dance instruction:

> Quiet unmotivated students seem to open up [while] active boys are able to channel their activity, because of the symbols, in a positive manner and shy children were not so shy... Children became aware of movement and were able to identify it in both professional performances and in their peer projects.

She continues, "[Dance] was enjoyable for all involved, the symbols allowed for creative interpretation ... for various learning styles, and for the usually unsuccessful student to be successful." Students participating in these classes had greater focus and heightened participation in class and overall enthusiasm for dance, which also spread to other students throughout the school. Other classroom teachers concurred with these statements.

The objective written structure and the unbiased acceptance of students' creative efforts and kinetic empowerment bring about this curriculum success. Motif assists sensitive children, older students without previous dance experience, non-athletic children who might queue into the logical sequencing involved, and boys who view dance as "feminine." Students experience major changes, learning the rigorous physical challenges, creative expressive potential, and special symbolic language found in dance. The Literacy in Motion framework renders meaning from classroom curricular experience and provides a link between the kinesthetic and other forms of literacy.

Motif Writing Vocabulary

Listed below is the Motif Writing vocabulary covered within the Literacy in Motion curricular framework. It includes the three major direction symbols, the six basic actions of the body, the three dimensions of level, the four pathways in space, and the four concepts of weight shift. The chart is organized into five categories: action verbs, pathways, directions, levels, and changes in support. It is followed by the essential principles of Motif Writing, such as scoring, duration, sequential action, and simultaneous action.

Action	Symbol	Definition	Imagery	Descriptive
Basic Movement Action				
An action stroke		A single movement of any kind	Freedom in choice of movement	An action, a gesture or whole body movement as in a wave of the arm, a turn of the head or movement with the whole body
Stillness	ó	The absence of action	Hiding trying not to be, noticed, playing freeze tag	Pause, hold, freeze
Expand	▬	Actions of lengthening away from the center of the body	A turtle stretching his head out of his shell, vine growing, frog leaping for fly	Opening and reaching out growing, lengthening, unfolding, extending, stretching
Contract	! •	Form of flexion; drawing the limbs toward center of the body	Curled up kitten, folded rug, closed flower bud	Squeezing, shrinking, bending, folding, making smaller
Rotation Turn		A general rotation of the body, as a whole or parts of the body	Cartwheel, pirouette, rolling like a ball, spinning like a top	Spinning, revolution, rolling, circling, gyration, orbit
Rotation Twist		Specific form of rotation in which the extremity produces the turning action from a fixed base	A plant reaching to find the sun	Spiral, intertwine, corkscrew, curve, torque

Pathways in Space				
Any path		Any pathway which moves from one place to another	Any and every path is available to the mover	Any kind of path, all different paths, a combination of all paths
Curving path		A pathway describing a rounded and irregular floor plan	Walking around a pond, a winding road, water draining from tub	Turning, twisting pathway; spiraling path; curving or bending pathway; snaking
Straight path		A pathway that is composed of straight lines.	Balance beam, walking the plank	Zigzags, direct, uninterrupted, undeviating
Circular path		A pathway that describes a full circle, clockwise or counterclock-wise, large or small	Native American Round dance	Equidistant from the center, hoop-like; ring-shaped path, spherical path
Directions in Space				
Forward		Movement traveling, or a gesture which advances the body	Running in a marathon, pushing a shopping cart full of groceries	Frontward, advancing
Backward		Movement traveling or a gesture which is retreating	Tiptoeing back out of danger, retreating from an attack	Rearward, backing up, retreating
Sideward		Movement traveling or a gesture which is to the right or left side of the body	Hermit crab, Lipizzaner horses, sidewinder snake, travel sideways	Laterally, sideways, sliding

Levels				
High / rise		Upward movements against gravity in the process of rising	Jump for joy, bread dough, growing plants. Steam	Rise, elevated, towering, aerial, light
Middle		Horizontal movement a neutral place	Regular walk,	Level with the earth,
Low / sink		Downward in the direction of gravity, with actions in the process of lowering	Prowling animals crouching before a tiger pounces, a withering plant	Sink, depress, on the ground, submerge decline and lower
Change of Support				
Stepping		An action ending in a new support, stepping, a transfer of weight	Crossing a river on slippery rocks, penguins on ice, hopscotch	Stride, footprint, footfall, gait, walk
Balance		Equilibrium, center of gravity over a moving or static support	A bird on a wire	Equilibrium, stasis, stability, steadiness
Falling		The center of gravity moving beyond the base of support	Lava flows, raindrops, Waterfall	Dropping, collapsing, sinking, plunging
Jump		Any aerial step leaving the ground and returning to it	Frogs, victory celebration, bouncing off the diving board	Spring, bounce, rebound, leap, hurdle, hop

LITERACY in MOTION
curricular framework for dance education

UNIT ONE—LESSONS 1–8
BASIC MOVEMENT ACTIONS AND THE ARCTIC

LESSON 1	LESSON 2	LESSON 3	LESSON 4
Glaciers and icebergs Share a short video clip of the Arctic habitat, develop shape dances positive & negative shape sequences	Iceberg dances Show photographs of ice flow & glaciers and develop Shape relationships with partner	Penguin play Show video of penguins and young, create penguin movements, "Name that Dance"	Penguin dances Design dances using themes from Arctic environment: weather, rocks, holes in ice, nesting in small groups
movement concepts Basic actions and stillness	*movement concepts* shaping, weight sharing & buoyancy	*movement concepts* sequencing and symbol recall	*movement concepts* Basic actions, collaborative learning
symbols covered an action, stillness, shrink, grow, sequencing of actions, beginning & ending marks	*symbols covered* rise, sink, and sequencing of symbols	*symbols covered* wiggle jump, turn, twist simultaneous actions	*symbols covered* all from lesson 1-3; balance, falling and levels
LESSON 5	LESSON 6	LESSON 7	LESSON 8
Prey and predators Watch short video on Arctic environment & concept of camouflage; create prey & predator pair dances	Travel the tundra Discuss human & animal migration, create small group dances based on traversing the tundra in relation to the hunt	A harsh environment Explore elements of weather, including harsh, temperatures, freezing, wind, ice, snow, rocks	Arctic Dancing Have an Arctic environment celebration; from use themes the previous classes to design and form small group dances
movement concepts time, speed, shape, weight shift	*movement concepts* pathways	*movement concepts* dynamics and weight sharing	*movement concepts* sequencing, weight sharing
symbols covered shrink and grow, three levels, pause	*symbols covered* levels straight and curved pathway	*symbols covered* more complex sequencing using all known symbols	*symbols covered* use all known Motif symbols

LITERACY in MOTION
curricular framework for dance education

UNIT TWO LESSONS 1–8
PATHWAYS AND NATIVE AMERICAN INDIANS

LESSON 1	LESSON 2	LESSON 3	LESSON 4
American Indian community dances Dance themes and function, Round dance Group formation Arm, head isolations toe-heel footwork	American Indian dance movements Green Corn dance harvest Actions: picking, digging, seeding, carrying, watering, tending, growing, and eating	American Indian journeys Seasonal travel across long distances. Consider traditional roles in the family/NAI tribe	Mapping of American Indians Create terrain map of migration across the country; actions and challenges in one the of journey in small group dances
movement concepts sequencing and storytelling in dance	*movement concepts* structure, building individual dances	*movement concepts* directions, sustained & sudden time	*movement concepts* sequencing pathway and levels
symbols covered review basic movement actions and sequence in straight or curved pathway	*symbols covered* traveling on meandering pathways, rising and sinking	*symbols covered* sequence, jump, turn, rise, sink while moving on a pathway	*symbols covered* pathways straight, curved, meandering in round dance
LESSON 5	LESSON 6	LESSON 7	LESSON 8
Dancing Teepees Improvise to NAI children's poetry in small groups Action-to-Symbol trio quiz	Dance Ceremonies Deer, Eagle & Fire dances create ceremonial dance.	Indians of the River Storytelling & creating a map for a perilous adventure	Powwow dances Name that movement in circle Indians of the flowing water dances & drawings
movement concepts sequencing, elements of time: sustained and sudden	*movement concepts* strong/light weight, formation/ duration	*movement concepts* directional movement, force, speed.	*movement concepts* review all previous
symbols covered duration of pathway dynamics on pathway	*symbols covered* all symbols known concen- tration on timing	*symbols covered* all symbols, concentration on all 4 pathways	*symbols covered* all symbols known concentration on accents

LITERACY in MOTION
curricular framework for dance education

UNIT THREE—LESSONS 1–8
RELATIONSHIP AND PLANTS LIFE CYCLE

LESSON 1	LESSON 2	LESSON 3	LESSON 4
<u>Moving plants</u> Study the plant life cycle for changes in form, discuss contrasting species, watch time-lapse video of plants growing and changing shape; partner dances	<u>Root systems</u> Discuss plant life, role of roots, how they move, create individual plant dances in small groups sharing with name that symbol game	<u>Secret Garden</u> Video & photos of plant environments: forest, desert, wetlands; create representation of flowers, roots & leaves	<u>Seasons</u> Seasonal effects on plants including drying and decomposing investigate shape, color and functional changes in plants during life cycles
Movement concepts dynamics, duration, whole body action	*Movement concepts* dynamic elements of lightness & strength, timing, shaping	*Movement concepts* Storytelling, dynamics, levels, symbolism	*Movement concepts* sequential actions, bending, dynamic elements of quick and sudden time
symbols covered duration and review shrink, grow, and pause	*symbols covered* turn, twist, expand, pause & pathways	*symbols covered* all with focus on accent, duration and pathway	*symbols covered* scatter & gather wiggle, fall, balance
LESSON 5	LESSON 6	LESSON 7	LESSON 8
<u>Seasons</u> Spring growth and pollination; discuss connections to insects and form small group dances for partner notation	<u>Sensations</u> How sun, rain, wind assist or hinder plants, create & share dances with "Name that dance"	<u>Forest Life Cycle</u> Study influences of fire, flood, and lightning on trees, choose plant identity create dance	<u>Green Garden</u> Discuss ecosystems, life cycle, seasons, weather, groups choose plant topic create story and dances about plants
movement concepts duration, spreading elements of quick & sudden time	*movement concepts* dynamics strong/ light weight & free/bound flow	*movement concepts* dynamics, shaping, and storytelling	*movement concepts* review all previous lessons
symbols covered expand, rise, duration, simultaneous movements	*symbols covered* strong or weak accents and stillness	*symbols covered* all from previous lessons	*symbols covered* all from previous lessons

REFERENCES

Brown, A. K. (1986). An examination of motif description in children's dance. Unpublished master's thesis, University of Alberta, Canada.

Brown, A. K. (1989). The Laban system of notation: implications for the dance teacher. Special Issue on Dance, *Journal Canadian Association for Health, Physical Education and Recreation,* July–August 1989.

Brown A. K. (1987). Motif description and creative dance designing a teaching programme for children, *Action Recording! Newsletter, 47* and *48.*

Calvin, K. K. (1994). *Third Conference on Motif Writing*

Chilkovsky, N. (1976). Choreographer's jottings in a new perspective. *Dance Studies. Vol. I.* R. Lange (ed.). Channel Islands: Centre for Dance Studies.

Clausley. M. (1969). A language for movement. *Laban Art of Movement Guild Magazine.*

Dewey, J. (1938) *Experience and Education.* New York: Collier Books, Macmillan Publishing Company.

Dunlop, V. P. (1967). *Readers in kinetography Laban. Series B.* London: Macdonald and Evans.

Dunlop, V. P. (1966). Thoughts on teaching with Motif Writing. *Movement and Dance Magazine of the Laban Guild, 42,* 13–19.

Gardner, H. (1993). *Multiple intelligences: The theory in practice.* New York: Basic Books.

Greenblatt, C. Personal interview, 1997, Putnam Valley, New York.

Guest, A. H. (1995). *Your Move: A new approach to the study of movement and dance.* New York: Gordon and Breach.

Guest, A. H. (1989). *Choreo-graphics,* New York: Gordon and Breach.

Guest, A. H. (1984). *Dance notation.* London: Dance Books Ltd.

Guest, A. H. Personal interview, 1995, Torrington, Connecticut.

Guest, A. H. (1996). The development of language of dance. Unpublished manuscript.

Jacobs, H. H. (1989). *Interdisciplinary curriculum: Design and implementation.* New York, Teachers College Press.

Jenks, D. E. (1994). The application of symbol and scoring to the development of students' creativity through improvisation. Unpublished master's thesis, University of California, Irvine.

Joyce, M. (1973). *First steps in teaching creative dance to children.* California: Mayfield Publishing Company.

Laban, R. (1920). *Die welt des t☐nzers.* Stuttgart: Walter Seifert. (English Trans. Needed; used as source)

Laban, R. (1922). *Symbole des tanzes und tanz als symbole.* Cf. Die Tat. (English Trans. Needed used as source)

Laban, R. (1956). *Principles of dance and movement notation.* London: Macdonald & Evans.

Minnesota Guide for Arts Education. (1993). *Dance education initiative curriculum guide.* Minnesota: Minnesota Center for Arts Education.

National Dance Association. (1994). *National standards for dance education.* Reston, VA: NDA.

Piaget, J. (1973). *The child's conception of the world.* New Jersey: Rowman and Allenheld.

Redfern, B. (1978). The child as creator, performer, spectator. Paper presented at the *International Conference of Dance and the Child*, University of Alberta, Alberta, Canada.

Topaz, M. (1973). A different approach to the teaching of Labanotation. *Dance Studies.* Vol.1 R. Lange (ed.), Channel Islands: Center for Dance Studies.

Tuttle, F. B. (ed.). (1985). *Fine arts in the curriculum.* Washington, DC: National Education of the U.S.

Venable, L. (1994a). *What is motif description.* Unpublished manuscript.

Venable, L. (1994b). *What why Motif.* Unpublished manuscript.

Venable, L. Personal interview, 1996, New York City.

Voder, L. (1995). *Presentation at the Third Conference on Motif Writing.*

INDEX

Abstracting, 176
Action research project, 6
Action researchers, 9, 119
Actualization, 211
Adams, Carolyn, 135, 138,
    143, 144, 153, 160, 169
Alphabet of movement, 268
Alzheimer's disease, 208
American Dance Legacy
    Institute, 138

Balanchine, George, 178
Battle, Robert, 160
Berry, Wendell, 185
Bodily – Kinesthetic, 174
Body language and learning,
    203-220
Body Thinking Beyond
    Dance, 173-201
Boracszeski, Danny, 160
Bristow, Cathy, 186, 187,
    188
Brown University, 138, 163

Care-based thinking, 11
Charter School, 86
Civic humanist, 5
Coker College, South
    Carolina, 140, 143
Columbia College, South
    Carolina, 140, 141, 142,
    150, 163
Columbia University, 204
Concretization, 211
Connected Curriculum, 85-

133
Constructivist thinking, 10,
    11
Conventionalist, 5
Culminating dance
    experience, 111

Dance making, 68
Dance notation, 262
Dancing Out Loud, 233-243
Dance making, 68
Destiné, Jean Leon, 160
Differentiated learning, 120
Digital Improvisation, 59- 84
Dimensional thinking, 176
Drawings, 87-126

Early childhood education, 3
Elements of dance, 274
Emotional stress, 96
Empathizing, 176
Entomologist, 173
Ethical Decision-Making, 1-
    58
Etudes Project, 135-172
Examining Student Work,
    120
Expressivist, 5

Fantastic dance, 72
Feminist Pedagogy, 117
Forming patterns, 176

293